# POST-COLD WAR SECURITY ISSUES IN THE ASIA-PACIFIC REGION

# POST-COLD WAR SECURITY ISSUES IN THE ASIA-PACIFIC REGION

Edited by
Colin McInnes
and
Mark G. Rolls

FRANK CASS

First published in 1994 in Great Britain by
FRANK CASS & CO. LTD.
Newbury House,
890-900 Eastern Avenue,
Newbury Park,
Ilford, Essex IG2 7HH, England

and the United States of America by
FRANK CASS & CO. LTD.

c/o International Specialized Book Services, Inc.,
5804 N.E. Hassalo Street, Portland, Oregon 97213–3644

Library of Congress Cataloging-in-Publication Data
Applied for.

Post-Cold War security issues in the Asia-Pacific region/ edited by Colin
McInnes and Mark G. Rolls.
    Includes bibliographical references and index.
    ISBN 0-7146-4574-5. ISBN 0-7146-4131-6 (pbk).
    1. National security – Asia.   2. National security – Pacific Area.
3. World politics – 1989-   I. McInnes, Colin.   II. Rolls, Mark G., 1966-
UA830.P67 1994                                                   94-3570
355'.03305–dc20                                                       CIP

British Library Cataloguing in Publication Data

Post-Cold War Security Issues in the Asia-Pacific Region
I. McInnes, Colin II. Rolls, Mark G.
327.116095

    ISBN 0-7146-4574-5 (hb)

    ISBN 0-7146-4131-6

This group of studies first appeared in a special issue on 'Post-Cold War
Security Issues in the Asia-Pacific Region' in *Contemporary Security
Policy*, Vol. 15, No. 2 (August 1994), published by Frank Cass & Co.
Ltd.

**Printed in Great Britain by
Antony Rowe Ltd, Chippenham, Wiltshire**

# CONTENTS

List of Abbreviations

Post-Cold War Security in the Asia-       *Colin McInnes and*
Pacific Region: Trends and Issues             *Mark G. Rolls*       1

Changing US Force Levels and Regional
Security                                    *William T. Tow*     10

New Directions in Japanese Security Policy        *David Arase*    44

Security Co-operation in Southeast Asia:
An Evolving Process                          *Mark G. Rolls*    65

Vietnam, Cambodia and Southeast Asian Security    *Mike Yeong*    80

Thailand's Post Cold-War Security Policy
and Defence Programme                        *Mark G. Rolls*    94

Dragon's Fire and Tiger's Claws: Arms
Trade and Production in Far East Asia        *Susan Willett*   112

The ASEAN States' Defence Policies:
Influences and Outcomes                        *Tim Huxley*   136

China: Arms Transfer Policies and
Practices                                    *Gerald Segal*   156

Nuclearization or Denuclearization on the
Korean Peninsula                            *Darryl Howlett*   174

Notes on Contributors                                          194

Index                                                          195

# List of Abbreviations

| | |
|---|---|
| AEW | Airborne early warning |
| AFP | Armed Forces of the Philippines |
| AMM | Annual ministerial meeting |
| APEC | Asia-Pacific economic co-operation |
| ARF | ASEAN Regional Forum |
| ASEAN | Association of Southeast Asian Nations |
| AWACS | Airborne warning and control systems |
| C3I | Command, control, communications and intelligence |
| CBMs | Confidence-building measures |
| CFE | Conventional Forces in Europe (Treaty) |
| COCOM | Coordinating Committee for East-West Trade Policy |
| CRM | Congressional Research Service |
| CSBMs | Confidence and security-building measures |
| CSCE | Conference on Security and Co-operation in Europe |
| DMZ | Demilitarized zone |
| DPRK | Democratic People's Republic of Korea |
| EASI | East Asia Strategy Initiative |
| FPDA | Five Power Defence Arrangements |
| FSU | Former Soviet Union |
| GDP | Gross domestic product |
| GNP | Gross national product |
| IAEA | International Atomic Energy Authority |
| IISS | International Institute for Strategic Studies |
| INF | Intermediate-range nuclear forces |
| JNCC | Joint Nuclear Control Commission |
| LDP | Liberal Democratic Party (Japan) |
| LWR | Light water reactor |
| MDT | Mutual Defence Treaty (US-ROK) |
| MFA | Ministry of Foreign Affairs (Japan) |
| MLRS | Multiple launch rocket system |
| MoU | Memorandum of understanding |
| MRBM | Medium-range ballistic missile |
| MRC | Major regional conflict |
| MST | Mutual Security Treaty (US-Japan) |
| MTCR | Missile technology control regime |
| NPA | New People's Army |
| NPT | Non-Proliferation Treaty |
| NWFZ | Nuclear weapons free zone |

| | |
|---|---|
| **ODA** | Official development assistance |
| **P-5** | Permanent five members of the UN Security Council |
| **PECC** | Pacific Economic Co-operation Conference |
| **PEO** | Peace enforcement operations |
| **PKO** | Peacekeeping operations |
| **PLA** | People's Liberation Army |
| **PMC** | Post-ministerial conference |
| **PMO** | Peacemaking operations |
| **PRC** | People's Republic of China |
| **RDF** | Rapid deployment force |
| **ROK** | Republic of Korea |
| **SAF** | Singapore Armed Forces |
| **SDF** | Self-Defence Forces (Japan) |
| **SEATO** | Southeast Asia Treaty Organization |
| **SIPRI** | Stockholm International Peace Research Institute |
| **SLOC** | Sea line of communication |
| **START** | Strategic Arms Reduction Talks |
| **STH** | Singapore Technologies Holdings |
| **UNTAC** | UN Transitional Authority in Cambodia |
| **USDOD** | US Department of Defense |
| **USFJ** | US Forces, Japan |
| **ZOPFAN** | Zone of peace, freedom and neutrality |

# Post-Cold War Security in the Asia-Pacific Region: Trends and Issues

## COLIN McINNES and MARK G. ROLLS

This is a collection of essays on contemporary international security issues in the Asia-Pacific region. If the end of the Cold War has dominated and transformed the security agenda in Europe and the Atlantic, then its effect on the Asia-Pacific region has been somewhat more equivocal. Although this collection uses the term 'post-Cold War', the phrase has somewhat different connotations for the Asia-Pacific region: it is used less in terms of defining the security agenda than as a description of the contemporary era. But this is not to say that the Asia-Pacific region has been unaffected by the end of the Cold War. Post-Cold War military restructuring will have a major impact on the US presence in the region; the disappearance of the communist threat assisted in undermining the legitimacy and credibility of the previously dominant Liberal Democratic Party in Japan; and communist North Korea's growing international isolation may have helped to spur its nuclear programme. Nevertheless, many of the dominant trends and influences in Asia-Pacific security pre-date the end of the Cold War, and although they may have been affected by the collapse of communism in Europe (directly or indirectly) they were not decisively determined by events there, the region's security agenda has not been re-cast, nor have the major issues been redefined.

Asia-Pacific security is a complex web of domestic, regional and global issues, with a number of distinct sub-regional agendas (for example the fear of nuclearization in the Korean Peninsula). This can make the identification of regional trends and issues difficult. Nevertheless, a number of trends may be identified as affecting the region as a whole, albeit to varying degrees. These trends pre-date the end of the Cold War, and although they may not have been unaffected by the collapse of communism in Europe, neither have they been dominated by those events. Firstly, doubts over the US military commitment have been growing, reinforced by its withdrawal from Subic Bay. Although US economic and political interests in the region may be increasing, as demonstrated by the 1993 meeting of the APEC (Asia-Pacific Economic

Co-operation) forum in Seattle, US military strength in the region has declined and is set to fall yet further. Secondly, Soviet/Russian influence in the region has declined almost to the point of collapse, a result of both its growing domestic economic difficulties and its reduced naval presence in the region: forces at Cam Ranh Bay have been reduced since 1989, while the Pacific Fleet had fallen to such a state in 1993 that most of it was unseaworthy. As a result, Soviet/Russian political influence has also declined dramatically since its peak in the late 1970s/early 1980s. Clearly the decline in both Soviet/Russian influence and US military forces is linked to changes caused by the end of the Cold War; but both trends pre-dated and were to some extent independent of the collapse of communism in Europe.

A third trend is increased Japanese involvement in regional security affairs. Although the Japanese defence budget remains extremely low as a percentage of GDP (c. 1 per cent), the high level of economic growth in Japan over the past decade has meant that this translates into considerable military expenditure. This has been matched by a growth both in political assertiveness and in Japanese involvement in security affairs. Although Japan's security role is still constrained by domestic and international limitations, and the traditionally passive nature of Japanese security policy remains the dominant theme, a clear movement towards greater involvement and assertiveness is nevertheless apparent. Fourthly, China has continued in its role as a major arms producer, building weapons both for its own forces and for export purposes. This has caused considerable concern for regional stability both because of the states China appears willing to export arms to, and because the growth of Chinese military power has been matched by growing intransigence and assertiveness over territorial disputes. Finally, increased regional prosperity, particularly amongst the ASEAN member states has allowed much greater expenditure on weapons procurement, fuelling fears of a regional arms race. The growth of the regional arms market has coincided with a downturn in the global arms market (itself in part the result of the end of the Cold War, but also a consequence of economic recession in Europe and North America) making control of arms exports to the region that much more difficult. These five themes are explored in the following collection of essays each of which examines a specific security issue within the region.

The end of the Cold War has affected the United States more than any other major power in the region (the only possible exception being the Soviet Union/Russia, though its position in the late 1980s was already declining, and its influence never matched that of the United States). As William Tow argues, Washington's rhetoric has continued to stress the region's importance, and in particular US interest in its political and economic stability, but that US actions have failed to persuade states in the region of the depth of that commitment. Two issues in particular demonstrate this: US military restructuring, and Washington's failure to develop a satisfactory regional strategy. On the former, US force levels have been cut considerably since the end of the Cold War. Further, the strategy of in-place forces has been replaced by a greater emphasis on crisis response using forces based in the United States, and a greater reliance on regional allies. Although cuts in force levels were perhaps inevitable with the end of the Cold War (and with the enforced withdrawal from Subic Bay), the depth of the US commitment has nevertheless been questioned by the scale of cuts proposed by both the Bush and Clinton administrations, and by the direction of military restructuring. On the second issue, the United States has failed to develop a new strategy for the region to replace the Cold War strategy of containment. More damaging, however, has been the United States' failure to accept the need to develop a regional approach to post-Cold War security issues, rather than a global one. In particular the Clinton administration's liberal institutionalism appears ill-suited to a region more attuned to realist politics. As Tow points out, these two trends may undermine the United States's pivotal role as 'honest broker' in a region where the lack of a balance of power system threatens stability, with possible global consequences.

If US military involvement in the region is declining, then Japan has become more interested in taking an active role in both regional and world security. Its role, however, is constrained by the domestic and international limitations imposed after the Second World War. As David Arase argues, the result is that its new activism has focused upon non-military aspects of security (particularly economic aid) and contributions to UN-sponsored activities such as peacekeeping. Although its traditionally passive stance remains an important element in Japan's strategic culture, and self-imposed constraints are likely to remain in place for the immediate future, this new activism is acquiring considerable momentum and these limitations are increasingly being undermined. Japan's new assertiveness has led to a variety of disagreements with the West over security issues, while its military has continued its gradual build-up such that Japan is now a major regional military power.

Within the Asia-Pacific region security co-operation is limited, and even amongst the ASEAN states co-operation falls well short of that required for a security regime. Given the increased arms purchases and latent tensions in Southeast Asia, the potential for a security dilemma to emerge there appears high. As Mark Rolls argues, co-operation amongst ASEAN members has been limited by mutual suspicions and different strategic perspectives. Co-operation has tended to be bilateral rather than multilateral, and even then only of significance when linked to an outside power (such as the United States). From the late 1980s on, however, a number of trends began to affect this position: the sense of uncertainty engendered by a shifting balance of power, as US and Soviet/Russian power decreased and Chinese and Japanese influence began to increase; the change in attitude towards Vietnam; and increased arms spending as a result of high economic growth. These trends required a shift in security policies. Two types of proposal emerged: the use of arms control and confidence-building measures; and the establishment of a regional security forum. ASEAN members tended to prefer the latter, and by the early 1990s thinking had rapidly evolved with the establishment of a forum for security dialogue (the ASEAN Regional Forum) and movement towards expanding ASEAN to include all Southeast Asian states. Moreover, the traditional exclusionist ideal (symbolized by ZOPFAN) was being further undermined by attempts to maintain US involvement in the region as a balance to concerns over Chinese (and to a lesser extent Japanese) ambition. Nevertheless, ASEAN is unlikely to develop into a military alliance, despite some co-operation over piracy, and significant obstacles block the development of a Southeast Asian security regime, particularly the intra-mural tensions and suspicions between ASEAN members as evidenced in the various disputes within the sub-region. A wider, Asia-Pacific security regime is even less likely: major concerns exist over Chinese ambitions in the region; the United States is seen by many as an essential 'balancer', but crucially not by China; and for the ASEAN states regional co-operation has the potential to undermine their own efforts at sub-regional political and economic co-operation. As a result, despite some moves towards increased security co-operation in Southeast Asia, the situation falls well short of a security regime and latent tensions coupled to high defence spending may still trigger a security dilemma.

From the mid-1960s until the early 1990s, Vietnam and more recently Cambodia dominated Southeast Asian security concerns. The Vietnam War created a pattern of regional alignments which have only slowly changed, while the Vietnamese invasion of Cambodia was seen by many states in the region as but the first part of a wider ambition on the part of Hanoi. As Mike Yeong points out, however, the 1991 Paris peace agreement and subsequent 1993 elections in Cambodia have fundamentally changed this situation. Both Vietnam and Cambodia now appear more interested in internal security concerns, in promoting economic growth, and in developing relations with ASEAN. Although old fears remain – the Khmer Rouge are still fighting in Cambodia, the potential for Vietnamese intervention in Cambodia continues, and relations between Beijing and Hanoi are still strained – Vietnam and Cambodia appear unlikely to dominate post-Cold War security in Southeast Asia to the same extent as they had for over two decades previously.

Vietnam and Cambodia have, of course, been at the heart of Thai security policy throughout the Cold War, especially during the 1980s when Vietnam's occupation of Cambodia appeared to pose a direct military threat to Thai security. Although Indo-China remains a central focus of Thai security policy in the post-Cold War period, Mark Rolls argues that the emphasis has moved away from the political-military towards the economic aspect of security. Thailand is now concerned with the development of political relationships with these states so that its economic interests can be furthered and its security enhanced. Indeed, the promotion of economic security appears to lie at the centre of much of post-Cold War Thai security policy. Although there is a clear change in the issue emphasis of post-Cold War Thai securityi policy, there is a high degree of continuity in the conceptual approach of Thai security thinking. Thus, Thailand remains concerned with securing a favourable distribution of power in Southeast Asia. It is therefore anxious to develop its relationships with the United States and Japan, and to promote the establishment of a regional security framework in the light of fears about possible Chinese expansionism. Although Thailand's defence programme is influenced by long-standing factors, it also reflects the changed nature of the prevailing environment. Thus, there are plans to reduce the size of the army since there is no longer an immediate military threat from Vietnam, a large naval expansion programme has begun to help promote Thailand's maritime security, and there are the beginnings of an awareness of the ramifications of the prevailing relations-arms dynamic. Whilst there are differences between the civilian government and the military over the way in which arms purchases should be paid for this appears to be a rare example of divergence in the two group's aims. Unlike the past, there is now a high degree of convergence between the civilian administration and the military over the direction of Thailand's post-Cold War security policy and defence programme. The various aspects of continuity and change in Thailand's security policy and defence programme, and the areas of concern of much of this policy, also have a wider significance in the fact that, in many respects, they are illustrative of some of the characteristics of the other ASEAN states' policies and programmes.

The rapid economic growth in the region has helped to make it one of, if not the, most dynamic arms market in the world. At a time of global recession in the arms trade, the Asia-Pacific region is bucking the trend and spending more on arms than ever before. In some cases (such as Japan) economic growth has enabled major increases in arms spending while keeping the cost as a proportion of GDP relatively low; in others arms expenditure has increased in real and relative terms. This has led to fears of an arms race and regional instability as Western (and increasingly Russian) arms manufacturers, facing domestic recession, compete vigorously and with few international restraints for these growing markets. In the first of three essays on the arms trade, Susan Willett examines the structural changes which are taking place on both the demand and supply side. She notes that arms agreements in the region tend no longer to be simple weapons purchases, but often involve co-production and technology transfer as part of regional development strategies. Western defence technology is therefore being used to prime the pump for regional technological development, both civil and military. Furthermore, low factor costs (particularly skilled labour) have led Western defence manufacturers to use offshore production, enhancing regional defence industrial development. As a result, a number of states in the region are developing indigenous defence industries. Although these cannot always compete at the same technological level as Western manufacturers, they are demonstrating an ability to market at lower technological levels, and to niche market. In addition, the increasing use of civil research and development for military purposes (reversing the Cold War pattern) suggests that those states which can compete with the West in civil technologies (Japan, South Korea, Taiwan and Singapore) may be able to transfer this into the military sphere. In the long term, therefore, the development of an indigenous defence industrial base coupled to the increasing application of civil technologies for military purposes suggests that the West may face a very real rival in arms manufacturing terms. Thus a structural change is underway whereby the West is forced for short-term reasons to export to the area, but that the manner of these exports and the civil technological development of the region are helping to create indigenous defence industries which may prove to be competitors in the long term.

In the second essay on the arms trade, Tim Huxley examines the defence policies and arms purchases of the six ASEAN member states (Brunei, Indonesia, Malaysia, the Philippines, Singapore and Thailand). The ASEAN states have increased their defence expenditure and particularly their arms imports very considerably over the past few years. Although they appear determined to develop more substantial military capabilities, this does not appear to be driven by a sense of increased threat. Rather Huxley identifies a mixture of domestic and international factors at work: rapid economic growth, which has allowed defence budgets to increase in real terms without increasing as a percentage of GDP; the prominent role of the armed forces in political decision-making; internal security problems; the desire for national development and modernization via technology transfer and co-production agreements; widespread corruption amongst government officials; the declining role and influence of Britain and more recently the United States, while Japanese and Chinese influence is growing; and the increased importance of maritime issues, particularly territorial claims, smuggling and piracy. Interestingly, Huxley claims that the threat from Indo-China, which was often cited during the 1970s and 1980s as justifying increased arms expenditure, not only is no longer considered a threat to the region but may even have been more a public justification than a motivating factor. In outlining the defence programmes of the ASEAN states, Huxley identifies a number of important features. Firstly, the pattern of increased arms expenditure pre-dated the end of the Cold War, and was indeed relatively unaffected by the collapse of communism in Europe. Secondly, defence policies and arms purchases are shifting away from internal security considerations towards enhancing conventional warfare capabilities, especially air and naval ones. Thirdly, there is no evidence of co-operation in arms procurement by the six ASEAN members. Fourthly, the agreements and defence links between these states are more significant for their confidence building aspects than in terms of any practical measures agreed. And finally competition and latent conflict between the ASEAN states is probably more significant than the co-operation so far demonstrated, and may perhaps explain the cycle of weapons procurement – in other words that it is less an arms race than an 'arms dynamic', where prestige is as much a motivating factor as the security dilemma.

Whereas arms exports world-wide have decreased over the past few years, China has managed to increase its exports and thereby maintain its position as one of the world's four leading arms exporters. Chinese arms production, whether for export or domestic use, has had major regional repercussions. It is both a supplier of arms to states in the region and a major source of concern through its own arms build-up. As Gerald Segal points out, the motives for Chinese arms exports are uncertain, a complex blend of personal and national profit and political advantage. This makes arms control efforts aimed at limiting Chinese exports that much more difficult. Although China is not always hostile to conventional arms control, it is cautious and somewhat ambivalent, particularly in the Asia-Pacific region. Hopes of limiting Chinese arms production and exports therefore appear slim, though not impossible. But, as Segal suggests, the real problem China poses for regional security is not simply its arms production, but its revanchist and unco-operative behaviour *coupled to* its arms production.

Potentially the most destabilizing trend for the region, however, is that of nuclearization, particularly the possible development of nuclear weapons by the Democratic People's Republic of Korea. In the im-mediate aftermath of the Cold War, relations between the two Koreas underwent a marked improvement, and denuclearization of the Korean Peninsula appeared on course (helped by the United States unilateral decision to withdraw its tactical nuclear weapons from the area). By 1993, however, progress had been reversed, and nuclearization was once more on the agenda with the DPRK's 12 March 1993 announcement of its intention to withdraw from the nuclear Non-Proliferation Treaty. Darryl Howlett analyses the DPRK's declared nuclear programme, and the doubts which have arisen over it. Although there is considerable un-certainty both over the DPRK's motivations and the state of its nuclear programme (has it something to hide, or is it using the fear of nuclear-ization as a political lever?), the requirement to re-establish the process of denuclearization is clear for the sake of regional stability and security. Within the region there is a consensus that a diplomatic response is best to the threat of a DPRK nuclear capability, but outside powers are clearly worried over the precedents which might be set should the DPRK acquire nuclear weapons without more drastic international sanctions.

In conclusion, a number of themes can be identified concerning post-Cold War security in the Asia-Pacific region. Firstly, the changing balance of power, as Soviet/Russian and US military forces in the region fall, and as Japan and China become more militarily powerful and politi-cally assertive, has created a high degree of uncertainty. In a region temperamentally inclined to think in neo-realist balance of power terms, the current state of flux between the great powers causes concern. In particular the uncertain future role and military commitment of the United States coupled with increased Chinese capabilities are seen as worrisome. Second, tentative steps are now being taken along the road to security co-operation, particularly in Southeast Asia. These de-velopments, however, have so far failed to mitigate the latent tensions in the region, and hopes of developing a security regime or community lie in the distant future. Indeed, the current level of security co-operation is so fragile that a single crisis could rip it apart. Third, despite the recent recession in Japan, the area seems set to continue its dramatic economic growth, making it ever more important in global politics. Trade will in all probability continue to drive political relationships in the region, while at the same time increased wealth and the desire to develop high technology industries make the continued import of weapons, and increasingly their indigenous development and production likely, fuelling fears of an arms race. Finally, international politics will be affected by domestic political developments, most obviously the possible leadership crises in China and North Korea, but also the role of the Khmer Rouge in Cambodia, the sea change in Japanese politics and pressure on the Clinton administration to assist economic recovery by keeping defence spending low. As in Europe, so in the Asia-Pacific the end of the Cold War has not automatically led to an era of peace and stability; indeed, many of the old concerns remain, while new uncertainties have developed which may threaten the region's security.

# Changing US Force Levels and Regional Security

## WILLIAM T. TOW

The United States' Asia-Pacific security posture is being currently shaped by two countervailing factors. The importance of the United States as a regional security actor is enhanced by the unwillingness or inability of Asian states to trust each other sufficiently to forge a new regional balance of power on their own. This invests Washington, by default, with the status of 'honest broker' for Asian security issues. Its ability to fulfil that role, however, is impeded by domestic budgetary constraints. These will lead to substantial reductions in US defence forces by the end of this century unless a new global or regional adversary emerges to take the place of the now defunct Soviet military threat. As recently noted by one respected American security analyst, US force planning in the Asia-Pacific is shifting away from 'threat driven' calculations for military deployments to 'uncertainty-based models'.[1] These new criteria are being employed to rationalize cuts in US force deployments throughout the region, it is hoped without ceding regional strategic predominance in the process.

The major incentive for the United States to remain strategically engaged in the Asia-Pacific is to sustain that region's continued economic growth and political stability. Asian nations accounted for a third of all US exports in 1992 and are expected to produce a substantial amount of the world's wealth over the next half century (according to some estimates, well over half of the world's economy by the year 2050).[2] Yet the risk of continued strategic engagement for the United States in the Asia-Pacific is that those forces which do remain deployed there may undermine US strategy if their strength becomes so depleted as to render the American commitment to regional stability incredible. In the absence of adequate US force presence or, alternatively, effective regional multilateral arms limitation and confidence-building initiatives, Asia-Pacific governments may well succumb to a dangerous regional arms build up and to opportunistic geopolitics.[3]

The Clinton administration has moved quickly to project a 'dual track' policy to Asia-Pacific security. It supports exploratory dialogues to identify multilateral approaches to regional security, including transparency, confidence-building, and other arms control measures.

However, it simultaneously endorses the maintenance of US bilateral security treaties in the region as the 'foundation' for building new regional security arrangements or, in the worst case, to deter, or respond to, threats against Washington's Asian allies.[4] Despite this effort to reconcile the bilateralism which has dominated American global strategy with the multilateralism of future regional security politics, US force planning is still too reactive and too incremental for confronting the Asia-Pacific's emerging security problems. Many Asians remain deeply concerned that reaffirmation by US officials 'of Washington's commitments to regional security may not always be supported by an American Congress ever vigilant that allies pay an equitable share of mutual defence burdens. US domestic politics may not always facilitate the multilateral dialogue and strategic reassurance which are underwriting current negotiations about Asia-Pacific security politics.[5] For example, the extent to which the US supports new institutions such as the ASEAN Regional Forum as a building block for region-wide security collaboration is directly related to what force levels the United States is willing to maintain in the region.[6]

The major argument advanced here is that the United States will make a significant contribution to regional order and stability in the Asia-Pacific only if it is able to develop a credible and region-specific doctrine to replace the global containment posture of the Cold War. President Clinton has clearly stipulated his global strategic priorities: the development of rapid and effective crisis response mechanisms, slowing the proliferation of weapons of mass destruction, the promotion of democracy, and the development of economic security in the United States itself. These are all commendable as national security objectives but the extent to which they can be effectively applied to Asia-Pacific security problems is less clear. This is especially the case when American defence budgets and force capabilities are declining. The most critical challenge the Clinton administration faces in its Asia-Pacific security policy is to develop and implement more specific approaches to regional peace and stability than the fundamentally ambiguous dual track approach. In this article, initial efforts by the Bush and Clinton administrations to adjust changing US force levels to US national security objectives in the Asia-Pacific will be reviewed. The implications of the streamlining of US Asia-Pacific force postures with respect to the region's overall balance of power will then be addressed. Finally, observations will be advanced on how the United States can revise its current dual track policy to a more region-specific strategy.

TABLE 1

PHASED US TROOP REDUCTIONS

| Country Service | 1990 Starting Strength | Phase I Reductions 1990–1992 | Philippines Withdrawal | 1993 Strength | Phase II Reductions 1992–1995 | 1995 Strength (Approx) |
|---|---|---|---|---|---|---|
| JAPAN | 50,000 | 4,773 | | 45,227 | 700 | 44,527 |
| Army Personnel | 2,000 | 22 | | 1,978 | | 1,978 |
| Navy Shore-based | 7,000 | 502 | | 6,498 | | |
| Marines | 25,000 | 3,489 | | 21,511 | | 21,511 |
| Air Force | 16,000 | 560 | | 15,440 | 700 | 14,740 |
| Joint billets | | 200 | | | | |
| | | | | | | |
| KOREA | 44,400 | 6,987 | | 37,413 | 6,500[1] | 30,913[1] |
| Army Personnel | 32,00 | 5,000 | | 27,000 | | 27,000 |
| Navy Shore-based | 400 | | | 400 | | 400 |
| Marines | 500 | | | 500 | | 500 |
| Air Force | 11,500 | 1,987 | | 9,513 | 9,513 | |
| | | | | | | |
| PHILIPPINES | 14,800 | 3,490 | 11,310 | | | |
| Army Personnel | 200 | | 200 | relocated | | |
| Navy Shore-based | 5,000 | 672 | 4,328 | elsewhere | | |
| Marines | 900 | | 900 | in region | | |
| Air Force | 8,700 | 2,818 | 5,882 | | | |
| | | | | 1,000 | | 1,000[2] |
| Subtotal | 109,200 | 15,250 | 11,310 | 83,640 | 7,200 | 76,440 |
| Afloat or otherwise forward deployed. | 25,800 | | | 25,800 | | 25,800 |
| Total | 135,000 | | | 109,440 | | 102,240 |

[1] Korean troop reductions deferred in light of North Korean threat.
[2] Estimated relocations to Japan, Korea and Singapore. Does not include Guam.

## Changing US Force Postures

Under the Bush administration, the United States adopted the so-called 'Base Force' strategy for downsizing and reconfiguring its overall military strength while retaining a modest forward deployed force presence in both Europe and the Asia-Pacific. The US Defense Department implemented this posture in the latter region through the East Asia Strategy Initiative (EASI), first introduced in April 1990. A force strength reduction of approximately 32,000 personnel was scheduled for implementation between 1990 and 1995, bringing US forces down from 135,000 to 102,000–103,000 personnel (see Table 1).[7] Among the specific missions designated by EASI for US forces in this theatre of operations were the maintenance of a forward deployed force capability sufficiently strong to defend vital sea lines of communication (SLOCs) 'throughout the Pacific as well as the Persian Gulf, Indian Ocean, and East and

South China Seas' – the preservation of US politico-economic access to the region. The Base Force concept, it was argued, would guarantee regional stability and 'discourage the emergence of regional hegemony'.[8]

The concept of 'economy of force' underscored the Bush administration's adoption of the Base Force and EASI postures. Estimates prepared by the Center for Defense Information projected that approximately $US6.9 billion would be saved in US defence spending by withdrawing and demobilizing the c.45,000-strong US forces still deployed on mainland Japan and Okinawa. If all US forces were to be withdrawn from South Korea as well, the total savings would increase to an estimated $US12 billion.[9] While nothing so drastic was seriously contemplated by US defence officials, the United States nevertheless moved steadily throughout the first phase of the EASI force reduction timetable (1990–92) to realize a 25 per cent reduction of US forces in the Asia-Pacific theatre. Two thousand US military personnel were removed from Okinawa in 1991 with another 2,753 scheduled to depart by the end of 1992. Eighteen out of seventy-two F-15 jet fighters at Japan's Kadena Air Force Base were also scheduled to be withdrawn.[10] US ground force deployments in South Korea were reduced from approximately 43,000 to around 37,400. The only real setback to the force reduction timetable outlined by EASI was the imposition of a freeze in the withdrawal of a further 6,000 troops from South Korea in November 1991. American intelligence estimates indicated that North Korea's progress in developing nuclear weapons had advanced to a level where the military balance on the Korean peninsula could become threatened if all the projected US force cuts were actually implemented.

The Base Force strategy emphasized the rapid deployment of well-equipped, mobile and flexible US units for crisis response. Increased access to allied and friendly installations and ports throughout the region in lieu of fixed base deployments was deemed critical. Some US military units originally stationed in the Philippines (an airborne logistics support squadron, a special warfare squadron, and some personnel working with explosives or ship repair) were to be shifted to Guam with the remainder demobilized under EASI's downsizing programme. A November 1990 memorandum of understanding signed between the US and Singapore permitted the United States Air Force to use Singapore's Paya Lebar airfield for short-term rotations for squadrons of its F-16 jet aircraft. A small naval logistics unit (Command Task Force 73) was also redeployed to Singapore. At about the same time, the US Air Force training complex located at Crow Valley, near the Philippines' Clark Air Base, was transferred to Alaska. All of these measures represented

TABLE 2

MAJOR REGIONAL CONFLICT FORCE OPTIONS BY THE BOTTOM-UP REVIEW

| Strategy/ Force | Win one major regional conflict | Win one major regional conflict with hold in second | Win in two near simultaneous major regional conflicts (Pentagon's selected option). | Win in two near simultaneous major regional conflicts plus additional duties |
|---|---|---|---|---|
| US Army | 8 Active Divisions<br>6 Reserve Division equivalents | 10 Active Divisions<br>6 Reserve Division equivalents | 10 Active Divisions<br>15 Reserve Enhanced Readiness Brigades | 12 Active Divisions<br>8 Reserve Division equivalents |
| US Navy | 8 Carrier Battlegroups | 10 Carrier Battlegroups | 11 Carrier Battlegroups<br>1 Reserve/training carrier | 12 Carrier Battlegroups |
| USMC | 5 Active Brigades<br>1 Reserve Division | 5 Active Brigades<br>1 Reserve Division | 5 Active Brigades<br>1 Reserve Division | 5 Active Brigs<br>1 Reserve Division |
| US Air Force | 10 Active Fighter Wings<br>6 Reserve Fighter Wings | 13 Active Fighter Wings<br>7 Reserve Fighter Wings | 13 Active Fighter Wings<br>7 Reserve Fighter Wings | 14 Reserve Fighter Wings<br>10 Reserve Fighter Wings |
| | | | Force Enhancements | |

*Sources:* Les Aspin, US Secretary of Defense, *The Bottom-Up Review: Forces For a New Era* (Washington, DC: US Department of Defense, 1 Sept. 1993), p. 14 and Barbara Starr, 'Pentagon Planners Take on the Two-Region Challenge', *Jane's Defence Weekly* (Jane's Information Group) 20, No. 12 (18 Sept. 1993), p.19.

elements of a 'places, not bases' approach for maintaining a forward deployed American force presence in the Asia-Pacific.[11]

President Clinton was elected to office primarily to repair the United States' slumping economy. As a result, he was under even greater pressure than his predecessor to realize an increased 'peace dividend' from the end of the Cold War. This translated into further reductions in US defence spending, to release funds for rebuilding America's economic health and to strengthen its economic competitiveness abroad. Clinton's first Secretary of Defense, Les Aspin, had foreshadowed a $US100 billion reduction in defence expenditures for 1992–97 even before the new president took office. It soon became clear that the Base Force levels projected by the Bush administration would be undergoing further reductions.[12] In September 1993, Aspin announced the results of the 'Bottom-Up Review of Defense Needs and Programs' which would effectively replace the Base Force concept.[13] In justifying the new programme, the Defense Secretary noted that the world that existed in 1993 was significantly different from that of 1990, so 'naturally, the bottom up review is different from the base force'.[14] Less emphasis would be placed on forward presence and sea control, while more importance would be placed on moving forces rapidly over long distances and on mobile amphibious combat capabilities to cope with regional crises and conflicts. In an Asia-Pacific context, increasing US airlift capabilities, pre-positioning of equipment near possible crisis spots, stationing aircraft carriers and other surface ships in key locations to provide force presence and deterrence potential, and relying more on offshore naval and air strike assets appear to be integral components of the Bottom-Up

Review (see Table 2).[15] Allied burden-sharing is also integral to the strategy.

This new programme illustrates what Asians view as a general American tendency to convey ambivalent signals on overall US strategic intentions and doctrinal planning. Such a perception was reinforced in May 1993 when US Undersecretary of State for Political Affairs Peter Tarnoff speculated that limits would have to be set on the amount of American engagement in a post-Cold War world.[16] Yet during his visit to Korea in July 1993 President Clinton assured the South Koreans that US troops would stay in the ROK 'as long as the Korean people want and need us'.[17]

The Asia-Pacific theatre of operations will be less affected by the cost-cutting which is called for by the Bottom-Up Review than US deployments in Europe. US forces in Asia presently account for $US43 billion, or about 15 per cent of the overall US defence budget while Europe currently assimilates $US122 billion, or roughly 40 per cent, of total expenditure.[18] However, continuing economy-of-force measures will have significant ramifications on America's strategic posture in the Asia-Pacific. More importance will be assigned to projecting US ground forces in future Asian contingencies from bases within the continental United States.[19] To what extent these forces can be quickly transferred to future Asian crisis points, however, remains questionable. Setbacks experienced by the C-17 military transport aircraft project seem intractable. The Bottom-Up Review acknowledged that the C-17 falls far short of meeting requirements outlined by the US Defense Department's (USDOD's) 1991 Mobility Requirements Study (MRS).[20] A 'Strategic Lift Fund' has been created by Congress to explore 'alternative mixes' of ships and aircraft for developing an American long-range troop transport and long-range cargo capacity. It appears, however, unlikely that any viable alternative to the C-17 will be available over the five-year timeframe envisioned by the Bottom-Up Review.[21]

The readiness of US reserve forces is also at issue. Recent studies conducted for the USDOD have concluded that a reserve combat brigade needs 128 days of training and preparation to deploy overseas as opposed to the 90 days envisioned by the Pentagon as the optimum preparation time. The three US Army National Guard combat brigades activated for duty in the Persian Gulf conflict were never deployed because of their inexperience in training at the brigade-sized level.[22] Lack of surge capability and gaps in carrier presence represent two additional problems which must be overcome if the Bottom-Up Review's criteria for the US fighting and winning two 'nearly simultaneous' major regional conflicts (MRCs) are to be met. Surge capability is particularly important during the second phase of combat operations envisioned under the new US strategy, because most combat forces, equipment and supplies needed to sustain and prevail in an MRC would arrive by sea. However, according to the Commander-in-Chief of the US Pacific Command (CINCPAC), Admiral Charles R. Larson, the loss of the Philippines basing system will affect American forces' surge capability to respond to future regional conflicts in the Asia-Pacific. With less bases, more dispersed staging centres and fewer combat ships afloat in the region at any given time, greater American reliance upon reserve forces and allied support efforts is inevitable.[23]

During its first few months in office, the Clinton administration seriously considered reducing the number of active duty US carrier battle groups from twelve to ten or lower. American naval officials warned that any further streamlining of the US carrier force would detract from US capabilities to project power into distant regions and would affect force readiness by lengthening overseas deployment tours for naval personel to an extent where manpower retention would become difficult.[24] The Bottom-Up Review announced that the US would retain twelve carriers, although one would operate on a reserve status. It acknowledged that 'some gaps in carrier presence' would be experienced in Southwest Asia, Northeast Asia and elsewhere, but argued that large-deck amphibious assault ships, Aegis cruisers, guided-missile destroyers, submarines and surveillance aircraft could temporarily compensate for this deficiency. The type of firepower and sea lanes coverage and control needed to establish time-relevant maritime superiority with the sudden outbreak of an MRC of the scale of the two scenarios envisioned by the Botton-Up Review, however, is carrier-dependent.

A shrinking defence resource base will mean that the most likely contingencies will be accorded greater priority in advance, risking an erosion of confidence by those bilateral allies in the Asia-Pacific often afforded less priority in American strategic planning. Even those allies afforded greater US attention, such as Japan and South Korea, will question a strategy which calls for the 'primary responsibility' of initial defence efforts to be assigned to the allied country threatened or attacked because US forces are being tailored downward. The Japanese and South Koreans are both being asked to contribute more to the costs of increasingly modest US military capabilities deployed on their soil with the bland American reassurance that 'forces already in the theatre would move rapidly to provide assistance'.[25] South Korean policy officials, in particular, can hardly be blamed from asking themselves 'how much of a residual US force commitment is still enough?' South Korea responded warily to the Clinton administration's proposed modifications in the US force readiness posture. The revised criteria had envisaged the United States fighting and winning two regional conflicts simultaneously. In June 1993 Aspin's military and civilian advisers recommended that the United States adopt a 'win-hold-win' strategy. This change anticipated that if the United States were confronted with two major regional conflicts simultaneously it would 'hold' the second conflict's adversary by employing air power and a limited number of ground forces. After prevailing in the first conflict, US forces would be redeployed to reinforce the ally under siege in the second theatre until the conflict was terminated on favourable terms. South Korean leaders quickly concluded that the win-hold-win strategy set the context for the Clinton administration to reduce US ground forces once more in South Korea.[26] Their concerns were only slightly assuaged with the formal announcement of the Bottom-Up Review three months later. The win-hold-win strategy had given way to a 'win-win' doctrine which revised the Base Force emphasis on fighting two regional conflicts successfully at the same time, instead calling on US forces to win two such conflicts 'nearly simultaneously'. The Review alluded to eventual US plans to withdraw the two Army brigades still stationed in the ROK although emphasizing that current forces would remain in place for halting any North Korean invasion.[27] Both Secretary of Defense Aspin and Joint Chiefs of Staff Chairman Colin Powell cited cost factors as hindering the US development of sufficient air transport capacity to dispatch forces to both conflict theatres at the same time. South Korean officials interpreted this to mean that if US troops were tied up in combat somewhere in the Middle East, their own defence self-reliance would be critical in deterring or initially defending against a North Korean invader intent on exploiting the United States' strategic preoccupation in another region.[28]

Washington's efforts to formulate a coherent post-Cold War strategy have drawn attention to the relative strategic importance of the Asia-Pacific. Intensified financial and resource constraints have compelled the United States to rely more upon Japan, South Korea and other regional allies to translate American strategic doctrines into policy realities by assuming increased defence burden-sharing responsibilities. If the allies achieve greater defence self-reliance, however, they may just as easily seek more strategic independence from the United States. US military power may, however, still be a catalyst for future collective defence actions in the Asia-Pacific. The Bottom-Up Review's rhetoric about sizing and structuring US forces 'to preserve the flexibility and the capability [for the US] to act unilaterally, should we choose to do so' must be weighed in the context of US domestic political constraints.[29] As US Deputy Secretary of Defense William Perry noted in Tokyo during a mid-May 1993 address, the US will deal with regional threats 'in concert with our allies and friends' as long as those friends and allies are willing to support a continued US forward presence in the Asia-Pacific through cost-sharing and by allowing the US regional access during both peacetime and in times of crisis.[30] The more relevant question is how realistic the Asia-Pacific states regard these commitments to be, given the reduced US force capabilities available to meet future security challenges.

## Regional Security Implications

The key factor underlying the ability of Asia-Pacific states to develop a stable and enduring regional security order is the extent to which they can overcome their historical animosities and interests as American military power gradually declines in their region. Prospects for hegemonic competition between the region's larger powers, the lingering ideological tensions between socialist and market economies, resurgent problems of irredentism, various ethnic cleavages, and the persistence of classical security dilemmas emanating from dangers of nuclear proliferation and intensified arms racing all loom as threats to regional stability. The US still remains the most obvious conduit between a region which is only now by virtue of its economic growth assuming centre-stage in world politics and the larger international community. Regional instability seems certain to materialize if the Americans are perceived as losing strategic interest in the region and the will to act as a regional balancer.[31]

### Hegemonic Competition

Those who support the United States assuming the role of a benign power balancer in the Asia-Pacific envision that by doing so it will assure 'hegemonic stability' there. The hegemonic stability thesis argues that the United States, as the world's benign hegemon, moved to liberalize the world's economy and to promote a *laissez-faire* international trading system during the early post-war years by underwriting the rebuilding of Western Europe and Japan with its military power.[32] With the revival of the Japanese economy assured and with other East Asian states becoming more prosperous, the American marketplace nevertheless remained critical for integrating the Asia-Pacific region into an increasingly interdependent global politico-economic system. American military power, it is argued, can be gradually withdrawn if the co-operation which has taken place in the economic sector can be translated into long-term global stability, pursuing comprehensive regional arms control arrangements, creating regimes for monitoring and curbing weapons transfers, and pressing for greater human rights in developing societies.[33] Many of those who are formulating the Clinton administration's international security policies identify with this perspective, although deferring to the need for maintaining post-war US alliances and security commitments.

The majority of Asia-Pacific policy elites and analysts are 'realists' as opposed to the 'liberal/institutionalists' described above. Realists believe international relations is inherently competitive and that national security postures are best served through implementing power balancing strategies.[34] In the absence of a US 'honest broker', potential regional hegemonists such as the People's Republic of China (PRC) and Japan, they believe, would move unchecked to pursue relative gains and to neutralize each other. Some analysts argue that this process is already under way as China has moved to procure advanced weaponry from Russia and to upgrade its navy to defend its irredentist claims. In the meantime, China views Japan's efforts to modernize its own armed forces with increased alarm.[35] Neither Japan or Russia are regarded by their Asian neighbours as conforming to the hegemonic stability model. They instead fear that they will be forced to compromise their own economic development and political independence by accommodating Tokyo's and Beijing's geopolitical prerogatives in a highly anarchical and largely self-contained post-Cold War regional security environment.[36]

The Clinton administration has not effectively addressed the potential problem of regional hegemonic competition. It has instead lumped Asia-Pacific security problems into an amorphous perspective of global security which fails to adequately differentiate Asia from other regions. Security politics in Europe and the Middle East are now more susceptible to multilateral security dialogues and agreements because the major factors of conflict which have dominated these regions for so long have been either removed (the Soviet threat to Europe) or modified (Israeli-Arab hostilities). The Asia-Pacific region constitutes a greater diversity of cultures, aspirations and tensions, still far too unwieldy and too heterogeneous for imposing universalist solutions to problems of conflict resolution. While multilateralist approaches can be explored, US security interests in this part of the world are still best pursued through realist strategies: specifically, creating sufficient leverage and equilibria via selective power balancing and the tangible pursuit of bilateral security relations to check the geopolitically opportunistic behaviour of aspiring regional hegemonists. In this context, US concerns about blocking missile sales to developing states, renewing the nuclear Non-Proliferation Treaty (NPT), and underwriting regional peacekeeping operations may be important concerns but not always relevant ones for achieving Asia-Pacific security interests.

US analysts who are increasingly concerned that their country's pre-occupation with domestic issues and fiscal constraints has resulted in foreign policy drift and strategic decline are especially critical that the Clinton administration's liberal/interdependence adherents have lost sight of those security threats in Asia that are most dangerous to American interests.[37] China's uncompromising irredentism, backed by its increased military spending, could lead to its eventual challenging of US transit rights to critical sea routes between Japan, Southeast Asian straits and the Middle East. Increased military co-operation between Russia and China could lead to a new strategic coalition between these two countries which, in turn, could threaten to isolate Japan and to neutralize American power in the region. Either a renewed Korean con-frontation or a premature unification of the Korean peninsula could also lead to an increasingly insecure Japan and gradual Chinese pre-dominance on the peninsula. Any of these developments would affect US access to and influence within the region.

*China*

China's military spending, according to US Central Intelligence Agency estimates, has increased by 60 per cent between 1988 and 1993.[38] If accu-rate, this rate of military modernization raises the question as to whether Beijing thinks its interests are best served by encouraging a regional balance of power or by seeking to take advantage of declining American miliary power in the region. In the absence of national disin-tegration or civil war following the passing of its ageing communist leadership, China's national security architects may well become con-fident that they can wear down the United States or other, intra-regional, forces who would oppose the expansion of Chinese power. Indeed, President Clinton's stated desire to include China in new regional security architectures signals an American recognition that China must be taken into account as the key factor in any regional power balance that may emerge. This reality affords Beijing greater leverage in its differences with the United States over human rights issues and weapons export policies.[39] No matter how onerous American politicians and public opinion may find Chinese behaviour to be, the PRC cannot be excluded from any regional security order in the way it was when the post-war American containment network isolated it during the early post-war years. The United States' position is further complicated by the difficulty it would have in reversing the momentum of strategic disengagement from Asian forward positions unless a major conflict were to occur in the region.

China therefore appears destined to challenge a 'less powerful' United States in the Asia-Pacific in several critical ways. First, it is projecting military capabilities ever further beyond its own political frontiers through a naval modernization programme as its land borders become more secure.[40] By developing greater naval capabilities, the Chinese are moving to combine their always formidable potential for waging an Asian continental war with a powerful maritime supplement which could harass (although never dominate) US offshore power.[41] Secondly, China is proceeding with the development of a relatively advanced weapons technology and is procuring sophisticated defence systems from abroad. This trend is likely to accelerate if the Chinese economy continues to experience rapid growth. China's naval modernization programme has achieved impressive breakthroughs in shipbuilding and high technology, especially electronics. While reports of Chinese efforts to buy an aircraft carrier from Ukraine proved to be premature, it is committed to developing the type of high technology weapons which were employed so effectively by the US during the Persian Gulf conflict.[42] China is also procuring enough SU-27 jet fighters and AS-15 air-launched cruise missiles from Russian stockpiles to pose an increasingly serious offensive threat to Taiwan and Japan. These weapon systems can be applied to enforce the Chinese Parliament's February 1992 Territorial Waters Act which authorizes the Chinese military to secure China's territorial claims by the use of force. It is clearly directed toward enforcing China's sovereign claims to both the Spratly Islands and the Senkaku Islands chain (the latter which China contests with Japan). Mid-air refuelling tankers, reportedly developed with Iranian assistance, would enable Su-27s and other Chinese combat aircraft to sustain air support for future naval and amphibious operations in these contested areas.[43] Moreover, China's acquisition or purchase of production rights for *Kilo*-class conventional submarines and S-300 air-defence missile systems has been discussed with Russian suppliers. If completed, such a sale could allow China to provide greater protection for its naval surface units operating in distant waters as well as against incoming ballistic and cruise missiles.[44] Such Chinese capabilities would clearly make the US Pacific Command's strategic planning tasks more difficult.

Thirdly, China's ballistic missile programme and modest nuclear arsenal factor into both American and regional security calculations. As the Chinese moved during the mid-1980s to develop solid-propellant ballistic missiles for deployment in land-mobile and sea-based delivery systems, they began to present US force planners with several problems.[45] By deploying tactical ballistic missiles (most probably armed with conventional rather than nuclear warheads), they could better provide rapid fire support to the People's Liberation Army (PLA) units deployed over long distances to compensate for their lack of aircraft carriers and air-refuelled aircraft operating in the East and South China Seas.[46] China's nuclear power projection capabilities, and therefore its ability to contest US Seventh Fleet operations, will increase even further as the PLA consolidates its hold on various offshore littorals, allowing it to construct air and naval facilities in areas well beyond its homeland. This expanded regional military presence will be supported by the development of what one Chinese analyst has termed 'a newer generation of [Chinese] sea-based nuclear weapons' with increased ranges, strengthened target penetration features and greater yield-to-weight ratios.[47] A more diverse and sophisticated Chinese second-strike nuclear force will enhance the credibility of China's deterrence posture which has until now been characterized by Western analysts as only a 'tentative second-strike capability'.[48]

Fourth, China's ability to shape the outcome of small and medium wars in the region will increase because its forces could confront the United States and other regional adversaries with counter-offensives designed to establish military supremacy through the rapid deployment of highly mobile forces and the application of decisive firepower in a highly concentrated conflict zone. At the very least, China's enemies would have no prospects for a quick victory over Chinese forces such as that achieved by the United States over Iraqi contingents during the Persian Gulf war.[49] Recent PLA military exercises in Guangdong province have involved combined force operations which have demonstrated an increasingly formidable Chinese ability to sustain conflict outside its sovereign boundaries. China's ability to apply force against Taiwan or against those contesting its claims over the Spratly Islands cannot be doubted if Beijing's interests cannot be realized through diplomatic negotiations or coercion.[50]

All of these factors will give US policy planners and military commanders far greater pause before escalating future Asian regional crises in ways which could involve Chinese forces. Recent US threats to obliterate North Korea if it introduced nuclear weapons in a renewed Korean conflict, for example, may prove to be ill-considered if China were to decide to intervene once more on behalf of its North Korean ally.[51] Previously viewing US forces on the Korean peninsula as a stabilizing element against Soviet influence in Pyongyang and against North Korean bellicosity, Chinese leaders may now question the continued utility of US forces in Northeast Asia if they are viewed in Washington as an instrument of nuclear brinkmanship. Moreover, Beijing may also question the ability of a reduced US force presence to constrain Japanese remilitarization.[52]

## The Korean Peninsula and Japan

The collapse of the Soviet Union and the emergence of China as a formidable military power has prompted increased speculation about America's ability to manage the changing power balance in Northeast Asia. Some proposals have been advanced for gradually supplanting the US bilateral security treaties in Northeast Asia with confidence-building measures eventually leading to a Northeast Asian security community.[53] However, intensified nationalism in Japan and South Korea and still unresolved ideological differences between North and South Korea render any hopes for the imminent 'Asianization' of security politics in the Northeast Asian sub-region premature. Until these factors are more effectively addressed, Tokyo and Seoul are better off coping with an American 'honest broker'.[54]

The extent to which the United States continues effectively to underwrite its post-war bilateral security relationships with Tokyo and Seoul will largely determine what security roles Japan and South Korea will opt to pursue, even as the United States reduces its force presence in the Asia-Pacific region. The policy risk for Washington in maintaining these alliances is that their purpose and focus may become increasingly obfuscated as strategic change accelerates in Northeast Asia. Prospects are slim that Japan would be able to fill the power balancing gap left by a total American strategic disengagement in ways which would be acceptable to its neighbours or that either a unified or divided Korea could finesse a series of *modus vivendi* with Japan, Russia and China without avoiding confrontation with one or more of these powers. The Clinton administration thus faces the policy dilemma of coming to terms with both Japan and Korea assuming more responsibility for alliance defence burdens without precipitating greater regional tensions in the process.

Despite continuing trade tensions between the United States and Japan, efforts to posit their relations as adversarial in any geopolitical sense are misguided.[56] The two countries' security interests are now so linked by their mutual adherence to free markets and fear of an uncertain post-Cold War international security environment as to discount military rivalry. However, the US–Japan Mutual Security Treaty (MST) must be predicated more clearly upon politico-strategic equivalence rather than on Japan's continued strategic subservience to the United States if Japan is eventually to succeed in becoming a 'normal power'.

Japanese analysts have called for a revitalization of the MST in ways which would better enable Washington and Tokyo to co-ordinate their efforts against future regional threats. Over the long term, they argue, Japan's strategic perspective on Article 5 of that accord needs to be re-cast from Japan *supporting* the United States in maintaining regional peace and security to it *complementing* American forward deployed forces in the Asia-Pacific.[56] The acceptability of any such policy shift would ultimately rest upon a continued American willingness to stay engaged in Japan to a level where other Asian states will be reassured that Japanese military power does not become projectionist in its own right. The Clinton administration needs to address regional apprehensions about Japan's future military role by reinforcing the United States' determination to sustain a viable US military capability in and around Japan.

The United States will need to strike a balance between maintaining an adequate force presence in that country and assisting Japan's Self Defence Forces (SDF) to become something more than a local auxiliary force to US deployments in the region.[57] Modest qualitative improvements in the strength of US Forces Japan (USFJ) address the first requirement while increased SDF procurement of US defensive weapon systems and increased high-technology collaboration between the two allies relate to the second imperative. The USFJ was augmented in September 1991 by the deployment of the Forrestal-class USS *Independence* aircraft carrier to replace the ageing *Midway*. Ship refit facilities, recently transferred from Subic Bay, have also been assimilated by the port facilities at Yakusuka and Sasebo.[58] The United States is selling or is scheduled to sell to the SDF Airborne Warning and Control Systems (AWACs), Aegis-class destroyers, and Patriot air defence batteries. These force enhancements should help the Japanese overcome serious deficiencies in airborne early warning, shipborne anti-air capabilities, and especially in air missile defences.[59]

South Korea is the US regional ally which has the most direct stake in the strategy outlined by the Bottom-Up Review. The very few US forces deployed in forward positions close to South Korea's demilitarized zone (DMZ) would be subject to combined North Korean artillery barrages and infantry attacks. Their major function is to provide the deterrence 'trip wire' signalling Washington's readiness to augment US and South Korean defences with troops from the continental United States. Such reinforcements need to arrive before North Korean forces could seal off key airfields and seaports of debarkation (most of North Korea's offensive conventional force capabilities are deployed near the DMZ and thus constitute a major short-warning conventional threat).[60] If

American force planning was complicated by the United States having to wage another regional conflict 'nearly simultaneously', the planning and logistics required to overcome a North Korean *blitzkrieg* would be even more formidable. Another problem is that any US effort to impose escalation control in a future conflict would be complicated by a possible North Korean nuclear capability. American pre-emptive strikes designed to eliminate this factor run the risk of missing concealed nuclear weapons stockpiles and/or delivery systems which could then be delivered by a vengeful North against South Korean and Japanese targets.[61] President Clinton's recent warning that if North Korea uses nuclear weapons in combat it would mean the end of that country thus rings somewhat hollow. As it now exists, North Korea's command and control system is fragmented between the national leadership and various field-grade military officers. There is no real certainty that a unified command system can be implemented by the North Koreans to overcome this structural anomaly during times of escalating crisis. Moreover, uncertainties remain about North Korean military prowess, especially in regard to overcoming logistical problems such as integrating equipment and ammunition stockpiles with combat forces efficiently or moving large amounts of personnel and material over key battle areas. The North Korean leadership's ability to implement a credible crisis escalation strategy of its own in response to an 'American threat' could become increasingly questionable as a beleaguered Pyongyang leadership weighs options for intensifying a renewed Korean conflict.[62] In this context, American extended deterrence strategy is most viable if it is employed to buy time for negotiators to elicit North Korean restraint on nuclear strategy rather than activated as a crude strategic bludgeon to coerce the North Koreans into submission.

Of most concern to US strategy is what role a continued American strategic presence in Northeast Asia may play to facilitate and sustain a unified and peaceful Korea. It is unlikely that a newly unified Korean state would favour a posture of either armed or unarmed neutrality, because their country would then become more vulnerable to penetration by China, Japan or Russia. Nor would a shift of major alliance relationships necessarily work to a unified Korea's interest because the United States, as the most distant power, is less likely to influence the course of domestic Korean politics.[63] Korean nationalism, intensified by successful unification, could be better assimilated into a revised Northeast Asian power balance by integrating the bilateral US-ROK Mutual Defence Treaty (MDT) with an evolving multilateral regional security framework incorporating confidence-building and conflict resolution. The multilateral process, however, could not replace the MDT completely at the outset of Korean unification. At least a symbolic US troop presence serving as a basis for short-term strategic reassurance on the peninsula would still be required.

At present, adjustments in both the MDT and US-ROK Combined Forces Command (CFC) are under way to accommodate South Korea's growing status as a full security partner to the United States while still preserving a viable US operational status on the peninsula. South Korean commanders, for example, are gradually assuming control over their country's major defence and security missions. ROK armed forces now guard much of the Joint Security Area in Panmunjom and the transfer of peacetime operational control of South Korea's armed forces to Seoul should be completed by the end of 1994. By the following year, one-third of the South Korean won-based stationing costs for US Forces, Korea (USFK) will be met by Seoul. Other defence burden-sharing measures are being implemented, including the storage and management of US war reserve stockpiles in South Korea, the construction costs of US military facilities, and the maintenance of US military equipment.[64]

However, the danger of assigning the ROK predominant responsibility in defending itself too soon must be avoided. Korea's still uncertain fate renders a stable Northeast Asian balance of power tenuous. The strategic intentions of China, Japan and Russia towards Korea are still unknown and both Pyongyang and Seoul fear that any of these three states are capable of imposing their own agenda on Koreans at some future date, permanently compromising Korean independence and sovereignty in the process. If the United States remains strategically engaged on the peninsula, American officials could work with their Chinese, Japanese, and Russian counterparts to provide a breathing space for the Koreans to work out their own political destiny in ways which could facilitate regional confidence building. In this regard, the precedents of the Joint Declaration of the Denuclearization of the Korean Peninsula (January 1992), the Agreement of Reconciliation, Nonaggression and Exchanges and Cooperation between the North and South (February 1992), and the Agreement to Establish a North-South Joint Military Commission (May 1992) are illustrative. Without sufficient US input and the United States sustaining its politico-military commitment to Korean stability, the prospects of these declarations ever materializing would have been remote.

The key to American alliance relations with South Korea thus lies more with the Clinton administration's ability to integrate the US-ROK alliance into a comprehensive strategy for regional security rather than in the President offering *ad hoc* reassurances to the South Koreans that US forces will stay as long as they want them. The latter policy course would relinquish too much control to Seoul over the timing and dynamics underpinning the deterrence strategy still underlying US-ROK security relations while doing nothing to reassure the South Koreans that American force capabilities will be sufficient to defend them if future regional crises escalate into regional conflicts.

*Southeast Asia*

Recent US security initiatives efforts directed toward Southeast Asia have signalled Washington's commitment to exercise strategic influence there but not at the expense of draining American resources in ways which have undermined past US policies in this part of the world. The enforced departure of American forces from the Philippines in 1992 reinforced the Bush administration's policy shift from relying upon fixed bases for maintaining a forward presence in the Asia-Pacific region to favouring less controversial and commercially acceptable access arrangements with other ASEAN states. As Paul Wolfowitz, US Under Secretary of Defense for Policy explained during a June 1992 press conference, 'from the US perspective, one of the advantages of access as opposed to bases is you have much more flexibility about who you are operating with at any particular time'.[65]

A more qualified American strategic posture and the reduction or dispersal of US military resources in the ASEAN sub-region is congruous with the ASEAN states' traditional preference for regional nonalignment as embodied by the concept of a Zone of Peace, Freedom, and Neutrality (ZOPFAN).[66] Initially posited by the ASEAN foreign ministers in their 1971 Kuala Lumpur Declaration, ZOPFAN was the antithesis of American post-war containment strategy. It envisaged that Southeast Asia could eventually become insulated from great power rivalries by the formalization of ASEAN neutrality.[67] As dedicated supporters of the Non-Alignment Movement, Indonesia and Malaysia have always been ZOPFAN's main proponents, cultivating close bilateral defence ties since the early 1970s. ASEAN was viewed as serving their economic and diplomatic interests and both the Indonesians and Malaysians were determined to disassociate ASEAN from the US war effort in Vietnam. Thailand, by contrast, has regarded its formal defence ties with the United States (the 1954 Manila Pact which formed SEATO and the 1962 Rusk-Thanat communiqué) as vital, although the US response to Bangkok's recent overtures to upgrade US-Thai bilateral defence ties have been low-key. Singapore and Brunei both welcome a US presence as the best insurance against a regional or sub-regional power vacuum.[68] After four decades of strategic subordination to the United States, the Philippines has expressed its determination to forge an independent national identity; however, the question remains whether the United States or any other important regional security actor really cares. The United States has distanced itself from Manila's territorial disputes over part of the Spratlys and over the Sabah (now under Malaysian control). The result of these varying Southeast Asian attitudes is an asymmetry between the increasingly qualified US interest in the region and the various degrees of individual ASEAN member-state support for a continued US balancing role.[69]

This asymmetry has been illustrated by the development of the US 'access strategy' in Southeast Asia since Singapore initially offered to host rotational US forces in August 1989. The offer was justified by the Singaporean government as a gesture to compensate for the pending US departure from the Philippines and thus to preserve a regional power equilibrium. It was initially criticized by Indonesia and Malaysia in an effort by both of those states to reinforce their non-aligned credentials. In reality, both of them had concluded or were in the process of concluding their own access agreements with the United States for upgraded defence co-operation. None of these arrangements begins to approach the scope or visibility of previous American basing operations in the sub-region, however. Singapore now hosts the Command Task Force 73 naval logistics facility at the Sembawang port facility. American F-16 aircraft would also be deployed several times a year to the Paya Lebar airport to engage in joint air combat training with the Republic of Singapore Air Force (RSAF) in the South China Sea.[70] After initially fearing that US operations in Singapore may have developed into a full-scale basing operation to replace the US installations in the Philippines, Malaysia and Indonesia gradually shifted their attitudes as Washington's access strategy became better understood. Their apprehensions were modified, in part, by Singapore launching an 'education campaign' in early 1992 which underscored its determination to limit US military operations in the city-state to logistical support.[71]

Malaysia subsequently moved to expand a Bilateral Training and Education Cooperation agreement, initially signed with the United States in 1984 to broaden the scope of exercises between Malaysian and US army units from command-post to field-training exercises, and to allow the US navy access to Lumut Base in western Malaysia.[72] Indonesian leaders also reiterated their 'strong desire . . . for a continued US military presence [in the Asia-Pacific region] which will ensure the smooth process of establishing a new[power] configuration'. Permanent US bases were deemed to be unacceptable and unnecessary but a US forward presence was still needed, the Indonesians argued, to counterbalance the growing economic predominance of Japan and future prospects for Chinese expansionism.[73] In early 1992, Indonesian military officials announced that joint naval and air exercises with the United States would be 'intensified' and that US naval units would also be serviced at Indonesia's PT PAL shipyard in Surabaya.[74] Brunei has also announced plans to step up military exercises with the United States and to host two or three ship visits a year.[75]

Alliance relations between the United States and its two other bilateral allies in the sub-region, Thailand and Australia, remain healthy, despite Thai domestic political turbulence intensifying in early 1992 and notwithstanding intermittent US-Australian trade tensions. US-Thai defence co-operation was temporarily suspended by Washington following the Thai military's violent suppression of political demonstrators in May 1992 but were restored in September when Thailand held a general election, returning a civilian government to power in that country. American military aircraft regularly use the U-Tapao air base as a staging post and utilized that facility as a refuelling centre during the Gulf War. The annual 'Cobra Gold' joint US-Thai military exercise and other manoeuvres concentrate on amphibious and special warfare tactics, aerial minelaying and minesweeping operations, and logistical co-ordination in the Gulf of Thailand and at other sites along Thailand's eastern and southern seaboards.[76] Australia contributes to Southeast Asian stability by assuming a leading role within the Five Power Defence Arrangements (FPDA) which include New Zealand, Malaysia, Singapore and the United Kingdom along with itself and by conducting close military-to-military relations with the Indonesian armed forces.[77] Both sets of relations contribute to regional confidence building and transparency by encouraging closer interaction in the formation of each country's formulation of national security doctrines and at the operational level of force projection.

On the whole, Southeast Asia and the Southwest Pacific will not be as critical to US regional strategy as is Northeast Asia, where access to Japan, relations with China and deterrence of a North Korean nuclear threat dominate American calculations. By emphasizing conflict scenarios which assign a premium to firepower, air defences, and rapid reinforcement, American defence planners have relegated the Southeast Asian conflict environment to a lower order of priority. US access to the China Sea and Malacca Straits is still deemed crucial but could be compensated for during wartime. An American defence of the Spratly Islands against Chinese occupation is unlikely. As US military presence outside of the Asia-Pacific's northeast sector winds down, even defending Taiwan becomes more questionable.[78]

The evolving post-Cold War US defence posture, however, at least partially correlates with the ASEAN states' national security interests. Access to Southeast Asian ports and airfields are regarded by US force planners as a cost-effective means to ensure continued American access to the Asia-Pacific's key SLOCs during peacetime but still less critical than a sustainable US strategic presence in Northeast Asia. This outlook coincides with the preference of most ASEAN states for a low-key 'over-the-horizon' US presence, sufficiently active to serve as a buffer between themselves and the potentially assertive Northeast Asian greater powers but dispersed to the point that it could be withdrawn if it were to become perceived as a catalyst for conflict spilling over into their sub-region from Northeast Asia.[79]

### Revising the Dual Track Approach

Region-specific security challenges are rapidly supplanting Cold War geopolitics in framing the Asia-Pacific's new regional security environment. The Clinton administration's blueprint for dealing with international change, however, remains tied to the post-war legacy of 'indiscriminate internationalism'.[80] In an address to the United Nations on 29 September 1993 the president declared that the 'enlargement' of democratic institutions and market-based democracies would be the overriding purposes of American foreign policy.[81] This American tendency to combine global and region-specific security policies is also evident in recent US policy statements on the Asia-Pacific region. Washington views Japan as a 'global partner' in economics and security, perceives Korean nuclear intentions and Chinese missile sales behaviour as integral to the overall problem of nuclear/mass destruction weapons proliferation, regards APEC and ASEAN relations as part of a US international free-trading agenda, and sees the promotion of democratization and human rights as universal values.[82] While acknowledging that 'Asia is not Europe', the current American policy orientation nevertheless epitomizes a Eurocentric approach for dealing with Asia-Pacific security problems. Encouraging confidence-building dialogues while simultaneously pursuing a power-balancing strategy to underwrite such processes is very reminiscent of the dual track strategy pursued by NATO policy planners in the early 1980s designed to compel Moscow to eliminate its theatre-specific nuclear weapon system (the SS-20 intermediate-range ballistic missile) deployed against Western European targets. Both China and Japan recognized the potential global ramifications of this strategy by noting that any such agreement could not apply exclusively to Europe. The Soviets could merely redeploy the SS-20 to Asia-Pacific sites, threatening them directly, unless a complete disarmament of that particular weapon system was negotiated. Fifteen years later, the Bottom-Up Review has asserted that the United States should 'promote new regional security arrangements and alliances to improve deterrence and reduce the potential for aggression by hostile regional powers'. This, again, leads Asian policy planners to ask to what extent the United States has assigned precedence to other regions' security problems at the expense of their own where the existing US defence network is still valued as a stabilizing influence by most Asian states. The new US policy emphasis thus is in danger of being perceived as strategically insensitive to specific Asia-Pacific security requirements.[83]

The residual US presence in the Asia-Pacific region, in fact, has little to do with any overriding American vision about what future security values and arrangements must shape their region's emerging strategic environment. Indeed, US and Asian perspectives about security issues are often sharply at odds. The United States' imposition of limited trade sanctions against China in June 1993 was designed to retaliate against the PRC's sale of missile technology to Pakistan. The Clinton administration argued that such transactions were in violation of the Missile Technology Control Regime (MTCR) guidelines. The US response highlighted growing differences between Washington and Beijing over how the transfer of weapon systems and defence-related high technology should be viewed within the context of international security management.[84] North Korea's continued rejection of unlimited IAEA inspections of all its suspected nuclear weapons production sites further illustrates the readiness of various Asian security actors at odds with the American global security agenda to contest its applicability in a region-specific context. Even Japanese and South Korean policy-makers are increasingly uneasy about the continued relevance of international security mechanisms to their own evolving national security concerns. While publicly reaffirming his country's 'unqualified support' for an indefinite extension of the NPT, Japanese Foreign Minister Kabun Muto recently speculated at an ASEAN-PMC session that Tokyo may have to reconsider its own long-standing anti-nuclear policies and take advantage of 'escape clauses' in that treaty if the US nuclear umbrella proved to be ineffective against a North Korean nuclear threat.[85] Japan's territorial dispute with a Russia that is still a formidable nuclear power also appears to be influencing Japanese strategic perceptions in ways which appear increasingly at odds with the United States' determination to fund Russia's economic reconstruction. Intermittent American efforts to create incentives for North Korea to become a more 'reasonable' power are viewed in Seoul as not necessarily compatible with South

Korea's determination to withstand North Korean ideological and military pressure.[86] South Korean policy officials would instead concur with Paul Bracken's observation that 'treating the North Korean nuclear program purely as a problem in non-proliferation may be convenient in forming policy but it fails to take into account the interdependencies that exist among important – and dangerous – parts of the problem'.[87] Washington's plans for strengthening international controls on arms procurement has yet to affect the national security postures of most Asia-Pacific states significantly. Steady rises in their gross national products has led them to allocate major expenditures toward the modernization and expansion of their military forces. Between 1985 and 1991 the Philippines' defence spending increased by 42.86 per cent; Singapore's by 30.95 per cent; Malaysia's by 23.36 per cent; and Thailand's by 12.05 per cent. Straddling the East and South China Seas, Taiwan's defence spending increased 24.59 per cent. Taiwan now rivals South Korea as the region's most sophisticated middle power producer of advanced weapon systems.[88] In the absence of a formal consultative process where their respective military doctrines could be reviewed and ceilings for their weapons procurements might be negotiated, the potential for intra-ASEAN or Southeast Asian sub-regional security disputes intensifying appears high. If still outstanding territorial disputes, rival interpretations of economic enterprise zones (EEZs), or leadership changes precipitate nationalist tensions and invite extra-regional intervention, the appeal of access arrangements for the United States would decrease commensurately.[89]

American intentions to press for global democratization have also been challenged by many Southeast Asian elites as irrelevant to their greater concern for achieving social stability and economic prosperity. Unleashing the forces of social dissent, they believe, could only impede this process. The views of Singapore Senior Minister Lee Kuan Yew typify this outlook: the United States should not insist that capitalism and democracy must co-exist but must realize that Asians are fully capable of blending market-economics with the enlightened authoritarianism which has historically shaped their cultural development.[90] Other examples of the ASEAN states' resentment over perceived US efforts to export Western values to their sub-region include Malaysia's recent (although unsuccessful) campaign to restrict Asian regional economic membership to 'non-Western' Pacific Rim states by forming an East Asia Economic Caucus (EAEC) separate from the broader Asia-Pacific Economic Community (APEC) forum, and increased tensions between the United States and Indonesia over the latter's policies on East Timor, human rights and labour relations.[91]

The United States urgently needs to weigh how it can replace the dual track approach with more region-specific policies in the Asia-Pacific region. In doing so, it must develop a new policy agenda relating its own national security interests more closely to distinctly Asian security issues. This policy reformulation process may not necessarily coincide with the Clinton administration's plans for expanding democracy throughout Asian societies, and it may involve extending short-term concessions to potential adversaries to circumvent unwanted or unnecessary American involvement in future regional conflicts. Any US power-balancing strategy directed toward the region must be implemented only with very specific and delimited policy objectives in mind. The ultimate objective must be to cultivate a regional security order which is increasingly self-sustaining but which is still capable of accommodating fundamental American strategic interests in the Asia-Pacific rim: access to regional lines of communication, markets and emerging diplomatic frameworks. US policy must also signal a clear determination to earmark a specific level of American military power toward the region which will consistently be available for crisis resolution, even though other contingencies may, at times, divert Washington's attention to other regions.

Within this policy framework, the United States can work to facilitate multilateral security dialogues but only as a means of reinforcing those bilateral defence relationships it desires to retain with selected Asia-Pacific allies. Multilateralism's viability in an Asia-Pacific context remains uncertain because there is not as yet any real consensus in the region on what security norms should be institutionalized or what region-wide benefits would be generated as a result. Moreover, fledgling and ill-defined security regimes can be too easily compromised by intraregional tensions. Democratization and 'nation building' are less central to contemporary Asia than the ideological competition which initially shaped post-war American strategy there. The most appealing dimension of the United States' future strategic involvement in the Asia-Pacific region is the US potential for serving as a distant arbitrator, defusing those regional disputes which otherwise may escalate into widespread regional conflict.[92]

The United States can exercise direct influence with its formal bilateral defence partners in Northeast Asia and exercise informal diplomatic and strategic leverage with various Southeast Asian states. It must reassure the South Koreans that the United States will maintain its current force levels in their country and reinforce its forces there *without exception* if North Korean sabre-rattling ever transforms into actual military aggression. It must communicate to Pyongyang that the intensity and scope of future American military co-operation with the

ROK will be determined largely by North Korea's future willingness to comply with IAEA nuclear safeguards and to honour the confidence-building treaties it signed with the ROK during late 1991 and early 1992. The replacement of any US troops that are withdrawn with UN contingents, until reunification of the peninsula occurs, may be an option to reinforce this policy approach. The most important American task is to condition the North Koreans into gradually accepting that simply developing their own nuclear force cannot ensure their leadership's political survival.

Washington can also pressure both Japan and South Korea to collaborate more intensively in their defence planning. This is especially important for implementing a common strategy against the emerging North Korean ballistic missile threat. The Japanese and South Korean defence establishments can work together with US defence officials to develop and deploy a viable anti-missile defence system in Northeast Asia as quickly as possible. Japanese-South Korean co-operation leading to other joint regional defence responsibilities, as envisioned by Article 5 of the US-Japan Mutual Security Treaty, can also be pursued.

The United States should endeavour to use all of its diplomatic leverage to keep Russia from playing a destructive role in the Asia-Pacific region. It should work to restrict Moscow's *laissez-faire* weapons sales policies toward Asian states and to push both the Russians and Japanese toward resolving their dispute over the Northern Territories. Achieving some moderation in Russian arms sales policy would remove a major shortcut for China to acquire excessive military power. US national interests would be served by encouraging Chinese restraint in that Japan would be less likely to regard China as a hegemonic threat justifying its own arms build up. Conversely, a Russian-Japanese settlement of their territorial dispute would unquestionably be one of Northeast Asia's most significant and desirable confidence-building measures.

Over the remainder of this decade it is China which will pose the most serious challenge to the Asia-Pacific security order. It is beyond the United States' strategic capabilities to neutralize the Chinese threat completely, either unilaterally or in concert with regional friends and allies. The United States, however, can instil greater caution in China's more expansionist factions without putting undue strain on its own defence budget by formulating an extended deterrence posture explicitly directed against the PRC. US defence officials must specify for Congress and for the American public those specific regional contingencies where the United States would need to confront China militarily. These might include contesting Chinese intervention on North Korea's behalf in a renewed Korean conflict, resisting China's

assimilation of Taiwan by force, and preventing Chinese nuclear in-
timidation of other Asia-Pacific states. China should also be strongly
warned that if it incorporates the Spratlys, apart from negotiations with
that island group's other claimants, the US Seventh Fleet elements will
be strengthened sufficiently to guarantee continued US access to the
South China Sea and key Southeast Asian sea lanes of communication.

Washington should directly link concessions to the Chinese such as
most-favoured-nation trading status, to Beijing's future willingness to
adopt and sustain more co-operative regional security postures. This
linkage should apply to region-specific Chinese behaviour rather than
becoming tied solely or principally to broader international security
issues such as nuclear non-proliferation, interregional arms sales
questions or human rights. By separating its Asia-Pacific security policy
from its global security objectives, the United States would be less vulnerable to Chinese tactics of divide and rule by appealing to Japanese
and ASEAN instincts to side with other Asians against 'Western' imposed security agendas.

In Southeast Asia the United States should encourage the ASEAN
states to formulate their own national security doctrines clearly as a condition for receiving continued American military assistance and as a
basis for the United States to determine what specific security commitments it will extend to the region. This process may enhance regional
confidence building, but the primary American interest would be to
determine how feasible a US 'honest broker' role would be relative to
the local threat perceptions and defence-spending rationales which
emerged from such doctrinal development. Given their different
strategic priorities, the ASEAN states cannot hope to enter into a
formal defence alliance supported by a common doctrine and a joint
military command. They can, however, identify specific strategic interests in common which can then be reasonably supported by the
United States through adjustments in its own sub-regional force commitments and security diplomacy. Multilateral consultative mechanisms
can then be designed to facilitate both ASEAN common security objectives and US efforts to support them.

**Conclusion**

Prior to his inauguration, President Clinton was advised by numerous
commentators and observers of Asia-Pacific security affairs to reaffirm
American interest in the region but not to risk strategic uncertainty
there by revising US strategic postures too quickly. The president conducted a well-received tour of Japan and South Korea in July 1993 as

part of his effort to meet the first requirement. However, US security interests in the Asia-Pacific region have been compromised by the defence posture subsequently introduced by his administration. Strategic deterrence and defence, forward presence, crisis response and force constitution, which made up the basic components of the Bush administration's Base Force concept, are still all highly relevant to Asia-Pacific stability and to US security interests in that region. Only the third component was addressed in detail by the Bottom-Up Review, and the crisis response options weighed by that document did little to inspire the confidence of Asian allies.

US security policy in the Asia-Pacific region is in danger of failing because of Washington's inability to revise its post-war legacy of indiscriminate internationalism with a determination to implement a new and more stable regional balance of power. US officials in the new administration have thus far misrepresented policy ambiguity and strategic retraction as enlightened multilateralism and alliance recommitment. Rather than promoting new regional security arrangements and alliances to underwrite security interests that have yet to be systematically identified, the United States would do better to reaffirm and implement existing commitments and resources to an Asia-Pacific region which is far less interested in or amenable to conforming to the American global agenda than its policy planners have assumed.

## NOTES

1. Jonathan Pollack, 'The United States in East Asia: Holding the Ring', in *Asia's International Role in the Post-Cold War Era: Part 1*, Adelphi Paper 275 (London: Brassey's for The International Institute for Strategic Studies, 1993), pp.72–3.
2. Urban C. Lehner, 'Asian Economic Growth May Change World Order', *Asian Wall Street Journal Weekly*, 17 May 1993, pp.1, 24; and Robert B. Oxnam, 'Asia/Pacific Challenges', *Foreign Affairs*, Vol.72, No.1 (1993), pp. 58–9.
3. Chin Kin Wah has argued that since 'the local sources of instability are not so directly related to the cold war . . . states in the Asia-Pacific . . . will find that they need to spend far more resources on force upgrading and expansion to enable them to play more effective and meaningful national security roles when the reassuring US presence is no longer to be taken for granted.' See his 'Changing Global Trends and their Effects on the Asia-Pacific', *Contemporary Southeast Asia*, Vol.13, No. 1 (June 1991), p.12.
4. 'Lord Lays out 10 Goals for US Policy in Far East', United States Information Service (hereafter cited as USIS), *Official Text*, 5 April 1993, p.4.
5. Author interviews with various Asian government officials and defence analysts, June–July 1993. The State Department's reaffirmation of US commitments to its regional bilateral treaties is contained in testimony by Winston Lord, US Assistant Secretary of State for East Asia/Pacific Affairs to the US House of Representative's Foreign Affairs Committee, 6 May 1993 as reprinted by the USIS, *Wireless File* EPF406, 6 May 1993, pp.9–10.

6. The ubiquitous Lord has again led the way. Just prior to President Clinton's atten-
   dance at the Group of Seven summit in Tokyo, the Assistant Secretary of State
   pledged that the United States would not allow its bilateral security ties to the area to
   become frayed or fragile and that a 'substantial forward [US] military presence'
   would be maintained. Lord, 'The United States is, and will remain, a Pacific power',
   USIS, *Wireless File* EPF 404, 1 July 1993, p.7.
7. See the Statement by Admiral Charles R. Larson, Commander-in-Chief, United
   States Pacific Command before the Asian and Pacific Affairs Subcommittee, Foreign
   Affairs Committee, US House of Representatives, *Implications of the US With-
   drawal From Clark and Subic Bases* 102nd Cong., 2nd Sess., 5 March 1992, p.4 and
   US Department of Defense, *A Strategic Framework for the Asian Pacific Rim*
   (Washington, DC: US GPO, 1992), p.23.
8. The Directorate for Force Structure, Resources, and Assessment (J-8), The Joint
   Staff of the US Joint Chiefs of Staff, *1992 Joint Military Net Assessment*, Unclassified
   Version (Washington, DC: US Department of Defense, 21 Aug. 1992), pp. 3–7; 8–6
   through 8–7; 9–4 through 9–6; 9–10 through 9–11.
9. Center for Defense Information, *The Defense Monitor*, Vol.21, No. 3 (1993), p. 6 as
   cited by Paul Dibb, *The Future of Australia's Defence Relationship With The United
   States* (Sydney: The Australian Centre for American Studies, 1993), pp.32, 76.
10. Research Institute for Peace and Security, Tokyo, *Asian Security 1992–93* (London:
    Brassey's, 1992), p. 52.
11. *A Strategic Framework for the Asian Pacific Rim*, pp.14–16 and Larson's testimony in
    *Implications of the US Withdrawal*, pp.18, 24–25.
12. A comprehensive account of the transition process and the relevant expenditure
    figures involved is offered in Dibb, op. cit., pp.23–27. For a background on Aspin's
    pre-election estimates, see Alan Tonelson, 'Superpower without a Sword', *Foreign
    Affairs*, Vol.72, No.3 (Summer 1993), pp.170–8 and Dov. S. Zackheim and Jeffrey
    M. Rainey, 'Matching Defense Strategies to Resources: Challenges for the Clinton
    Administration', *International Security*, Vol.18, No.1 (Summer 1993), pp.72–5.
13. Les Aspin, Secretary of Defense, *The Bottom-Up Review: Forces for a New Era*
    (Washington, DC: US Department of Defense, 1 Sept. 1993). Also see 'Transcript of
    Aspin's Address on "New Force for a New Era"', USIS, *Wireless File* EPF406, 2
    Sept. 1993, p.25 and Thomas E. Ricks, 'Military Unveils Plan to Reshape Armed
    Forces', *Wall Street Journal*, 2 Sept. 1993, pp.3, 7.
14. *The Bottom-Up Review*, p.17; 'Transcript of Aspin's Address . . .' , p.26; and Paul
    Horvitz, 'US Forsees a Tight but Highly Lethal Military Force', *International Herald
    Tribune* (hereafter IHT), 2 Sept. 1993, pp.1, 6.
15. *The Bottom-Up Review*, p.14 and Susumu Awanohara, 'Regroup and Relaunch: US
    Unveils New War Planning Strategy', *Far Eastern Economic Review* (hereafter
    FEER) Vol.156, No.37 (16 Sept. 1993), pp.12–13. On the role of naval presence and
    deterrence in this context, see Jack McCaffrie, 'Surface Warships: All Ahead Flank',
    *Business Times* (Singapore), ISEAS 'Trends' Section, 26–27 June 1993, p.iv.
16. Daniel Williams and John M. Goshko, 'A Lesser US Role in the World?' IHT, 27
    May 1993, pp.1, 2, and Morrison, p.1908. Prior to joining the government, Tarnoff
    wrote 'America's New Special Relationships', *Foreign Affairs*, Vol.69, No.3 (1990)
    pp.67–80 in which he advocated the United States, Germany and Japan forming a
    global triumvirate for international security management as opposed to the US
    becoming a unipolar hegemonist.
17. 'Clinton Says Spread of Nuclear Weapons Must Not Replace Cold War', USIS, *Wire-
    less File* EPF110, 12 July 1993, p.22. Also see Jonathan Friedland *et al.*, 'Clinton's
    Clarion Call', FEER 156, No.29 (22 July 1993), pp.10–11.
18. Dibb, op.cit., p.76.
19 *Bottom-Up Review*, pp.7–8. Also see Cameron Stewart, 'Clinton to Cut Pacific
   Forces but Lift Mobility', *The Australian*, 20 Oct. 1992, p. 5 and 'Aspin Outlines '94
   Clinton Defense Plan', USIS, *Wireless File* EPF104, 29 March 1993 p.10, which notes
   that a major initiative 'geared to regional dangers' includes 'special emphasis on
   strategic mobility and military power projection'.

20. *The Bottom-Up Review*, pp.11–12.

21. Pat Towell, 'Surprises are Unlikely as Hill Tackles Defense Budget', *Congressional Quarterly Weekly Report*, 14 Aug. 1993, pp.2232, 2237.

22. Eric Schmitt, 'Under 2-War Plan, Pentagon Sees Role for Part-Time Troops', IHT, 4–5 Sept. 1993, p.3. This article cites a RAND Corporation study on combat readiness.

23. See *Implications of the U.S. Withdrawal From Clark and Subic Bases*, op.cit., pp.35–6.

24. 'Proposed US Warship Cuts Worry Admiral', *Mainichi Daily News* (English language edition), 20 June 1993, p. 3 citing remarks by US Chief of Naval Operations Admiral Frank Kelso, Jr. and Michael R. Gordon, 'Pentagon Seeks 12-Carrier Fleet as World Peace Patrol', IHT, 12 Aug. 1993, p.3 which reports that the US has recently experienced intervals where it had no carrier in the Persian Gulf for about a month.

25. *The Bottom-Up Review*, op. cit., p.7.

26. 'Win, Hold, Confuse', FEER Vol.156, No.28 (15 July 1993), p.12.

27. *The Bottom-Up Review*, op. cit., pp.14, 18 and Barbara Starr, 'Pentagon Planners Take on the Two-Region Challenge', *Jane's Defence Weekly*, Vol.20, No.12 (18 Sept. 1993), p.19. US forces currently earmarked for duty at the outbreak of a new Korean conflict include one division (2 brigades), 2–4 fighter wings, a carrier battle group, and a pre-positioned Marine Expeditionary Force. Starr notes that 'prepositioning' is the real key to the Bottom-Up Review strategy's success or failure with assets afloat available for deployment to either the Middle East or Northeast Asia in a crisis situation.

28. 'Regroup and Relaunch', p.13 and author interviews with Korean defence analysts in Seoul, 28–29 June 1993.

29. *The Bottom-Up Review*, op.cit., p.6.

30. 'Perry: "Democracy is an idea whose time has come"' (Transcript of an address to the Asia Society, Tokyo, 13 May 1993) as reprinted by the United States Information Agency, *Wireless File*, EPF406, 13 May 1993, pp.50, 52.

31. This point is developed more fully by Douglas M. Johnston, 'Anticipating Instability in the Asia-Pacific Region', *The Washington Quarterly*, Vol.15, No.3 (Summer 1992), pp.103–6, 109–12 and by *Asian Security 1992–93*, op. cit., pp.21–22, 50–51. Also see Daljit Singh, 'East Asian Security Means Dialogue and US Will', IHT, 27 July 1993, p.6.

32. Robert O. Keohane, *After Hegemony: Cooperation and Discord in the World Political Economy* (Princeton: Princeton University Press, 1984). For a penetrating critique of this argument, consult Duncan Snidal, 'The Limits of Hegemonic Stability Theory', *International Organization*, Vol.39, No.4 (Autumn 1985), pp.580–614.

33. The seminal work anticipating this approach is by Joseph Nye, *Bound To Lead* (New York: Basic Books, 1990). Recent commentary on the need for America as a more 'normal' power to engage other states on the basis of liberal values in a more interdependent world include a careful essay by Jerry W. Sanders, 'Democratic Engagement', *World Policy Journal*, Vol.9, No.3 (Summer 1992), pp.367–87 and Doug Bandow, 'Avoiding War', *Foreign Policy*, Vol.89 (1992–93), pp.156–74, who warns that residual US military power should be removed from lingering regional collective defence and potential global collective security commitments. For specific perspectives dealing with the Asia-Pacific, see Richard J. Ellings and Edward A. Olsen, 'A New Pacific Profile', *Foreign Policy*, Vol.89 (Winter 1992–93), pp.116–36, who advocate a residual US military presence to safeguard what are increasingly economic US policy priorities in the region (especially p.130) and Steve Chan, 'National Security in the Asia-Pacific: Linkages among Growth, Democracy, and Peace', *Contemporary Southeast Asia*, Vol.14, No.1 (June 1992), pp.13–32, who argues that national security has become a multidimensional concept moving beyond 'military and ideological preoccupations' to incorporate 'trade protectionism, industrial adjustment, technological diffusion, regime transition, and domestic stability in an era of rapid socio-economic change' (p.13).

34. Samuel Huntington has recently endeavoured to apply this thesis in a post-Cold War context, focusing especially on US-Japan relations. See his 'America's Changing Strategic Interests', *Survival*, Vol.33, No.1 (Jan./Feb. 1991), pp.3–17.

35. Derek da Cunha, 'Strain Ahead between China and Japan', IHT, 21 July 1993, p. 6; Tai Ming Cheung, 'China's Buying Spree', FEER Vol.156, No.27 (6 July 1993), p. 24; and 'Citing Foes, Japan will Build up its Forces', IHT, 31 July/1 Aug. 1993, p.4.

36. These points are discussed in-depth by the Brookings Institution's analyst Thomas L. McNaugher in 'US Military Strategy in East Asia: From Balancing to Bargaining', Unpublished Paper, Aug. 1993 especially pp.12–22.

37. See, for example, Philip Bowring, 'On China, America Misses the Point', IHT, 4–5 Sept. 1993, p.6; an interview with William H. Gleysteen, Jr., President of the Japan Society in New York, published as 'Japan Society Head says US Security Interests Shouldn't be Obscured by Current Trade Heat', *The Asian Wall Street Journal Weekly*, 21 June 1993, p.12; and the observation by Robert Oxnam that Asian leaders are most concerned that 'the long history of instability in the Pacific' tends to generate power vacuums which 'tempt tyrants or promote crisis' in Oxnam, op. cit., p.62.

38. See the remarks of Martin Peterson, director of the CIA's East Asian analysis section as reported in 'Chinese Military Spending Soaring, CIA Reports', IHT, 31 July – 1 Aug. 1993, p.4. China's official defence spending figure is now approximately $16–17 billion but officially disclosed outlays reflect only about half that total ($6.8 billion in 1992). China's increased defence expenditures raise the apprehensions of other Asian countries that China is driving to become the region's dominant power. Background on the implications of China's defence spending as it relates to that country's force build-up is provided by Michael Richardson, 'China's Military Secrecy Raises Suspicions', *Asia-Pacific Defence Reporter* (June–July, 1993), p.24.

39. When speaking to the Korean National Assembly in July 1993, the president argued that 'China cannot be a full partner in the world community until it respects human rights and international agreements on trade and weapons sales. But we are also prepared to involve China in building this region's new security and economic architectures. We need an involved and engaged China, not an isolated China.' 'Transcript: Address to Korean National Assembly, July 10', as reprinted in USIS, *Wireless File* EPF 110, 12 July 1993, p.15. Also see Friedland *et al.*, p.11.

40. This point is addressed by Rosita Dellios, 'China', in *Asian Defence Policies: Great Powers and Regional Powers* (Geelong, Victoria: Deakin University Press, 1992), p.113.

41. See Jim Mann and David Holley, 'China Builds Military: Neighbors, US Uneasy', *Los Angeles Times*, 13 Sept. 1992, pp.1, 8.

42. A Chinese account of how impressed China's military was with the array of exotic weapon systems the Americans had at their disposal in this conflict is by Lo Ping, 'Notes on Northern Journey: Old Generals Complain about Deng Delaying Improvement of Weapons Equipment', *Cheng Ming*, 1 May 1991, pp.6–9 as translated and reprinted in Foreign Broadcast Information Service (hereafter FBIS), *China*, 7 May 1991, pp.51–55. For concise accounts of Chinese naval modernization, which includes the acquisition of helicopter carriers to support missions distant from China's own shores, see *Asian Security 1992–93*, op. cit., p.94 and You Ji and You Xu, 'In Search of Blue Water Power: The PLA Navy's Maritime Strategy', *The Pacific Review*, Vol.4, No.2 (1991), pp.137–149.

43. Nicholas D. Kristof, 'Experts Fret over Reach of China's Air Force', *New York Times* (International Edition), 23 Aug. 1992, p.11.

44. de Cunha, Tai Ming Cheung, op. cit., p.26; and Michael Richardson, 'China's Build-up Rings Alarm Bells', *Asia-Pacific Defence Reporter*, Vol.19, No.8–9 (Feb./ March 1993), pp.10–11.

45. The most authoritative background on China's development of nuclear delivery systems is by John Lewis and Hua Di, 'China's Ballistic Missile Programs: Technologies, Strategies, and Goals', *International Security*, Vol.17, No.2 (Fall 1992), pp.5–40.

40 SECURITY IN THE ASIA-PACIFIC REGION

46. Ibid., p.31.
47. Zheng He, 'Submerged-to-Land Carrier Rockets', *Bingqi Zhishi [Ordinance Knowledge]* No.3, 15 May 1989, pp.18–19 as translated and reprinted in Joint Publications Research Service, *China*, 6 Sept. 1989, p.53.
48. Avery Goldstein, 'Robust and Affordable Security: Some Lessons from the Second-Ranking Powers during the Cold War', *Journal of Strategic Studies*, Vol.15, No.4 (Dec. 1992), p.502.
49. In-depth analysis on China's doctrinal rationales in this context is offered by Arthur S. Ding, 'War in the Year 2000: Beijing's perspective', in Bih-jaw Lin *et al.*, *The Aftermath of the 1989 Tiananmen Crisis in Mainland China* (Boulder, CO: Westview, 1992), pp.174–87.
50. A report on the Guangdong military manoeuvres is provided by Tai Ming Cheung and Nayan Chanda, 'Exercising Caution', FEER Vol.156, No.35 (2 Sept. 1993), p.20. The release of a Chinese 'white paper' on Taiwan which insists that the PRC has the right to assimilate that island back into the Chinese mainland by force is covered by Frank Ching, 'Peking's Taiwan Paper Shows its Ultimate Reliance on Force', FEER, Vol.156, No.37 (16 Sept. 1993), p.28.
51. President Clinton visited the demilitarized zone between North and South Korea on 10 July 1993 and observed that 'It would be pointless for them [the North Koreans] to try to develop a nuclear weapon because if they use it, it would be the end of their country.' Cited by Shim Jae Hoon, 'Socking It To Them', FEER, Vol.156, No.29 (22 July 1993), p.12.
52. These points are considered by David Shambaugh, 'China's Security Policy in the post-Cold War Era', *Survival*, Vol.34, No.2 (Summer 1992), p.98.
53. Illustrative examples include Geoffrey Wiseman, 'Common Security in the Asia-Pacific Region', *The Pacific Review*, Vol.5, No.1 (Spring 1992), pp.42–59; Andrew Mack, *Reassurance Versus Deterrence Strategies for the Asia/Pacific Region*, Working Paper No. 103 (Canberra: Peace Research Centre, Research School for Pacific Studies, The Australian National University, February 1991); Yuji Miyamoto, 'Towards a New North East Asia', *The Pacific Review*, Vol.6, No.1 (1993), pp.1–7; and James T. H. Tang, *Multilateralism in Northeast Asian International Security: An Illusion or a Realistic Hope?*, North Pacific Cooperative Security Dialogue Working Paper Number 26 (Toronto: York University, April 1993).
54. Chung-Min Lee, 'What Security Regime in North-East Asia?' in *Asia's International Role in the Post-Cold War Era: Part II*, Adelphi Paper 276 (London: Brassey's for the IISS, April 1993), pp.5–20; Douglas M. Johnston, 'Anticipating Instability in the Asia-Pacific Region', pp.103–12; and Gerald Segal, 'Keeping East Asia Pacific', *The Korean Journal of Defence Analysis*, Vol.5, No.1 (Summer 1993), pp.9–26.
55. Samuel Huntington's commentary is illustrative: 'The issue for the United States is whether it can meet the economic challenge from Japan as successfully as it did the political and military challenges from the Soviet Union. If it cannot, at some future time the United States could find itself in a position relative to Japan that is comparable to the position the Soviet Union is now in relative to the United States'. Huntington, p. 16. A Japanese version of this zero-sum outlook of US-Japan bilateral relations is Shintaro Ishihara's *The Japan That Can Say No*, English language edition (New York: Simon & Shuster, 1991).
56. Masashi Nishihara, 'New Rules for the Japan-US Security Treaty', *Japan Review of International Affairs*, Vol.5, No.1 (Spring/Summer 1991), pp.25–6.
57. The modest force capabilities of the SDF have often been misrepresented as a far more powerful entity. Takashi Inoguchi has correctly observed that the SDF's force structure makes clear that the Japanese military could not fight a war in Japan or beyond that country's boundaries without direct US intervention and support on its behalf. See Takashi Inoguchi, 'Japan in Search of a Normal Role', in *Asia's International Role in the Post-Cold War Era: Part I*, pp.59–60. Also see Andrew K. Hanami, 'The Emerging Military-Industrial Relationship in Japan and the US Connection', *Asian Survey*, Vol.33, No.6 (June 1993), pp.593–5 who notes that 'Japan is

assigned to provide local defence without offensive capability that does not threaten nervous Asian neighbours, notwithstanding the possibility that the Asian states are using the Japan military issue to retain an American presence in the region. When specific details are examined, it can be seen that the SDF's current capabilities are quite minimal'.

58. Larson testimony in *Implications of the US Withdrawal From Clark and Subic Bases*, pp.29, 41; Shigekatsu Kondo, 'The Maritime Priorities of Japan', in Ross Babbage and Sam Bateman (eds.), *Maritime Change: Issues for Asia* (St. Leonards, Australia: Allen & Unwin, 1993), p.148; and Japan Defence Agency, *Defence of Japan 1992*, English language edition (Tokyo: The Japan Times, 1992), pp.46–7.

59. Robert Holzer and George Leopold, 'US Pacific Rim Presence will Key on Alliances', *Defence News*, 10–18 Aug. 1992, p.8 and Takahiko Ueda, 'Defence White Paper Takes Aim at Arms Programs', *The Japan Times Weekly International Edition*, 9–15 Aug. 1993, p.3.

60. This problem is discussed by James C. Wendt, 'Conventional Arms Control for Korea: A Proposed Approach', *Survival*, Vol.34, No.4 (Winter 1992–93), pp.112–13.

61. William J. Taylor, Jr. and Michael J. Mazarr, 'North Korea and the Nuclear Issue: US Perspectives', *The Journal of East Asian Affairs*, Vol.4, No.2 (Summer/Fall 1993), pp.367–8.

62. An excellent analysis on these points is offered by Paul Bracken, 'Nuclear Weapons and State Survival in North Korea', *Survival*, Vol.35, No.3 (Autumn 1993), pp.142–5.

63. Taylor and Mazarr, 'US-Korean Security Relations: Post-Reunification', *Korean Journal of Defence Analysis*, Vol.4, No.1 (Summer 1992), p.159 and Mark T. Fitzpatrick, 'Why Japan and the United States will Welcome Korean Unification', *Korea and World Affairs*, Vol.15, No.3 (Fall 1991), especially pp.424–35.

64. Ministry of National Defence, Republic of Korea, *Defence White Paper 1992–1993*, English Language edition (Seoul: Korea Institute of Defence Analysis, 1993), pp.143–4.

65. 'Wolfowitz Says US Performs Same Security Role with Smaller Force [Transcript: Press Conference in Kuala Lumpur, 23 June 1992]' reprinted in USIA, *Wireless File* EPF 205, 23 June 1992, p.38.

66. Amitav Acharya, *A New Regional Order in South-East Asia: ASEAN in the Post-Cold War Era*, Adelphi Paper 279 (London: Brassey's for The International Institute Strategic Studies, Aug. 1993), pp.54–7.

67. Background and evaluation of ZOPFAN is offered by Acharya, pp.54–7.

68. Acharya, pp.56–8 and Leszek Buszynski, 'ASEAN Security Dilemmas', *Survival*, Vol.34, No.4 (Winter 1992–93), pp.104–5.

69. For further evaluation of this point, consult Donald Weatherbee, 'ASEAN and evolving patterns of regionalism in Southeast Asia', *Asian Journal of Political Science*, Vol.1, No.1 (June 1993), pp.51–2.

70. David Boey, 'USA Takes Singapore Option in Hunt for New SE Asian Home', *Jane's Defence Weekly*, 18 Jan. 1992, p.83.

71. 'Transfer of US Naval Team within Terms of MOU, Says Chok Tong', *Straits Times Overseas Weekly Edition*, 1 Feb. 1992, p.4; 'Singapore Premier Rules Out US Military Base (Kuala Lumpur Radio Malaysia Network, 25 January 1992)', FBIS, *East Asia*, 27 Jan. 1992, p.1 'Discusses Issue with Indonesia (Jakarta Radio Republik Indonesia Network in Indonesian, 27 January 1992)', in ibid.; and 'No Question of US Setting up Base in Singapore, ASEAN Envoys Told', *Straits Times Weekly Overseas Edition*, 11 Jan. 1992, p.11. *A New Straits Times* editorial argued in May 1992 that 'Malaysia's vehement initial objection to the placing of US Navy Logistic Command in Singapore arose largely from miscommunication than anything else as the republic neither consulted nor briefed its ASEAN neighbours beforehand. Once it was made clear that the republic would not provide a permanent base but only facilities for repairs, maintenance, and supplies and the 200 personnel under the Logistic Command

would deal with matters pertaining to this arrangement, it no longer became an issue.' 'No Objection to US Presence', *New Straits Times*, 1 May 1992, p.10 as reprinted in FBIS, *East Asia*, 6 May 1992, p.27.

72. 'Pact for KL to Service US Ships "Will Boost Navy Ties"', *Straits Times Weekly Overseas Edition*, 18 April 1992, p.10; 'Malaysia and US to Raise Status of Joint Exercises', *Straits Times Weekly Overseas Edition*, 21 Feb. 1992, p.10; Acharya, op. cit., p.57; and Buszynski, op. cit., p.104.

73. *Kompas* (Jakarta) interview with Indonesian Foreign Minister Ali Alatas as reported in an editorial, 'What Kind of US Presence Continued to be Needed in Asia?' *Kompas*, 1 May 1992, p.4 as translated and reprinted in FBIS, *East Asia*, 26 May 1992, pp.30–31.

74. Michael Richardson, 'Indonesia-US Get Together', *Asia-Pacific Defence Reporter* 18/10–11 (April–May 1992), p.31 and Michael Vatikiotis, 'Spreading the Load', FEER, Vol.154, No.45 (7 Nov. 1991), p.35.

75. Buzynski, op. cit., p.104 and 'Regional US Military Presence Supported', FBIS, *East Asia*, 4 May 1992, pp.14–15.

76. Jeffrey D. Young, *US Military Interaction with Southeast Asian Countries*, Congressional Research Report for Congress 92-241-F, 27 Feb. 1992, pp.5–6; Sheldon Simon, 'The Regionalisation of Defence in Southeast Asia', *The Pacific Review*, Vol.5, No.2 (1992), p.115; Rodney Tasker, 'Security Embrace', FEER,, Vol.156, No. 7 (18 Feb. 1993), p.12; and Cynthia Owens, 'Thai General Plays Down Military Threat from China', *Asian Wall Street Journal Weekly*, Vol.15, No.3 (June 1993), p.21.

77. Acharya, op. cit., p.5 and Simon, op. cit., p.120.

78. This question is treated in some detail by Parriss H. Chang and Martin L. Lasater, *If China Crosses the Taiwan Strait* (Washington, DC: University Press of America, 1992).

79. Aspects of evolving US defence posture planning correlating with or diverging from those of Southeast Asian states are addressed in James A. Winnefeld *et al.*, *A New Strategy and Fewer Forces: The Pacific Dimension*, R-4089/2-USDP (Santa Monica, CA: RAND), 1992, p.71.

80. The term 'indiscriminate internationalism' has been applied by Robert Art in his discussion on 'A US Military Strategy for the 1990s', *Survival*, Vol.34, No.4 (Winter 1992–93), p.7.

81. 'Clinton: US Committed to Making UN Vision a Reality', USIS, *Official Text*, 29 Sept. 1993, pp.3–4.

82. The specific US policy objectives outlined by Assistant Secretary of State for East Asia/Pacific Winston Lord at his April 1993 confirmation hearing reflects the global-regional linkage. See 'Lord Lays out 10 Goals for US Policy in East Asia', passim.

83. The quote is from *The Bottom-Up Review*, op. cit., p.2.

84. 'US Levies Trade Sanctions against China in Arms Flap', *Asian Wall Street Journal* 30 Aug. 1993, pp.3, 4 and Marcus W. Brauchli, 'Beijing's Qian Calls US Move Unfair, Says China Won't Alter its Policies', ibid., pp.3, 5. General background on China's recent arms sales policies is provided by Eric Heyer, 'China's Arms Merchants: Profits in Command', *China Quarterly*, Vol.132 (1992), pp.1101–18.

85. Sam Jameson, 'Japan Rattles Nuclear Sabre at North Korea', IHT, 30 July 1993, p.4.

86. Author interviews with South Korean defence analysts in Seoul, 27–28 July 1993.

87. Bracken, op. cit., p.148.

88. Michael T. Klare, 'The Next Great Arms Race', *Foreign Affairs*, Vol.72, No.3 (Summer 1993), pp.138–40, 146–7. Also see Ball, 'The Military Build-up in Asia-Pacific', *Pacific Review*, Vol.5, No.3 (1992), pp.197–208. The sale price of the Indonesian purchase was not immediately disclosed. It was assessed as an opportunity for Jakarta to procure the units needed for expanding its navy's capabilities to patrol that country's extensive archipelagoes more effectively for 'bargain basement prices' and to counter the Chinese naval build-up in the South China Sea. See Michael Richardson, 'Indonesia's Big Naval Buy No Threat', *Asia-Pacific Defence Reporter* (April–May 1993), p.9.

89. Sheldon W. Simon, 'US Strategy and Southeast Asian Security: Issues of Compatibility', *Contemporary Southeast Asia*, Vol.14, No.4 (March 1993), pp.305–6.
90. 'Let Asia be Asia', *Straits Times* (Singapore), 14 May 1992, p.28 as reprinted in FBIS, *East Asia*, 18 May, p.31. Also see Kishore Mahbubani, 'The Dangers of Decadence', *Foreign Affairs*, Vol.72, No.4 (Sept./Oct. 1993), pp.10–14. Mahbubani is Deputy Secretary of Singapore's Ministry for Foreign Affairs.
91. Background on the US differences with Indonesia on these issues is provided in remarks by Winston Lord, US Assistant Secretary of State for East Asia and Pacific Affairs to Indonesian journalists during a USIA 'Dialogue' session and reprinted as 'Lord: "New Pacific Community" is Important to US Interests', USIS, *Official Text*, 24 Aug. 1993, pp.4–5 and by Susumu Awanohara, 'Hard Labour', *Far Eastern Economic Review*, Vol.156, No.19 (13 May 1993), p.13.
92. Larry Niksch describes this preferred US posture as 'managed diplomatic and security cooperation, but, in some cases, at lower levels than at present and coexistent with increased strains and disputes'. See his 'Keeping US, East Asia within Arms Length', *Asian Wall Street Journal Weekly*, 9 Nov. 1992, p.12.

# New Directions in Japanese Security Policy

## DAVID ARASE

This article will indicate how Japan is adapting to its changing security environment. Although discussions of post-Cold War security have legitimately broadened to include such non-military threats as population growth, ecological disaster and global economic imbalances, this discussion will be more narrowly focused on contingencies where Japan's interests might be targeted or collaterally affected by threats of the use of force within East Asia. The critical question in Japanese security policy today is whether or not Japan will assume expanded military roles; and East Asia is where Japan's interests are vital enough to force change in this direction. While it is fairly clear that the Japanese government wishes to be more active in protecting its security interests, contemporary domestic and international factors inhibit Japan from taking an active military role. As a result, Japanese security policy is characterized by increasing non-military contributions to international security, the introduction of Japan's Self-Defence Forces (SDF) into UN-sponsored collective security activities, and a prudent emphasis on widening the scope of longer term military security options for Japan.

### Japan's Post-war Policy

The destruction of the Japanese military as a domestic political actor and the drawing-up of the 1947 Peace Constitution were fundamental changes imposed on post-war Japan by the American occupation. The intention was to demilitarize Japan, but after the US 'lost' Nationalist China in 1949, the United States reversed course and pressed Japan to remilitarize. The then Japanese prime minister, Shigeru Yoshida, successfully resisted this pressure, but he did grant the United States the right to station troops in Japan. In return he gained a US security guarantee in the form of the 1951 US-Japan Security Treaty without having to make any reciprocal or third-party military commitments. Since then, this arrangement has provided the foundation for Japanese security policy. Japan modified this passive stance under US demands for defence burden-sharing in the early 1980s. Japan assumed a sea-lane defence mission that extended 1,000 miles from Japan, which implicitly aimed to offset increased Soviet naval deployments. The Constitution and domestic opinion, however, still prevented Japan from explicitly committing the Japanese Self-Defence Forces to anything but local defence of the Japanese homeland. To broaden its contributions to Western security, Japan began to portray economic assistance as a security contribution. It extended sizeable loans to South Korea and increased official development assistance (ODA) to such front-line states as Thailand, Pakistan, Turkey, Egypt and Jamaica. This economic contribution to Western security relieved pressure on Japan to expand the scope of its military commitments, but the question now is whether this strategy will continue to secure Japan's interests in the post-Cold War period.

The Japanese concept of 'comprehensive security' (*sogo anzen hosho*) was developed at the start of the 1980s to support this subtle shift in post-war Japanese security policy. Comprehensive security called for the co-ordinated application of economic, political and military measures at three levels: the global level; within selected groupings of countries; and in national self-help efforts. Key security objectives identified at each level were: at the global level, arms control, better North–South relations, and free trade; at the intermediate level, maintenance of good relations with political allies and key economic partners; and at the national self-help level military defence as well as economic productivity and export competitiveness.[1] Comprehensive security was not so much creative as pragmatic. It identified policy goals that fitted within existing domestic and international political frameworks, and it implicitly assumed that regional and global armed conflict would be managed by the United States. In this sense, it was premised on the US-Japan Security Treaty. As a result, comprehensive security differed from conventional Western concepts which centre on the state's ability to use force.[2] Insofar as Japan saw no need to go beyond local military sufficiency, not unexpectedly comprehensive security emphasized non-military efforts to sustain national security. It made the preservation of friendly relations with the United States and other countries a core policy objective, and it gave its own economic competitiveness the importance of a national security goal. It might be noted that success in the latter objective affects the former to a much greater degree in the post-Cold War era. Be that as it may, this concept continues to structure the foci and limits of contemporary Japanese policy thinking.

## The Impact of the Second Gulf War

Japan's initial response to Iraq's invasion of Kuwait in August 1990 was another example of its traditionally passive stance towards international security. It took Japan three weeks to formulate a positive commitment to help the United States and the Western allies restore the *status quo ante*, and there was disappointment when Japan announced only a monetary contribution of one billion dollars. A financial contribution had also been the Japanese response to the earlier threat to Gulf oil access during the 1987–88 Kuwaiti oil tanker reflagging crisis. At that time Japan gave only economic assistance to construct shipping navigation aids in the Persian Gulf. In August 1990, however, Japan misunderstood the new expectations it faced after the end of the Cold War.

The Iraqi invasion of Kuwait raised the issue of how regional conflicts could be controlled after bipolar superpower competition had ended. The strength of the Iraqi army and the desire by a fiscally overburdened United States for a 'peace dividend' meant that a military solution would be far too costly for the United States to impose by itself. Thus the crisis was the first test to see how the Western allies could address out-of-area regional conflicts jointly when their collective interests were at stake. The Japanese government under Prime Minister Toshiki Kaifu did not grasp the issue, or if it did, its response signalled that Japan expected the United States to continue to protect Japan's interests without Japanese participation. This aroused both heated international criticism of Japan and quiet arm-twisting by Washington, which sparked off a domestic debate over Japan's international security role. The debate was only sharpened by Kaifu's withdrawal in November 1990 of proposed legislation in the Diet (the Japanese parliament) that would have authorized a civilian unit staffed by SDF personnel to participate in UN Peacekeeping Operations (PKO). A storm of international criticism, and the danger of permanent damage to relations with the United States, ultimately extracted some $13 billion from Japan to defray the costs of Operation 'Desert Shield/Desert Storm', as well as the belated despatch of four small wooden minesweepers two months after the hostilities ended. But these measures earned Japan little credit because they risked no Japanese lives, nor were Japan's actions perceived to be spontaneous and voluntary.

Japan learned important lessons from this episode. The Japanese leadership and public recognized that Japan needed to participate directly in resolving international security issues. For the first time Japan's 1991 *Diplomatic Blue Book* called for going beyond 'cheque-book diplomacy'. Weaknesses in Japan's political leadership and crisis decision-making capacity were also identified, and reforms are now under domestic study and debate. Finally, Japan began to work for greater participation in existing international security decision-making structures, and towards the creation of new ones, especially in Asia. These lessons explain Japan's later effort to participate in UN collective security efforts. In June 1992 the Japanese Diet authorized the despatch of SDF forces to participate in UN-sponsored peacekeeping operations (PKO). Although the Ministry of Foreign Affairs (MFA), conservative Liberal Democratic Party (LDP) leaders, business leaders, as well as elements of the LDP's political opposition agreed that Japan needed to go beyond cheque-book diplomacy, they disagreed over how far Japan should go. From a legal standpoint, the Japanese government decided that SDF participation in PKO would not violate the Constitution. The reasoning behind this was that although Article 9 of the Constitution forbade the threat or use of force to settle disputes with other nations, this did not exclude the overseas dispatch of SDF forces *per se*. Further, PKO activity was not a constitutionally proscribed active threat or use of force. From a political standpoint the attraction of PKO to the left and centre was participation in international security efforts through the United Nations, and not at the behest of the United States, while it offered the right a mechanism for expanding the SDF's role. These views developed in the context of 60–70 per cent public approval ratings of measures to increase Japan's contributions to international security following the Gulf crisis.

The MFA's own motives for supporting PKO are worth mentioning. The United Nations promised to be a central actor in helping to wind down Cold War regional conflicts and controlling future regional conflicts. Yet Japan lacked a permanent seat on the Security Council – a lack of parity with its Western allies that was keenly felt during 'Desert Shield/Desert Storm'. To build a case for inclusion, the MFA wanted Japanese involvement in PKO to demonstrate Japan's participation in managing international security. It also wanted to participate in the United Nation's effort to resolve the Cambodian conflict which would help establish Japan's political leadership credentials in Asia. By the autumn of 1992 over 600 SDF logistics and engineering personnel were sent to participate in the Cambodian PKO mission that ended successfully in 1993 after a democratically elected Cambodian government was formed. Japan followed this up by sending SDF personnel to Mozambique for PKO. Despite the misgivings of some of its neighbours, Japanese participation in PKO marked the cautious start of an overseas Japanese military role in international peace and security activities.

## Present Military Force Posture and Missions

Japan's Defence Agency limits the missions of the SDF to local defence and sea-lane patrols extending 1,000 miles from Japan, but in the longer term there may be both external pressures and national capacities to increase patrol ranges. The SDF, though, has a few immediate problems. The current manpower level is under 250,000 and is likely to remain there so long as the SDF has low status and poor pay. In addition the growth in military spending is likely to slow slightly from its rate of 5 per cent in 1992, due to Japan's recession. On the other hand, Japanese military forces will acquire an impressive array of hardware under the current 1990–95 defence plan. The SDF already has 64 major surface combatants, 16 attack submarines, 100 long-range patrol aircraft, some 200 F-15 air superiority fighters, and a large anti-submarine warfare capability, all equipped with advanced weapon systems. By the end of the decade it intends to have in place in-flight refuelling capabilities, over-the-horizon radar, airborne AWACS systems, seaborne Aegis air defence systems, a new FSX surface attack fighter, and a missile defence system which is currently under development. There are also plans to acquire a small helicopter carrier in the near future, but there is no indication that fixed-wing aircraft carriers, bombers, or amphibious capabilities are being contemplated at the moment.

In assessing the threat environment which Japan faces the overall stance of the Japan Defence Agency's 1993 Defence White Paper was cautiously optimistic. It reported that international security was improving despite a trend toward territorial and ethnic conflicts. The report did single out North Korea's development of the recently tested Rodong-1 missile with an estimated range of 1,000–1,500 km, together with its suspected development of nuclear weapons, as potentially 'dangerous'. China and Russia were viewed as potential threats, but the report went on to favour increased security dialogues with China, Russia, South Korea and the Southeast Asian nations. With regard to multilateral security issues, it favoured continued participation in PKO and regional multilateral security fora, but it stated that a NATO-style multilateral organization for Asia would be inappropriate. In an interesting sideline, for the first time the report identified a business slump in Japan's defence industries as a security problem. This indicates a concern about the need to develop Japan's defence industrial base that first came to light when Japan decided to develop the FSX fighter in the mid-1980s. This could mean new weapons development programmes and possible pressure to remove the current ban on weapons exports as steps to sustain a growing defence industry.

In contrast to the low-key approach of the Defence White Paper, other assessments of the threat environment show greater concern. The International Institute for Strategic Studies' (IISS) *Military Balance 1993–1994* argued that a number of issues in East Asia could escalate to hostilities in the absence of regional security or arms control arrangements. In the *National Military Strategy of the United States* published in January 1992, General Colin Powell gave the following assessment of East Asia: 'Logic dictates that change is inevitable, but the transition period is likely to be fraught with great risk.' And Professor Seizaburo Sato of Keio University recently wrote: 'if the EC and the US continue to shift their attention towards internal affairs and Japan continues to hesitate in exercising greater world leadership, the possibility of collapse of the existing multilateral co-operative system cannot be lightly dismissed'.[3] Such assessments raise the question of whether Japan should prepare for these risks. To answer this question, the particular security issues that Japan confronts in East Asia need to be addressed.

## East Asian Security Issues

Japan presently defines its international role in terms of a continuing partnership with the United States and Europe, lending its economic strength to promote development, and supporting United Nations and other multilateral fora.[4] Nevertheless, there are specific issues and disputes that could force Japan to augment its regional and global military roles.

### The Russo-Japanese Islands Dispute

The subsidence of the Cold War has highlighted the disputed ownership of the Kurile Islands between the Russian coast and the Japanese homeland. The islands themselves are of marginal military and economic significance to either side, but they have become pawns in a zero-sum game of national pride and political prestige. Japan insists Russia must admit that all four islands are Japanese before it will give substantial economic assistance to the former Soviet Union (FSU). Although there is some willingness to reach an accommodation on the part of Russian academics such as Konstantin Sarkisov, the problem is that Russian nationalists prevent President Yeltsin from meeting Japan's conditions.[5]

The legal principles behind a just resolution of this matter are unclear since both sides' claims have merit. The Russo-Japanese commercial treaty of 1855 recognized the four islands to be Japanese, and its sovereignty over these islands was not in dispute until Japan was defeated in the Second World War. On the basis of a secret agreement signed by Stalin, Roosevelt and Churchill on 11 February 1945, the Soviet Union was promised the entire Kurile Islands archipelago in return for entering the war against Japan. The Soviet Union occupied the four islands in question following Japan's surrender, but only the northern two were part of the Kurile Islands chain. The 1951 San Francisco

Peace Treaty did not recognize Japan's sovereignty over the disputed islands, but the Soviets were not among the signatories. In 1956 the Soviets offered to return the southern two islands in return for a peace treaty, but the United States intervened to prevent Japan from accepting. In 1960, however, the Soviets withdrew this offer owing to the renewal of the US-Japan Security Treaty. During his October 1993 visit to Tokyo, Boris Yeltsin did agree to discuss the dispute, but the problem was that Japan wanted Yeltsin to pay a territorial and political price that was beyond his capacity to deliver.

The dangers of this impasse are both direct and indirect. The direct danger is a local military confrontation at some point in the future with consequences which could be out of all proportion to the issue at stake. The indirect danger to international security is that this creates a difference of opinion between Japan and the West over the need to help stabilize the FSU – a matter of vital concern to Western Europe. Thus, Japanese indifference to whether or not there is stability in the FSU may invite European indifference over Japan's security interests in East Asia.

### The Threat Posed by the Break-up of the Soviet Union

The unintended consequences of the break-up of the Soviet Union present Japan with the problem of weapons proliferation. The need for hard currency to finance short term imports spurs Russian sales of advanced conventional weapons to East Asian states. Moreover, the general breakdown of economic and social order facilitates secret or black market sales of advanced missile technologies, nuclear devices, nuclear materials and transfers of production technology. Since Prime Minister Nakasone's insertion of Japan's security interests into the West's negotiating strategy on INF in 1983, Japan has been concerned about the impact of the European theatre on Asian security. The linkage of European and Asian interests is heightened by the situation in the FSU. A failure by the United States to persuade the three nuclear armed republics outside of Russia to give up their nuclear weapons could affect the indefinite extension of the nuclear Non-Proliferation Treaty (NPT) in 1995. As one Japanese arms control expert delicately put it: 'If Ukraine, Belarus, and Kazakhstan join [the NPT] as nuclear weapons states . . . the number of nuclear weapons states will jump from five to eight instantly, provoking an outcry from non-nuclear weapons states.'[6]

Moreover, the loss of European and Central Asian buffer zones, and European arms control through the Conventional Forces in Europe (CFE) process impacts on East Asia to the extent that Russian naval, air and ground forces have been transferred east of the Urals to Siberian or Far Eastern military districts. The movement of Baltic and Black Sea naval units to the Far East is one conspicuous example of how a re-deployment of forces meant to improve security in Europe could inadvertently affect Asian security. Finally, the implementation of the START agreements and the resultant elimination of tactical nuclear devices and the destruction of thousands of larger nuclear bombs and warheads need to be adequately financed and monitored to prevent a large scale diversion of weapons and materials on to the black market. Japan is willing to help Russia dismantle missiles and nuclear warheads, but there is some Japanese doubt that targets can be met and illegal pro-liferation prevented.

*The Korean Peninsula*

There are two analytically distinct issues here which are joined by cir-cumstance. The first is Korean reunification and the second is nuclear proliferation. Although both North Korea and South Korea wish for peaceful reunification, the risk of conflict between the two Koreas per-sists. The South's strategy is slowly to 'absorb' the North through widening North–South exchanges in political, cultural and economic areas. If this strategy fails and conflict on the peninsula should occur, Japan would probably have to absorb refugees and give considerable economic assistance to ensure that the South prevailed. Whether reuni-fication occurred quickly through conflict, or slowly through absorption, Japan would still face the long-term problem of a heavily armed, reuni-fied Korean nation that has historic as well as current economic grievances to settle with Japan. And then there is the nuclear issue. Owing to its increasingly dire economic circumstances and international isolation, North Korea has little ability to resist the South Korean absorption strategy. This is the context in which the North has purport-edly been pursuing a nuclear option. North Korea has not allowed international inspection of all suspected nuclear facilities as provided for under the Non-Proliferation Treaty (NPT) which it signed in 1985. The refusal to allow inspections may hide a genuine weapons programme, or it may only be a bluff used as a bargaining chip to break its international isolation and resist the South's absorption strategy. It has already suc-ceeded in using the nuclear inspection issue to open official bilateral talks with the United States.

Japan moved to penetrate the diplomatic processes that were dis-mantling the Cold War in the Korean peninsula when LDP leader Shin Kanemaru visited North Korea in September 1990. Japan used the pros-pect of large-scale economic assistance in an effort to gain a role in

regional peace diplomacy. While it has not succeeded in gaining a leading role there, Japan has been satisfied to be an informed participant in
the Korean question.[7] The North's recent nuclear gambit, however,
changes the Korean question into something much more serious for
Japan. The North has tested a modified nuclear-capable Scud missile
that can strike the South and most of western Japan. If South Korea or
Japan believes the North has nuclear warheads, then one or the other
may feel compelled to develop a nuclear deterrent capability.

*The South China Sea and Asia's Conventional Weapons Build-up*

In the South China Sea, conflicting territorial claims over the Paracel
and Spratly Islands involve China, Taiwan, the Philippines, Malaysia,
Vietnam and Brunei. China is the focus of attention because it claims
both island groups and because it used force to remove Vietnamese
deployments on disputed islands in the Spratly's chain in March 1988.
This created a degree of tension, and other claimants became eager to
stake out their possessions.[8] To relieve tension and suspicion of China,
Chinese premier Li Peng pledged to defer the issue of sovereignty and
offered peaceful joint development of disputed territories in the South
China Sea during a visit to Singapore on 13 August 1990. Indonesia subsequently sponsored informal talks among the claimants in 1991 that
resulted in an agreement to avoid unilateral actions in disputed areas
and to settle issues peacefully. This conciliatory direction was reversed
in February 1992 when China passed a law on territorial waters and adja-
cent areas that renewed 'irreproachable' claims over the Paracel and
Spratly Islands, as well as a dormant claim over the Japanese-
administered Senkaku Islands. The law gave the Chinese military the
right to remove by force any incursion in these territories.[9] In May 1992
China leased an undersea section to a US oil exploration firm in an area
that is geographically and bathymetrically separate from the Spratly
Islands and on Vietnam's continental shelf.[10] Chinese officials pledged
to use force if necessary to protect the firm's personnel.[11]

Perhaps not coincidentally, this new Chinese assertiveness came just
after the United States announced its withdrawal from the Philippines.
China's claims to the Paracel and Spratly Islands would give it access to
fisheries and valuable undersea petroleum resources, not to mention a
stranglehold over vital East Asian sea lanes. China has the ability to
mount amphibious operations as far south as East Malaysia. Recently
acquired SU-27 combat planes operating from Hainan Island could support amphibious operations in the Spratlys, and with recently obtained
air-to-air refuelling technology and an air base currently under construction in the Paracels, air support could be extended to cover all of
China's claims.[12]

In the event of a dispute in the South China Sea, US intervention would be guaranteed neither by the United Nations (where China could exercise a veto in the Security Council), nor by a regional security regime (there is none). There are bilateral ties with Japan and the Philippines that might serve as a basis for US intervention, but there is scope for a flexible interpretation of US obligations in the case of small disputed territories. As a practical matter, Japan could exercise a veto since intervening US forces would be based there, and US reluctance to become involved with direct Japanese participation would be understandable. The question of the US commitment to Asian stability is raised in a parallel fashion by the Chinese threat of the use of force to 'recover' Taiwan. There are a number of scenarios under which China is expected by Taiwanese authorities to use force, but the most likely is any declaration of sovereign independence from China.[13] The United States views this matter as something the Chinese people should settle peacefully, but it has recently sold F-16s to Taiwan to help maintain a military balance in the Taiwan Straits. But what the United States would do in the event of hostilities is unclear. Here again, the role of Japan could be critical.

The end of a militarily predominant United States willing to intervene unilaterally to maintain stability is an important background factor behind the build-up of conventional forces in the region.[14] According to the Stockholm International Peace Research Institute, Asia's share of global arms imports increased from one-quarter in the mid-1980s to one-third at the start of the 1990s.[15] Regional arms purchases could be explained by factors such as normal modernization schedules, a reorientation of military missions from internal to external security, the availability of advanced weapons at bargain prices, the rapidly growing wealth of the East Asian states, and the power of military elites in setting budget priorities. But the perception of an emerging power vacuum in Asia and uncertainty over the long-term intentions of key actors threatens to spark off arms races.

Although mainstream policy-makers in Japan have discounted China as a threat due to its limited economic capabilities and troubled domestic politics, there has been growing suspicion of China's intentions. Japan had hoped to cement relations with China by being helpful and conciliatory towards it when the West imposed sanctions after the Tiananmen incident in 1989. But since then China has increased its military budget by 50 per cent, challenged Japan's claim to the Senkaku Islands, and raised questions about the security of Japan's vital sea lanes through the South China Sea. This has led respected strategists such as Hisahiko Okazaki to lay most of the blame for Asia's arms build-up on China and to worry about China's 'unpredictability'.[16]

## Japan's Regional Security Strategy

From the Japanese perspective, the two most important stabilizing factors in East Asia today are the US presence and rapid economic
development. These points can be gleaned from Prime Minister Miyazawa's policy speech in January 1993. But looking to the future, this same
speech made clear that a more collective Asian approach to security was
needed to reinforce these factors. On both counts Japan expects to
make a significant contribution while giving itself a central role in
regional security discussions. To support a broader Japanese security
role in the region, there are basic issues of trust and acceptance that
must be addressed. First, in an attempt to resolve bitterness in the
region towards Japan for its colonialist and wartime behaviour both the
Japanese prime minister and the new Emperor have voiced regrets to
members of the Association of Southeast Asian Nations (ASEAN), the
Korean people and China during official trips to these countries in
1990–93. A coming to terms with this wartime legacy is necessary before
Japan can expand its regional security role. Prime Minister Hosokawa's
admission of Japanese wrongdoing in the Second World War was a step
in the right direction, but there are now difficult compensation issues
that will have to be resolved.

Secondly, a rising standard of living supports the political stability of
many East Asian regimes, and the possibility of growth orients Asian
states towards positive-sum international economic co-operation instead
of negative-sum military conflict. Japan has moved aggressively to support this, as well as to profit from Asian economic dynamism, through
its bilateral trade, investment and ODA activity. To provide policy co-
ordination Japan has worked to strengthen formal and informal institutions such as the Asian Development Bank, the Asia-Pacific
Economic Co-operation (APEC) conference, and the Pacific Economic
Co-operation Conference (PECC). Japan has also moved to create
Japan-ASEAN co-operative frameworks such as the Japan-Asean Development Fund and a variety of other bilateral consultative
mechanisms. These economic mechanisms address Japan's security interests indirectly, but there are suggestions by the Japanese that
APEC's agenda be amended to raise security matters.[17]

Thirdly, Japan is cultivating the role of an honest broker in region
peace and security issues.[18] Japan hosted a meeting of the Cambodian
factions in Tokyo in May 1990, and had a Japanese UN official named as
head of the United Nations Transitional Authority in Cambodia (UN-
TAC). It also became chair of an international committee formed to
promote the reconstruction of Indo-China after resolution of the Cambodian conflict and has promised to help finance future economic

co-operation between ASEAN and Indo-China. In order to permit greater transparency and cohesion, Japan also floated the idea of turning the ASEAN Post-Ministerial Conference (PMC) into a forum for regional security discussions in 1991, an idea that was initially met with suspicion but approved by the ASEAN Summit in January 1992. Japan expects the PMC to help manage the South China Sea questions and to formulate a collective approach to regional security in which Japan can play a central role. With these arms control and confidence-building measures, economic co-operation and peace-brokering contributions Japan is starting to build a regional security role, especially in Southeast Asia.[19] This kind of 'soft' security role could lead to a legitimate and sustainable SDF presence in the South China Sea based on multilateral arrangements, without incurring hard and fast obligations that could raise difficult Constitutional questions or elicit Chinese hostility.

Japan is concerned about nuclear proliferation arising from the situation on the Korean Peninsula and the FSU, and that probably explains growing sentiment in the government and conservative elements to preserve a nuclear option for Japan.[20] Japan was unwilling to agree to the unconditional and indefinite extension of the NPT in 1995 during the 1993 G-7 Summit in Tokyo. The general position of the Miyazawa government is that Japan should sign the NPT in 1995 only if the nuclear states pledge to disarm at a certain future date.[21] Following the summit, a Japanese MFA official confirmed at a 23 July press conference that the government had not decided on indefinite extention of the NPT. At about this time Foreign Minister Kabun Muto assured the ASEAN PMC that Japan would sign the NPT, but afterwards he said to Japanese reporters: 'if it comes to the crunch, possessing the will to build nuclear weapons is important'.[22] The new prime minister, Morihiro Hosokawa, announced shortly after taking office in August 1993 that he supported signing the unconditional and indefinite extention of the NPT, but three of his cabinet ministers who are not of his party favour conditional extension.

A nuclear option for Japan is not out of the question. From a legal standpoint, if nuclear weapons are defined as a defensive deterrent, they could be consistent with Article 9. From a political standpoint, the collapse of the left and the new moderate-conservative centre of gravity in Japanese politics – coupled with the threat of a nuclear-armed Korea – makes this legal interpretation sustainable. The technical issues are not difficult for Japan. Japan imported 1.7 tons of weapons grade plutonium from France in late 1992 and has additional shipments of this size to schedule.[23] It has the right to purchase and import the material until its own reprocessing facility of Rokkashò is completed. In terms of delivery systems, the new Japanese H-2 rocket will be comparable to advanced US ICBMs in everything but guidance technologies. The strategic doctrine for Japanese nuclear weapons would be limited by two factors: its vulnerability to counter-value strikes and the adverse effects of nuclear weapons possession on Japan's economic relations with its neighbours. The most feasible accommodation of these factors would be a secure second strike capability with an Israeli or South African style posture of denial and ambiguity. In pursuing this line Japan could ask the West for the same consideration it has given to these other countries' nuclear efforts.

### Waning American leadership and US-Japan Relations

While it is evident that Japan faces serious regional security issues, in the final analysis the health of the US-Japan relationship may be the strongest factor determining the overall direction of Japanese security policy. Without a sound bilateral security relationship the foundations of Japanese security policy will have to be rebuilt. The phased drawdown of US forces in the region, called the East Asian Strategy Initiative, first announced in April 1990, has long-term implications. While the United States has been careful to emphasize that its unplanned withdrawal from the Philippines and a small drawdown of forces in Korea and Japan are not signs of a reduced commitment, few states in the region are fully convinced by this.[24] What they see are: US military cutbacks; a growing US preoccupation with domestic issues; persistent US fears of getting into 'another Vietnam', failures to deal effectively with Bosnia, Somalia, and smaller problems such as Haiti; and increasing friction with Asian countries over trade and human rights. All this does not augur well for continued US sponsorship of Asian security. Moreover, there is a growing sentiment in the United States which opposes continued interventionism. The expressions of this sentiment in policy recommendations for East Asia, with which the United States has chronically imbalanced economic relations, can be harsh: 'there is no need for the US to be policeman for the region, self-appointed or elected by default. Asian-Pacific dynamics should be unleashed to be dealt with by regional players.'[25]

Others, with more cautious instincts, foresee an end to US forward basing and the US-Japan Security Treaty after Korea is reunified and China is on a stable reform path.[26] In any case, it is conceivable that the United States could opt for the role of a less engaged regional balancer that need not commit itself to Japan.[27] This current in American strategic thinking casts doubt on the future of the US-Japan security relationship.

As in the United States, so in Japan there are signs of longer term doubt over whether the present strategy will remain adequate. Yukio Okamoto calls for rearmament and preparation for an independent security policy because emotions are nearing the breaking point in US-Japan relations.[28] Seizaburo Sato asserts: 'It seems almost impossible in the long run to limit Japan's military role to host-nation support in coping with regional conflicts . . . it will become necessary to revise the present official interpretation of the Constitution which makes it unconstitutional to exercise the right to collective self-defense.'[29] Commenting on the open debate over long-range security options, another Japanese analyst worries:

> If Japan does not trust the US to maintain its military commitment, or if Japan is to consider the necessity of a multilateral security system . . . Japan should carry out such a project within its government ranks, or through the use of a think tank so as not to attract attention.[30]

Nevertheless, the security establishments in Japan and the United States view continued close co-ordination under the US-Japan Security Treaty as vital to their respective interests and strategic postures. The Pentagon and State Department still badly want the forward deployment of US forces in Asia.[31] For its part, the Japanese government simply does not have an international security role outside of the Security Treaty framework, and leaving it now would lead only to international isolation. A recent RAND study notes that the strongest argument sustaining bilateral security relations today is 'the difficulty of envisioning a plausible alternative.'[32]

While this ensures no change in basic policy in the short term, both sides are now starting to think about plausible alternatives, because the economic and political relations underwriting the security relationship are troubled. The end of the Soviet threat, rapid Japanese penetration of the US economy in the 1980s, Japan's huge bilateral trade surplus and continuing difficulties in bilateral trade negotiations have widened the range of US domestic actors and their Japanese counterparts interested in the bilateral relationship. No longer do a handful of political and military experts on both sides manage relations. The entry of manufacturers, agricultural producers, labour interests, trade negotiators, politicians and intellectuals into debates over bilateral economic ties has restructured the debate over US-Japan relations in ways that dilute the influence of the security establishments of both countries. The impact of this new situation on public opinion by the summer of 1993 had been dramatic. A joint survey conducted by Yomiuri Shimbun and

Gallup found that only 8 per cent of US respondents thought Japan was a trustworthy country, and another joint poll conducted by *The New York Times*, CBS News and the Tokyo Broadcasting System showed that 64 per cent of Japanese thought bilateral relations were 'unfriendly'. Only 4 per cent of Japanese responents thought relations would improve. The Japanese government's reaction to chronic US criticism of Japanese policies has been pragmatic. During his visit to Washington in July, 1992 Prime Minister Kiichi Miyazawa committed Japan to pay 70 per cent of the non-salary cost of supporting US forces in Japan by 1995. This move ensured that the Pentagon and State Department could be relied upon to offset criticisms of Japan. At the same time, however, Japan is increasing its reliance on a wider range of mechanisms to reduce its overdependence on an increasingly fragile bilateral security relationship.

Aside from building up the SDF, Japan now says it is willing to use its economic power unilaterally to influence the security policies of other states. In April 1991 Prime Minister Kaifu announced the so-called 'four ODA principles' that would condition Japan's provision of ODA according to whether recipients develop, manufacture or transfer weapons of mass destruction, or respect democracy and human rights. Although the four principles seem to be more rhetorical than substantive, especially with regard to China, they do signal a new assertiveness in security affairs. Japan also views multilateral security fora as a means to assume greater international security responsibilities and participation.[33] At the regional level, Japan wishes to use multilateral fora such as the Asia-Pacific Economic Co-operation (APEC) conference, the ASEAN Post Ministerial Conference, and the newly established ASEAN Regional Forum to move itself and the United States into multilateral management of Asian regional security. Japan also became noticeably more interested in European security issues in 1992 when it hosted a high-level Japan-NATO seminar and joined the Conference on Security and Co-operation in Europe (CSCE) as an observer. This grew out of recognition that European security negotiations are more closely linked to Asian security after the Cold War.[34]

At the global level, Japan has let it be known that it wants to use the G-7 summit as a forum to discuss global security issues. This would allow Japan to co-ordinate policies with the main NATO countries, which could be helpful both in negotiating burden-sharing agreements as well as in managing global arms control. In this latter area Japan has become more activist. Japan chaired a meeting of the Missile Technology Control Regime (MTCR) in Tokyo, hosted a UN conference on arms control in Kyoto, and advocated a UN registry to record conventional weapons transfers in 1992. Japan's approach to the United

Nations is to pursue a permanent seat on the Security Council. To establish its credentials Japan points out that it contributes more money to the United Nations than do Britain, France and China combined, and that Japan has participated in PKO in Cambodia and Mozambique. There is also the prospect that Japan will use the UN to expand the role of the SDF. Peacemaking operations (PMO), where troops are introduced to facilitate negotiation of cease-fire agreements, could be permitted since, as in the case of PKO, the SDF would not be sent abroad with the intent to use force. There is also support in Japan for including non-combat SDF troops in UN peace enforcement operations (PEO).[35] This would allow the SDF to support a UN-sanctioned use of force to respond to unlawful aggression, but it would not require constitutional revision since the SDF would be in a non-combat role. Japan's new activism in regional and global security regimes is motivated, in large part, by a recognition that it needs to rely on a wider range of vehicles than the US-Japan Security Treaty to promote its security interests.

**Domestic Factors**

Recent domestic political developments will have a significant bearing on Japanese security policy. The electoral defeat of the LDP by conservatives, moderates and leftists, who have formed a new coalition government led by Morihiro Hosokawa, reflects an important structural change in Japanese politics. The key factors are the end of the Cold War and a 'rich Japan – poor Japanese' syndrome. The collapse of communism discredited the radical Japanese left and removed the external threat that supported the anti-communist LDP's electoral success. The removal of fear and Japan's superior economic performance freed the Japanese from psychological dependence on the United States. This resulted in such nationalist expressions of pent-up resentment against the United States as Shintaro Ishihara's 1990 bestseller, *A Japan That Can Say 'No'*. Domestically a desperate desire to enjoy better lifestyles and more leisure turned the LDP's traditional emphasis on hard work and GNP growth from an asset into a liability. The fall of the LDP in July 1993 opens Japan to a new direction. The debate over this direction will revolve around three questions: how to deliver a better quality of life for average Japanese; how to make politicians and bureaucrats more accountable to the people; and how to redefine Japan's international role.

Answers to these questions will be offered by a reorganized political spectrum that will offer a wider range of choices. With the collapse of the socialists and the weakening of the LDP on the one hand, and the emergence of more conservative and centrist parties on the other, Japanese society is constructing a reorganized and more differentiated party system that is likely to be more competitive than was the case during the 1955–93 period. The Hosokawa ruling coalition is not a permanent arrangement, but neither is the wounded LDP after the defection of elements led by Ichiro Ozawa and Tsutomu Hata. Further splits and mergers are inevitable. A stable party configuration will emerge only by the end of the decade. In the interim Japan's international role will come to have a central role in electoral politics. There is already broad agreement inside Japan that it should participate directly in international security efforts. The real debate is over modalities and the need to revise Article 9 of the Constitution.[36] As parties with different positions on these issues compete for power, Japanese policy will become more dynamic. One should bear in mind that Japan's conservatives have lived with self-imposed military limitations out of pragmatic calculations of national interest, not pacifism. As Shigeru Yoshida, the architect of mainstream post-war conservative foreign policy stated regarding military rearmament: 'The day will come naturally when our livelihood recovers. It may sound devious, but let the Americans handle [our security] until then.'[37]

It may be useful here to indicate how domestic politics could be restructured to facilitate policy change. Nationalists and domestically-oriented industrial and agricultural interests could gravitate towards policies that ranged from a non-provocative conventional defence posture, within a loose multilateral framework, to those of a fully rearmed Gaullist posture. Conventional internationalists, multinational industrial and financial interests, and pacifists would resist any revision of Article 9 and support the continuation of present policies. This scenario illustrates the dynamic of, and agenda for, policy change that could grow out of the continuing reorganization of Japanese politics. There are already signs that Japan's international role will be a central issue in domestic debates. While still a member of the LDP, Ichiro Ozawa organized a group of members of the Japanese parliament, the Diet, to study the issue of revising Article 9. He complained, however, that despite the fact that Japan faced serious long-term international threats, within the LDP 'the energy to take up reform now to deal with long-term issues is nowhere to be seen', and that his views were in the minority.[38] This frustration partly explains why he left the LDP to form a younger conservative opposition to the LDP. His party, Shinseito (Renaissance Party), formed a governing coalition with leftist and moderate parties under Hosokawa, but Ozawa is credited with organizing the government. To exploit differences of opinion inside the coalition and embarrass Ozawa, the LDP announced in October 1993 that it would not favour constitutional revision or an SDF role that went beyond PKO. Thus, the partisan debate over Japan's security policy may have begun. How this debate will evolve is impossible to foresee. One can predict, however, that security crises that occur while Japan struggles with its international role could have a great impact on Japanese domestic politics and foreign policy.

**Conclusion**

It is rather easy to sum up present Japanese security policy. Japan seeks to: retain a security relationship with the United States; promote dynamic economic growth in Asia; participate more actively in expanding global, regional and bilateral security discussions; and pursue these goals primarily through non-military means. The problem is that these policies may not be sufficient to preserve Japan's security interests regarding such problems as nuclear proliferation in Korea and the FSU, threats to its vital sea lanes from China or other regional actors, or waning US interest in Asia. This makes it difficult to predict where Japan will be by the end of the decade. Nevertheless, it is possible to point to certain issues and trends.

Japan's new assertiveness is beginning to reveal differences with Western sentiment and action in security-related areas that should be addressed. Japan is markedly less supportive of Russian President Yeltsin than is the United States or Western Europe; it is more supportive of China than are the United States and Europe; it wishes to change permanent seating arrangements on the UN Security Council that currently favour the United States and Western Europe; it wishes to make the United Nations more central to managing international security than does the United States; it places a far higher value on its non-military contributions to international security than does the West; and it refuses to acknowledge the political linkage between its trade and security policies. These are issues that will require effective two-way communication if they are to be managed effectively.

Another new theme is that Japan seeks to upgrade its military contributions to international security through multilateral mechanisms. The overseas deployment of the SDF in the post-'Desert Storm' minesweeping operation and PKO missions are important precedents that have expanded the role of the SDF. Japan's apologies for wartime behaviour, its ODA activities and the active cultivation of ASEAN-sponsored regional security dialogues prepare the way for SDF participation in regional security co-operation in areas such as information exchanges, maritime surveillance, joint training exercises and perhaps maritime police functions. Japan can make valuable contributions in these areas, but these aspects themselves are of only marginal significance to Japan's most basic security needs.

As for whether Japan will abandon its 'comprehensive security' policy framework and employ a kind of 'breakout strategy' from its self-imposed limitations, one can say that it is simply not politically or otherwise feasible in the next few years. Domestic and international opinion are unprepared for such a move, and Japan's political institutions are not configured at present to engineer such a change. But if we expand the time horizon to the end of the decade and beyond, these factors could change. Japan already wants to develop and produce its own advanced weaponry, and it is developing its own intelligence system.[39] Given the fluid and unpredictable state of international and Japanese domestic politics, it is hard to discount anything. The likely key determinants of Japanese policy toward the end of the decade will be the issues of nuclear proliferation, the presence of active threats to Japan's territory or vital sea-lanes, and the health of US-Japan relations.

## NOTES

1. Seisaku Kenkyûkai, Sôgô Anzen Hoshô Kenkyûkai Gurûpu, *Sôgô Anzen Hoshô Kenkyûkai Gurûpu Hôkokusho* [Report of the Research Group on Comprehensive Security] (Tokyo: Naikaku Kanbô, Naikaku Shingishitsu Bunshitsu, 2 July 1980), pp.23–4.
2. Stephen Walt, 'The Renaissance of Security Studies', *International Studies Quarterly*, Vol.35, No.2 (1991), pp.211–29.
3. Seizaburo Sato, 'Japanese Perceptions of the New Security Situation', in Trevor Taylor (ed.), *The Collapse of the Soviet Empire: Managing the Regional Fallout* (London: Royal Institute of International Affairs, 1992), pp.171–89.
4. Takakazu Kuriyama, *New Directions for Japanese Foreign Policy in the Changing World of the 1990s* (Tokyo: Ministry of Foreign Affairs, May 1990).
5. Graham Allison, Hiroshi Kimura and Konstantin Sarkisov, *Beyond Cold War to Trilateral Cooperation in the Asia-Pacific Region: Scenarios for New Relationships Between Japan, Russia, and the United States* (Cambridge, MA: Strengthening Democratic Institutions Project, Harvard University, 1992).
6. Ryukichi Imai, 'Disarmament and Arms Control in the Post-Cold War World', in Taylor (ed.), op cit., p.152.
7. David Arase, 'Japanese Policy toward the Two Koreas in a Changing Security Environment', in Robert H. Puckett (ed.), *The United States and Northeast Asia* (Chicago: Nelson-Hall, 1993), pp.179–203.
8. Chang Pao-Min, 'A New Scramble for the South China Sea Islands', *Contemporary Southeast Asia*, Vol.12, No.1 (June 1990), pp.20–39.
9. *FBIS Daily Report-China*, 'New Law Claims Sovereignty over Spratly Islands', 27 Feb. 1992, p.15.
10. Mark J. Valencia, 'The South China Sea: Potential Conflict and Cooperation', in

Rohana Mahmood and Rustam A. Sani (eds.), *Confidence Building and Conflict Reduction in the Pacific* (Kuala Lumpur: Institute for Strategic and International Studies, 1993), pp.55–69.
11. Nicholas D. Kristoff, 'China Signs US Oil Deal for Disputed Waters', *New York Times*, 18 June 1992, A8.
12. Paul H.B. Godwin, 'China's Asia Policy', in Sheldon W. Simon (ed.), *East Asian Security in the Post-Cold War Era* (Armonk, NY: M.E. Sharpe, 1993), p.135; see also Robert S. Wood, 'Naval Power in the Pacific in the Post-Cold War Era', in Robert H. Puckett (ed.), *The United States and Northeast Asia* (Chicago: Nelson-Hall, 1993), p.107.
13. *FBIS Daily Report–China*, 'Defense Paper Views Possibility of PRC Attack', 27 Feb. 1992, p.63.
14. Derek Da Cunha, 'Major Asian Powers and the Development of the Singaporean and Malaysian Armed Forces', *Contemporary Southeast Asia*, Vol.13, No.1 (June 1991).
15. *SIPRI Yearbook 1993: World Armaments and Disarmament* (New York: Oxford University Press, 1993), p.476.
16. Hisahiko Okazaki, 'Chugoku no gunkaku senryaku' ('China's Military Build-Up Strategy'), *Yomiuri Shimbun*, 8 Feb. 1993, p.1.
17. Satoshi Morimoto, 'Security in East Asia: Implications for Japan', *NRI Quarterly* (Spring 1993), pp.82–95.
18. David Arase, 'Japan in Post-Cold War Asia', in Chandran Jeshurun (ed.), *China, India, Japan and the Security of Southeast Asia* (Singapore: Institute of Southeast Asian Studies, 1993), pp.70–92.
19. Itaru Umezu, 'The Future Role of Japan in the Asia-Pacific', in Mahmood and Sani (eds.), op. cit., pp.79–86.
20. Selig S. Harrison, 'A Yen for the Bomb? Nervous Japan Rethinks the Nuclear Option', *Washington Post*, 31 Oct. 1993, C1.
21. Kumao Kaneko, 'A Japanese Perspective on Nuclear Non-Proliferation Treaty in Post-Cold War Era: Proposals for "Conditional" NPT Extension and International Plutonium Control', a paper presented to the *International Workshop: Nuclear Disarmament and Non-Proliferation: Issues for International Action*, Tokyo, 15–16 March 1993.
22. 'Official Says Japan Will Need Nuclear Arms if N. Korea Threatens', *Los Angeles Times*, 29 July 1993, p.A4.
23. 'Nuclear Watchdog for Asia Mulled', *Japan Times*, 14 Sept. 1993, p.3. See also *International Trade Reporter*, 14 July 1993, p.1156.
24. Office of International Security Affairs, Department of Defense, *A Strategic Framework for the Asian Pacific Rim* (Washington, DC: Jan. 1992).
25. Edward A. Olsen, 'A New American Strategy for Asia', *Asian Survey*, Vol.31, No.12 (Dec. 1991), pp.1139–54.
26. John E. Endicott, 'Can the US-Japanese Security Partnership Continue into the 21st Century?', in Dora Alves (ed.), *Change, Interdependence and Security in the Pacific Basin* (Washington, DC: National Defense University Press, 1991), pp.103–13.
27. Chalmers Johnson, 'Rethinking Asia', *The National Interest*, Vol.32 (Summer 1993), pp.20–8; Richard J. Ellings and Edward A. Olsen, 'A New Pacific Profile', *Foreign Policy*, Vol.89 (Winter 1992–93), pp.116–36.
28. Yukio Okamoto, 'Ningen kankei toshite no nichi-Bei kankei' (US-Japan Relations as a Human Relationship), *Chuo Koron*, Vol.106, No.7 (1991), pp.142–55.
29. Sato, op. cit., pp.185–86.
30. Yasushi Tomiyama, 'Doubts about Asian Security Plan Advocated by Prime Minister Miyazawa', *Chuo Koron* (Nov. 1992), p.72, quoted in Francis Fukuyama and Kongdan Oh, *The US-Japan Security Relationship after the Cold War* (Santa Monica, CA: RAND, 1993), p.46.
31. Dick Cheney, *Defense Strategy for the 1990s: The Regional Defense Strategy* (Washington, DC: Department of Defense, Jan. 1993).

32. Fukuyama and Oh, op. cit., p.46.
33. The Japanese Committee for a Post-Cold War Global System, Kazuo Takahashi (ed.), *Reconstruction of a New Global Order – Beyond Crisis Management: The Report to the Global Commission for a Post-Cold War System* (Tokyo: Sasakawa Peace Foundation, 1992).
34. Satoshi Morimoto, 'The Security Implication of Changes in the Former Soviet Union for Asia and Japan', in Taylor (ed.), pp.139–45.
35. The Japan Forum on International Relations, *The Strengthening of the UN Peace Function and Japan's Role* (Tokyo: The Japan Forum on International Relations, Oct. 1992).
36. Arase, 'Japan in post-Cold War Asia'.
37. Kenneth B. Pyle, *The Japanese Question: Power and Purpose in a New Era* (Washington, DC: AEI Press, 1992), p.26.
38. Ichiro Ozawa, 'Kokusai shakai ni okeru nihon no yakuwari ni tsuite' ('On Japan's Role in International Society'), in Research Bureau, Yomiuri Shimbun (ed.), *Kempo o kangaeru: kokusai kyocho jidai to kempo dai-kyu jo* [Thoughts on the Constitution: The Era of International Co-operation and Article Nine of the Constitution] (Tokyo: Yomiuri Shimbunsha, 1993), p.55.
39. David E. Sanger, 'Tired of Relying on US, Japan Seeks to Expand its Own Intelligence Efforts', *New York Times*, 1 Jan. 1992, A6.

# Security Co-operation in Southeast Asia: An Evolving Process

## MARK G. ROLLS

In biological terms evolution is 'widely regarded as a progressive force thrusting inexorably towards . . . improvement', although there are the qualifications that it is not automatically 'progressive' and that the time-scale can be very considerable.[1] These qualifications are pertinent in terms of a discussion of security co-operation as an evolving process. In terms of security co-operation between states, evolution as a progressive force can be identified with the establishment of a security 'regime' (in which states would seek to restrain their behaviour in order to lessen the effects of the 'security dilemma') and, ultimately, of a security 'community' (where states would obviate the security dilemma through a process of integration leading to a reliance on 'peaceful change').[2] Thus security co-operation should, perhaps, be seen more in terms of the creation of a sustainable regional order and of conflict resolution than in military co-operation. In Southeast Asia, even the members of ASEAN,[3] do not currently form more than a limited security regime, let alone a community. Despite the Association displaying some aspects of community (for example, its members' existing and growing economic ties), the fact that certain members still 'target each other with their armed forces' means that ASEAN fails the 'defining test' of the existence of a security community.[4] This is particularly evident in the case of Malaysia and Singapore.[5] There are simultaneously, however, elements of bilateral and trilateral military co-operation between various members.

Irrespective of ASEAN's classification as a security grouping, the Association represents the best medium through which to consider the evolving process of security co-operation in Southeast Asia. ASEAN not only demonstrates those aspects of co-operation which have occurred, but it also lies at the centre of current efforts to promote regional security co-operation including its extension beyond Southeast Asia to encompass the wider Asia-Pacific region. Moreover, it also illustrates some of the main obstacles to, and debates concerning, such efforts. In the main, this article will focus on the evolution of attempts to further regional security co-operation which have matched the changing

strategic environment in the post-Cold War era. However, it is important to understand that some of the underlying thinking behind current
efforts, especially in terms of ASEAN's approaches, is more long-
standing, and also that the regional strategic environment has, arguably,
been undergoing gradual change for many years now. This environment, Tim Huxley contends, has been 'evolving in the direction of
greater multi-polarity and uncertainty more or less continuously for the
last two and a half decades'.[6]

## The Origins and Directions of ASEAN Security Thinking

The 1967 Bangkok Declaration, ASEAN's founding document, stressed
that the Association's purpose was the promotion of economic, social
and cultural relations among its members. But the underlying political
purpose of ASEAN was to create an environment in which each state's
survival could be ensured through the fostering of regional stability and
the limitation of competition between them. These goals were of para-
mount importance because the then prevailing indigenous insurgencies
(primarily communist ones) threatened to undermine not only the states
themselves but also regional stability, with the possible consequence
that there would be unwanted external power involvement given the
prevailing superpower competition engendered by the Cold War.
ASEAN's founding purpose therefore had an undeniable 'security'
dimension to it; a dimension which was reflected in the development of
a highly sophisticated (though not entirely feasible) three-pronged
approach to the promotion of its members' – and therefore regional
security. The three prongs were: the pursuit of socio-economic development to alleviate the threat posed by communist insurgency
(represented by the concepts of national and regional 'resilience'); the
reduction or, ideally, elimination of external power involvement in the
region; and the limitation of competition and enhancement of relationships between members. The latter two aspects were reflected,
respectively, in the 1971 Zone of Peace, Freedom and Neutrality (ZOP-
FAN) Declaration and the 1976 Declaration of ASEAN Concord and
Treaty of Amity and Co-operation.

The Treaty of Amity and Co-operation was particularly significant in
promoting 'regional' security co-operation through its emphasis on the
desirability of peaceful relations with other states in the region (indeed,
the Treaty was open to accession by other states in Southeast Asia).
This emphasis included the need for signatories to avoid activities which
could be conceived by another signatory as representing a threat to it. In
addition the Treaty proposed a dispute resolution mechanism, the so-

called 'High Council', acknowledging the importance of intra-ASEAN disputes. In many respects, therefore, the Treaty of Amity and Co-operation can be equated with the principles, rules and norms which Jervis identifies with the creation of a security regime.[8] However, the evolution and expansion of the Treaty of Amity and Co-operation as a foundation for regional security co-operation was hampered by the ramifications of the Vietnamese invasion of Kampuchea (Cambodia) in December 1978. It was also adversely affected by the noted unwillingness of the ASEAN members to use the mechanism provided by the Treaty to resolve the various disputes amongst the members.[9]

The various intra-mural disputes and tensions in ASEAN (including not only territorial disputes, but also controversies over the alleged support by certain states for ethnic or religious insurgents in their neighbours)[10] have been widely contended as representing important obstacles to the development of ASEAN security co-operation. These disputes should not be seen as obstacles in themselves but, rather, as illustrative of more deep-seated tensions and suspicions between the Association's members. These tensions and suspicions often revolve around the fear that a state may be seeking to undermine its neighbour's security, evinced, for example, in aspects of the bilateral relationships between Malaysia and Singapore, and Malaysia and Brunei. Such tensions and suspicions, Tim Huxley notes, are a function of the low levels of socio-political cohesion which prevail in all the ASEAN states (except, arguably, Singapore), leading to their classification as so-called 'weak' states. Their 'weakness' can lead to either opportunities for interference by neighbours, perhaps through support for ethnic or religious insurgents, or the desire to obtain domestic political benefits through the continuance of existing disputes.[11]

A further obstacle to ASEAN security co-operation, particularly military co-operation, has been the divergent strategic perspectives held by the Association's members, especially during the 1980s. These divergences revolved around differing attitudes towards whether China or Vietnam constituted the greatest external threat to the Association's members. Thailand and Singapore deemed Vietnam to constitute the greatest threat, with Indonesia and Malaysia regarding China in this way (the Philippines regarded neither state as an overarching threat). These divergent strategic perspectives did not, however, prevent the Association from developing a common political front in response to the Vietnamese invasion of Kampuchea in order to provide support to Thailand as the front-line state.[12]

The existence of such obstacles as intra-mural tensions and divergent strategic perspectives is reflected in the very limited defence co-operation which has occurred amongst the Association's members. What has occurred has been on a primarily bilateral rather than ASEAN-wide basis, an emphasis which was stressed by the 1976 Declaration of ASEAN Concord.[13] ASEAN statements have eschewed any mention of the Association becoming a military alliance, and although a multitude of defence links appear to exist in the various bilateral (and sometimes trilateral) exercises which are held by the Association's members, in reality they do not enhance the members' defences and have little significance.[14] The only important examples of bilateral military co-operation concern counter-insurgency operations under the auspices of various General Border Committees, the most notable being that between Malaysia and Thailand during the time of the Communist Party of Malaya insurgency, and the continuing co-operation between Malaysia and Indonesia across their shared border in Borneo.

Where ASEAN members' defence co-operation has been able to help maintain their own security, and that of the region, is when it has occurred with external powers, primarily the United States. This is most evident with regard to Thailand and, especially, the Philippines, both of which have security treaties with America.[15] However, it is also evident in terms of joint exercises and the provision of military assistance by the United States (from which Singapore, Malaysia and Indonesia have benefited).[16] Such co-operation has, of course, been contradictory to the 'exclusionary' aspect of the ZOPFAN approach. These external defence links have also acted as a means of confidence-building through the creation of channels of communication and the exchange of information (particularly the Malaysian and Singaporean involvement in the Five-Power Defence Arrangements with Australia, Britain and New Zealand).[17] This role could also be attributed to much of the bilateral co-operation between ASEAN members.

### The Post-Cold War Strategic Environment: Characteristics and Responses

The post-Cold War strategic environment in Southeast Asia, heralded in 1991 by the Paris peace agreements on Cambodia and the Philippine Senate's decision to reject a new bases agreement with the United States, has been characterized by a sense of uncertainty created by the shifting balance of power in the region. This shifting power balance has seen the virtual elimination of Russia as a major player, a decline in the prevalence of US military power and doubts over its commitment to act as a stabilizing force in the region, and the increasingly influential roles played by Japan and China – roles which have been attributed with greater significance given both countries' increasing military strength.[18] Although this shift has been described as 'new', in reality the major trends had been emerging for some time. This was particularly true in the case of the big powers. Soviet involvement in the region, primarily through its *de facto* alliance with Vietnam, began to decline from the mid-1980s onwards as the Soviet Union's economic situation meant it could no longer afford to retain its existing military presence or provide the previous level of economic and military aid to Vietnam. Doubts also emerged over the future level of the US military presence in the region after the accession of Cory Aquino to the presidency of the Philippines in 1986. Increasingly influential nationalist sentiment began to demand the removal of the US military bases, reflected in the new Constitution which terminated the existing open-ended arrangement and required a new treaty for the period after 1991. The United States consequently sought alternative means of staying in the region, and by 1991 had begun to reconsider its commitment. Conversely Japan's and, especially, China's interest and involvement in the region began to increase during the 1980s. As well as supporting the Khmer Rouge in an attempt to contain Vietnamese domination of Indo-China, China began to focus increasingly on its territorial claims in the South China Sea, particularly the Spratly Islands. This focus was given greater significance because of China's military modernization programme (especially naval expansion). The combination of interest and capability was clearly demonstrated in 1988 when Chinese forces occupied six islands in the Spratlys chain claimed by Vietnam. Japan's increasing involvement in the region, on the other hand, has been more low-key, revolving around the expansion of trade links with the ASEAN states and the provision of large-scale investment funds. Japan has also been increasingly concerned about political developments in the region and the maintenance of stability (hence its involvement in attempts to foster the peace process in Cambodia). This concern has arisen not only because of its trade and investment links, but also because of fears about any disruption to its vital sea lanes of communication which pass through the region.[19]

For the ASEAN states, too, a number of trends concerning various aspects of their security were also becoming evident before the end of the Cold War. Most important was the gradually changing attitude towards Vietnam, highlighted by Thai Prime Minister Chatichai's attempt to resolve the Cambodian problem from 1988 on with his 'New Look Diplomacy'. The essence of this reorientation in Thai security policy was that Vietnam was no longer regarded as an overwhelming threat and that the focus of relations with it would now be centred on economics. Concurrently, Vietnam was reducing its military presence in

Cambodia and participating in the peace process. Other ASEAN states were also interested in the economic opportunities available in Vietnam and thus a climate of opinion was created in which Vietnam began to be perceived as potentially fitting into the ASEAN economic (and perhaps political) framework.

Another, albeit more long-term, trend driven by economics was the increasing level of defence spending and arms procurement of several of the ASEAN states during the 1980s. The high levels of economic growth which most of the ASEAN states experienced during the 1980s have enabled more resources to be devoted to defence expenditure. This, in turn, has led to the purchase of advanced weapon systems previously financially out-of-reach, enhancing in particular air and naval capabilities. Among the other major influences on the increased expenditure and procurement levels have been not only the need to modernize forces and defend increasingly important maritime resources but also the pattern of competition between the various members arising out of the tensions and suspicions between them.[20]

The long-standing nature of some of the trends affecting both the major regional powers and the ASEAN members has led to the recognition of the need either to adapt existing strategies, or to develop new ones, to manage the changed environment. The end of the Cold War has thus seen a variety of proposals put forward by both ASEAN members and the major regional powers (with the notable exception of China). These proposals can be grouped into two broad groups: those which concern arms control and the development of Confidence-Building and Confidence and Security-Building Measures (CBM/CSBMs); and those which favour the establishment of some form of regional security forum. Among the proposals for pursuing arms control and CBM/CSBMs were the Malaysian assertion that regional security could be enhanced by crisis management mechanisms and CBMs (including military ties and security dialogue); the call by the Malaysian defence minister for the establishment of a regional arms register; and the Thai proposal for a regional peacekeeping centre.[21] Proposals for the establishment of a regional security forum included Gorbachev's early suggestion of an 'Asia-Pacific' forum as well as those put forward subsequently by Japan and the ASEAN members themselves.[22]

On the whole the ASEAN members, certainly as a collective group, have preferred the idea of furthering Asia-Pacific-wide security cooperation through some form of dialogue process, despite it being something of a new approach for the Association, than that of establishing CBMs. This preference has arisen out of the ASEAN members' traditional aversion to any sort of 'institutionalized' arrangement (in the political and military spheres) as well as the fact that it is the approach which is favoured by Japan and the United States whose attitudes have been crucial in recent developments. Although ASEAN has sought to enhance and broaden the process of regional security dialogue through a series of developments concerning the ASEAN Post-Ministerial Conference (PMC), there was initially a marked reluctance to introduce the highly sensitive issue of security into the ASEAN framework.[23] Thus, whilst the 1991 Kuala Lumpur Annual Ministerial Meeting (AMM) agreed to the PMC being 'used as a forum for informal discussion on regional security'[24] there was an unwillingness to endorse the suggestion by Japan that senior officials should meet before the PMC to 'solely discuss security'.[25] Since 1991, however, ASEAN has been increasingly willing to further the process of security dialogue. This willingness has resulted not only from the members' awareness of the increasing volatility of the regional strategic environment (characterized by both territorial disputes and an arms build-up) and a desire to have some influence over the emerging pattern of regional security co-operation, but more importantly from the change in American attitudes. Prior to the Clinton administration, the United States had been hostile to the idea of any form of regional security dialogue, preferring instead to emphasize the importance of the stabilizing role played by its various bilateral security treaties and co-operation. Now, however, the US administration's Asia policy has begun to focus on the desirability of establishing multilateral security fora which can help to 'manage or prevent emerging concerns' (for example, the arms build-up or 'competing alignments').[26] For the United States, the ASEAN PMC, and its evolved form, the ASEAN Regional Forum (ARF), is seen as the security component of its plan for fostering stability and prosperity through the establishment of economic and security architectures.[27]

The evolution of ASEAN thinking on security dialogues has, consequently, been fairly swift. The 1992 Singapore summit declaration agreed that the PMC would include discussion of security issues,[28] and both the AMM and PMC in Manila later that year focused on security.[29] It was also agreed at the Manila AMM that the ASEAN members' defence officials (meeting at the Senior Officials Meeting before the AMM) would in future discuss regional security – a discussion meant, in fact, to act as a intra-ASEAN CBM. The 1993 Senior Officials Meeting subsequently focused on security issues, including discussions about preventive diplomacy and conflict management. More important, perhaps, was the recognition by the officials of the need to find some way of engaging other interested parties in the dialogue process, particularly Russia, China and Vietnam, who were not designated 'dialogue partners' and thus not part of the PMC.[30] The resulting solution was the decision of the following Singapore AMM that year to establish the ASEAN Regional Forum. The ARF involves nearly all those countries with a vital interest in regional stability (including China, Russia and Vietnam) and aims to assist in the development of a 'constructive pattern of political and security relationships' in the Asia-Pacific region.[31]

The ARF, which is due to hold its first meeting in Bangkok in 1994, is significant because it goes beyond ASEAN's traditional sub-regional approach to security co-operation, although this entails both problems and opportunities. ASEAN has, however, simultaneously sought to pursue its more traditional approach emphasizing the promotion of regional security in Southeast Asia through the establishment of 'peaceful and co-operative' relationships based on the Treaty of Amity and Co-operation. A primary feature of this sub-regional approach, it was noted earlier, is that it should encompass all the Southeast Asian states. An important step in this direction was thus taken at the Manila AMM in 1992 when Vietnam and Laos signed the Treaty and officials from Myanmar (formerly Burma) also signalled their willingness to sign.[32] However, merely acceding to the Treaty does not automatically enhance this form of security co-operation given the prevalence of disputes and suspicions amongst the signatories. Significantly, though, at the same time as they became signatories to the Treaty, Vietnam and Laos were also awarded 'observer' status by ASEAN enabling them to attend AMMs.

Vietnam's and Laos' accession to the Treaty of Amity and Co-operation, along with the awarding of observer status, have now been attributed with a greater significance than they might otherwise have been. Implicit in these moves was the assumption by ASEAN leaders that they were a step on the road to their eventual full membership of the Association and, concomitantly, to the furthering of regional security through the enhancement of relations between ASEAN's own members – one of the original ASEAN approaches to security. No timetable has, as yet, been openly discussed, though. Indeed, whilst Vietnam has expressed its desire to further defence and security co-operation with ASEAN, its leaders are fully aware that full membership is some time away and will require the removal of both 'conceptual' and 'practical' obstacles (including, for example, mistrust and different levels of development).[33] And if Vietnam's participation in ASEAN is problematic for the foreseeable future, then that of Myanmar or Cambodia is even more so.

If continuing significance and relevance is accorded to the Treaty of Amity and Co-operation and, especially, to the expansion of ASEAN as means of furthering regional security, then another aspect of ASEAN's traditional approach, revolving around ZOPFAN and its 'exclusionary' aspect, appears to be accorded much less importance. Of course, the credibility of this exclusionary approach had been seriously undermined by the Association's Cambodia policy which had actually increased the involvement of extra-regional powers and was thus contrary to the ZOPFAN idea.[34] The ASEAN members have come increasingly to view the exclusionary aspect of ZOPFAN as being undesirable because of the importance of involving the United States in the region to foster security and stability. This has been reflected in unprecedented public statements urging the United States to remain involved.[35] More importantly, it has also been reflected in the fact that the ASEAN states have sought to increase bilateral defence co-operation with the United States in response to the latter's enforced withdrawal from the Philippines.[36] The fact that the ASEAN members have sought to extend such links, when combined with the traditional importance which such links have had, increasingly illustrates the 'obsolescence of ZOPFAN as a framework for regional security'.[37]

A final point concerning ASEAN's responses to the post-Cold War strategic environment is that the Association has continued to eschew the idea of becoming a military alliance. Although ASEAN military chiefs have agreed to increase regional security co-operation they do not want to establish a military pact.[38] The goal of increasing security co-operation has resulted in an increase in the number and complexity of exercises but, by and large, they are still essentially bilateral and do not contribute significantly to the enhancement of members' defence capabilities.[39] One exception to this general pattern concerns the problem of piracy in the shipping channels between Malaysia, Singapore and Indonesia. These three ASEAN members have resolved to increase co-operation with each other through, for example, co-ordinated maritime patrols in an effort to address this growing problem.

### ASEAN's Responses: Obstacles and Debates

One of the continuing reasons for the absence of ASEAN-wide military exercises aimed at enhancing members' security is the continued existence of various intra-mural disputes between the members. Initiatives aimed at negotiated solutions to some of these disputes (for example, that between Malaysia and Singapore over Pedra Branca, and between Malaysia and Indonesia over Sipadan and Ligitan Islands) have been taken while in other cases there has been agreement to focus on promoting co-operation whilst 'side-stepping' contentious problems (for example, the Philippines' claim to Sabah).[40] However, it is difficult to foresee how these negotiations will succeed given the apparent unwillingness of any of the states to be seen to be backing down. This reluctance is generated by the continued weakness of the ASEAN states. In the case of Malaysia and Indonesia, for example, despite the onset of a process of dispute resolution (started by the establishment of a liaison committee in 1993) both sides have continued to emphasize publicly that the islands are an 'integral' part of their territory. Indonesia recently responded to apparent development on Sipadan Island by a Malaysian firm with increased naval patrols around the islands.[41]

The continued existence of tensions manifested in these various disputes represents a very real obstacle to any form of ASEAN-derived security co-operation. Indeed, the extension of the Treaty of Amity and Co-operation to the whole of Southeast Asia (let alone the expansion of ASEAN itself) will magnify the number of such disputes making this even more of an obstacle. This would particularly be the case with the latent suspicions between the existing ASEAN states (especially Thailand) and Indo-China, despite the recent onset of a *rapprochement* between them. Thailand and Vietnam, for example, have maritime disputes in the Gulf of Thailand, whilst Cambodia has long-running border disputes with Thailand and Vietnam, disputes which are at the forefront of the new Phnom Penh government's foreign policy.[42] In addition there are crucial problems regarding different levels of economic development, political outlook, and socio-political cohesion. Indeed, the Indo-China states, and Myanmar in particular, are extremely weak and could actually undermine ASEAN's existing limited security regime.[43]

The number of obstacles increases even more dramatically when considering any Asia-Pacific-wide approach to security co-operation. Ironically, although the multipolar nature of the post-Cold War strategic environment provides imperatives for regional security co-operation, it also makes such co-operation harder to achieve because of the wide-range of problems and concerns which exist. There are, moreover, important divergences in strategic perspective. These are particularly evident with regard to the perspectives of the ASEAN members, and those of China. While the ASEAN members may publicly prefer to stress the economic opportunities created by China's interest and involvement in Southeast Asia, downplaying the idea of it being a threat, one of the reasons for their desire to see the US remain engaged in the region is undoubtedly related to fears about China filling any 'power vacuum' that might emerge. China, on the other hand, will not regard a US role as crucial and would certainly be opposed to US regional dominance.

The role of China in any incipient Asia-Pacific-wide security regime is also problematic. Among the necessary conditions which Jervis identifies for the creation of a security regime is the need for the powers involved to 'prefer a more regulated environment to one in which all states behave individualistically'. Thus the status quo must be fairly satisfactory to all, as are alterations which can be achieved without recourse to the use of force.[44] It is far from clear that China, given its recent behaviour in regard to the Spratly Islands and its current military expansion, fulfils this condition. Furthermore, China is also, to some extent, a 'weak' state, and this weakness may be exacerbated in the event of a post-Deng power struggle. Such a power struggle could, of course, see competing power groups play upon nationalist sentiment through the pursuit of territorial ambitions.

The likelihood of divergent attitudes towards the form of a new multilateral security framework was evident within ASEAN prior to the announcement of the ARF. Indonesia believed that the situation did not warrant an 'immediate multilateral institutional thing', and Malaysia stressed the importance of existing arrangements.[45] Despite the proposed ARF it is not entirely clear that ASEAN favours an Asia-Pacific-wide approach over and above its more traditional sub-regional ones. For ASEAN, the debate over which approach to emphasize has implications not only for regional security and stability but also for the future of the Association itself. A major part of the rationale for ASEAN's initiative to promote the PMC/ARF has been the Association's desire to steer, or control, the development of a wider regional security process in order to preserve its identity. Paradoxically, however, it could find its identity becoming subsumed within a wider Asia-Pacific framework as the dialogue process is expanded, especially if the major powers take the lead. There is also the concern that moves towards a wider security framework in the Asia-Pacific – accompanied, perhaps, by an economic framework resulting from an 'institutionalized' Apec (Asia-Pacific Economic Co-operation) process – could be detrimental to the expansion and/or strengthening of ASEAN itself. An Asia-Pacific security framework could therefore undermine a crucial aspect of ASEAN's traditional security approach which focuses on the development of ASEAN itself.

Further, Acharya argues that attempts to create an Asia-Pacific-wide security framework could jeopardize the stability engendered by the prevailing status quo. He believes that there is a tension between any moves towards multilateralism and ASEAN's continued reliance on existing bilateral security arrangements with the United States. These arrangements contribute to a balance of power mechanism still deemed to be critical for the preservation of regional order.[46] Thus, the evolution of regional security co-operation on an Asia-Pacific basis may not automatically be progressive. It may rather be advisable for effective sub-regional security regimes to be established first, in more limited geopolitical areas, before attempting to extend the process into an Asia-Pacific-wide system.[47] This is of particular significance in the case of Northeast Asia which is widely perceived as requiring its own security mechanism because it is 'more of a powder keg than Southeast Asia, largely because of the unpredictability of North Korea and its nuclear ambitions'.[48]

## Conclusion

ASEAN's traditional approaches to security co-operation, with the exception of the exclusionary aspect of the ZOPFAN ideal, had some success during the Cold War. The Association's members (the Philippines excepted) were able to develop a sufficient degree of national resilience to end the threat posed by communist insurgencies. Moreover, they avoided confrontation with each other through adherence to the principle of the primacy of peaceful relationships, enshrined in the Treaty of Amity and Co-operation, and through the degree of restraint which they have exercised with regard to each other's internal affairs. Both of these have lessened the effects of the security dilemma. ASEAN has therefore operated as a limited security regime.

　　ASEAN's security thinking has evolved during the latter stages of the Cold War and in its immediate aftermath, particularly with the move away from a declaratory policy of excluding the major powers to an 'inclusionary' one. This involves both the provision of direct military co-operation (in the case of the United States) and the perceived requirement to involve all major regional powers in a security dialogue. The Association's failure to develop into a more effective security regime and, especially, into a security community, has resulted from the inability to alleviate tensions and resolve disputes brought about by the members' 'weak' statehood. If ASEAN's traditional sub-regional approach to security co-operation is to lead to the development of a stronger security regime and, eventually, security community, it needs the members to achieve a level of strength and 'maturity' whereby they can draw upon their own stability to enhance that of the region as a whole. This could be done through, for example, their willingness to adhere to 'a variety of . . . institutions for dealing with problems of a multinational scale',[49] one of which, in ASEAN's case, would be the High Council of the Treaty of Amity and Co-operation with its dispute resolution mechanism. In other words, a 'mature anarchy' would exist in which the 'importance' of the security dilemma can be reduced, an important consideration given the prevailing arms dynamic.[50] Thus a high level of security co-operation will require the evolution of the states themselves, which could take a long time.

The prospects for a maturing of the ASEAN states, and therefore for a future sub-regional security regime and community, will be assisted by the furthering of political and economic co-operation. The latter aspect is certainly being given a high priority at the moment with the intended ASEAN Free Trade Area and the various 'growth triangle' proposals. The pursuit of such co-operation will continue to remain a higher priority for the Association than extending the existing level of military co-operation. The difficulty for ASEAN, recognized in its attempts to involve the wider Asia-Pacific region, is that it cannot isolate itself from the wider region and establish an autonomous sub-regional security regime, whatever the merits of attempting to do so in the first instance may be. However, the prospects for developing Asia-Pacific-wide security co-operation are not particularly good and, in any case, the ARF should not be seen as the only solution. Indeed, it has been recognized that the ARF should actually be allowed to 'evolve' as part of a 'multi-faceted' approach to regional security co-operation.[51] The evolutionary process thus has some way to go at both the regional and sub-regional level.

## NOTES

1. Richard Dawkins, 'The Evolutionary Future of Man', The Future Surveyed: 150 Economist Years, The Economist, 11 Sept. 1993, p.103.
2. The 'security dilemma' exists when 'the military preparations of one state create an unresolvable uncertainty in the mind of another as to whether these preparations are for 'defensive' purposes only (to enhance its security in an uncertain world) or whether they are for offensive purposes (to change the status quo to its advantage)'. Nicholas J. Wheeler and Ken Booth, 'The Security Dilemma', in John Baylis and N. J. Rengger (eds.), Dilemmas of World Politics (New York: Oxford University Press, 1992), p.30. For detailed analyses of the concepts of security regimes and communities see: Robert Jervis, 'Security Regimes', International Organization, Vol.36, No.2, (Spring 1982), pp.173–95; K. Deutsch et al., Political Community and the North Atlantic Area (Princeton, NJ: Princeton University Press, 1957), esp. pp.5–6.
3. The founder members of the Association (which was established in 1967) were Indonesia, Malaysia, Singapore, Thailand and the Philippines. Brunei joined in 1984 after gaining independence from Britain.
4. Wheeler and Booth, op. cit. p.55.
5. See Tim Huxley, 'Singapore and Malaysia: A Precarious Balance?', Pacific Review, Vol.4, No.3 (1991), pp.204–13.
6. Tim Huxley, Insecurity in the ASEAN Region, Whitehall Paper 23 (London: RUSI, 1993), p.56.

7. For further details of these aspects of ASEAN security co-operation see: Mark G. Rolls, 'ASEAN: Where from or Where To?', *Contemporary Southeast Asia*, Vol.13, No.3 (1991), pp.324–6; Muthiah Alagappa, 'Regional Arrangements and International Security in Southeast Asia: Going Beyond ZOPFAN', *Contemporary Southeast Asia*, Vol.12, No.4 (1991), pp.269–305; Michael Leifer, *ASEAN and the Security of Southeast Asia*, (London: Routledge, 1989), Documentary Appendices, pp.160–74.

8. Jervis, op. cit., p.173.

9. Huxley, *Insecurity in the ASEAN Region*, pp.11–12.

10. The most notorious territorial dispute is that between the Philippines and Malaysia over Sabah in Borneo, although there are also a plethora of island disputes (for example, the one between Malaysia and Indonesia over the Sipadan and Ligitan Islands in the Sulawesi Sea). Allegations of support for insurgents being given by a neighbour have been made by, for example, Thailand against Malaysia (over Muslim separatists in the south) and by Indonesia against Malaysia (for similar support to separatists in Aceh, Sumatra).

11. Huxley, *Insecurity in the ASEAN Region*, pp.12–13. For the characteristics of weak states, see Barry Buzan, *People, States and Fear* (Hemel Hempstead: Harvester Wheatsheaf, 2nd ed., 1991), pp.96–107.

12. For an analysis of these divergent strategic perspectives, and of ASEAN's initial response to the Vietnamese invasion, see Leifer, pp.90–94.

13. 'Section E, Declaration of ASEAN Concord, 1976', cited in Leifer, Documentary Appendices, p.169.

14. See Amitav Acharya, *A New Regional Order in South-East Asia: ASEAN in the Post-Cold War Era*, Adelphi Paper 279 (London: IISS, 1993), Table 2 on pp.70–1.

15. These treaties are, respectively, the 1954 Manila Treaty (which also includes the Philippines) and the 1951 US-Philippine Mutual Defence Treaty. In the case of Thailand this defence co-operation has, since the withdrawal of US forces in 1976, taken shape in the form of both military assistance and joint training and exercizes. For the Philippines it has been most evident in the then US military bases at Clark Field and Subic Bay, along with the provision of large quantities of military aid.

16. See Huxley, *Insecurity in the ASEAN Region*, pp.22–25.

17. Ibid., pp.66–67.

18. For further details of the various changes in the major powers' roles in the region see the introduction to this volume and the relevant individual contributions.

19. For a more detailed analysis of the changing roles, and degree of involvement, of the major powers, see Huxley, *Insecurity in the ASEAN Region*, pp.21–49. (Although the author entitles this section 'The New Strategic Environment', he fully recognizes the long-standing nature of the shifting power balance).

20. The article by Tim Huxley in this volume provides a detailed examination and explanation of the ASEAN states' defence build-ups.

21. See respectively, *Straits Times*, 18 Dec. 1992, 10 June 1993 and 24 Feb. 1993.

22. See *Straits Times*, 18 April 1991.

23. The PMC is a meeting of the ASEAN members and their dialogue partners (Australia, New Zealand, the United States, Japan, the EU, Canada and South Korea) for discussion after the ASEAN Annual Ministerial Meeting, usually on economic matters.

24. *Straits Times*, 25 July 1991.

25. Rolls, op. cit., p.328.

26. The comments of Winston Lord, US Assistant Secretary of State for East Asian and Pacific Affairs, cited in *Far Eastern Economic Review* (hereafter FEER), 15 April 1993, p.10.

27. FEER, 18 Nov. 1993, p.17.

28. *Straits Times Weekly Overseas Edition*, 1 Feb. 1992.

29. *Straits Times*, 25 July 1992.

30. *Straits Times*, 22 May 1992.

31. Frank Ching, 'Eye on Asia', FEER, 12 Aug. 1993, p.27.
32. *Straits Times Weekly Overseas Edition*, 25 July 1992.
33. The comments of Vietnamese Deputy Foreign Minister Nguyen Dy Nien, at a seminar on ASEAN-Vietnamese co-operation. *Straits Times*, 7 Dec. 1993.
34. Rolls, op. cit., p.326.
35. See, for example, the comments of Malaysian Defence Minister Datuk Najib Tun Razak, in an interview with the *International Herald Tribune*, cited in *Straits Times*, 23 Dec. 1992.
36. For details of this co-operation see Acharya, pp.57–8.
37. Ibid., p.59. It has been contended, though, that in the post-Cold War strategic environment there has been 'new thinking' on ZOPFAN which has meant that it should now be regarded as being concerned with 'the establishment of ground rules for regional co-operation and security' and has thus undergone a repackaging. One element of this has been the recognition of the need to include extra-regional powers. The broadening of the ZOPFAN approach could accord it a continuing relevance, but only if it remains adaptable. However, the fact that current thinking on security co-operation is increasingly encompassing different aspects, notably the dialogue process, suggests that less attention will be focused on 'adapting' ZOPFAN to fit the realities of the changed environment. Thus, it will be difficult to prevent its obsolescence. ASEAN is unlikely, however, to declare publicly its abandonment of the ZOPFAN goal in the near future as it has held a symbolic position as the Association's primary declaratory security policy. Bilveer Singh, *ZOPFAN And The New Security Order in the Asia-Pacific Region* (Petaling Jaya, Selangor: Pelanduk Publications (m) Sdn Bhd, 1992), pp.100 and 114.
38. See *Straits Times Weekly Overseas Edition*, 9 Nov. 1991.
39. In the case of Singapore, for example, the Singapore Armed Forces (SAF) have conducted their first joint land exercise with the Armed Forces of the Philippines (in June 1993), and last year's naval exercise with the Malaysians continued the trend of these exercises away from 'shipboard tactical procedures of individual ships to larger operational matters involving planning at group level'. *Straits Times Weekly Edition*, 24 July 1993.
40. *Straits Times*, 10 Dec. 1993.
41. *Straits Times*, 14 Oct. and 24 Nov. 1993.
42. See FEER, 28 Oct. 1993, p.32.
43. Huxley, *Insecurity in the ASEAN Region*, p.75.
44. Jervis, op. cit., p.176.
45. The comment of Indonesian Foreign Minister Ali Alatas, *Straits Times*, 6 June 1993.
46. Acharya, op. cit., pp.77–8.
47. Singh, op. cit., pp.105–6.
48. Frank Ching, 'Eye on Asia', FEER, 11 Nov. 1993, p.42.
49. Buzan, op. cit., p.177.
50. Ibid., pp.176–7 and 324.
51. The comments of the Singapore Foreign Minister Wong Kan Seng, *Straits Times*, 16 Oct. 1993.

# Vietnam, Cambodia and Southeast Asian Security

## MIKE YEONG

The geopolitical landscape of Southeast Asia has been determined in large part by successive conflicts in Indo-China. If the Vietnam War shaped regional security concerns for a decade from the mid-1960s to the mid-1970s,[1] then the Cambodian conflict – arguably a continuation of the Vietnam War[2] – determined the security agenda from 1979 to 1991. Like the Vietnam War, so the Cambodian conflict reflected Cold War antagonisms, and the resolution of the conflict in 1991 heralded the post-Cold War era in Southeast Asia. But unlike the Vietnam War, the Cambodian conflict was in large measure a consequence of Sino-Soviet rivalry which had begun to intensify in Asia in the second half of the 1970s.[3] This essay briefly outlines the importance of the Vietnam War in shaping regional security alignments, before assessing the impact of the Cambodian conflict and its resolution on Southeast Asian security, and particularly on Vietnam and Cambodia.

### The Legacy of the Vietnam War

The Vietnam War shaped regional security not simply while it was being fought but in its aftermath. A number of points can therefore be made with regard to the legacy of the Vietnam War. Firstly, almost all Southeast Asian governments aligned themselves with the United States, albeit to varying degrees. US intervention was supported on the grounds that its professed aim was to prevent the spread of communism in the region. The 'domino theory' was accepted almost without question, particularly since many states in the region were themselves facing communist-inspired insurgency of one form or another.[4] The success of the communists in Vietnam and Cambodia therefore coloured relations with other Southeast Asian states for some time to come. Secondly, Beijing's support for Hanoi at the time when Mao was actively promoting the Cultural Revolution led to regional fears of China as the instigator of unrest and a potential source of instability. Its support of the Vietcong was proof of its willingness to support communist revolutions beyond its own borders, whilst the Cultural Revolution threatened to spill over from China into other states, particularly those with large ethnic Chinese populations. Thirdly, the military failure of the Tet offensive in 1968, when the Vietcong suffered heavy casualties and its underground network in the South was almost completely destroyed, led to a change in both the military and political relationships between the Vietcong and Hanoi. Previously the war had been fought by the largely South Vietnamese guerrilla army, the Vietcong, under the political leadership of the National Liberation Front and supported by the communist government of North Vietnam. Its objective was the liberation and independence of South Vietnam. With the failure of the Tet offensive, the North Vietnamese began to play a larger role in the conduct of the war and took greater control of the liberation movement in the South.[5] As a result, within a year of the fall of Saigon in 1975, Hanoi was able to impose unification upon the South, and the original nationalism of the Vietcong was replaced with socialism. More importantly this allowed the development in Hanoi of a policy of exporting revolution to neighbouring states.

While the Hanoi leadership had prepared the ground for eventual control of the South, it did not anticipate that the war would end with a swift military victory by the North Vietnamese army in 1975. The 1973 Paris peace agreement had in fact called for a peaceful transfer of power to an interim (neutral) government to be followed by self-determination by the South Vietnamese people. Were the terms of the 1973 Paris peace agreement allowed to be implemented, the Southerners would have stood a good chance of coming to power in view of the fact that they were nationalists and not Marxists. A series of fortuitous events, however, provided Hanoi with the excuse to resume military activities in the South, in particular the secret US bombing and then invasion of Cambodia in 1970[6] and the 1973 Watergate scandal which allowed Congress to exert a limiting effect on the US administration's support for the war effort.[7]

Emboldened by their victory over the Americans, Ho Chi Minh's successors next sought to export communism to the rest of Southeast Asia. Vietnam's regional ambition was revealed at the Non-Aligned Summit in Colombo in 1976 when the Vietnamese delegation, led by Prime Minister Pham Van Dong, sought the support of the movement for its proposal for the establishment of 'genuine independence' in the non-communist states of Southeast Asia. The implication was that these countries were not really independent since they were, in Hanoi's view, serving the interests of Western imperialist powers. In spite of its heroic reputation in the eyes of Third World governments, the Vietnamese delegation failed to persuade the Non-Aligned movement to endorse its resolution, largely because of opposition from the ASEAN members and Cambodia. In breaking with its Marxist neighbour, the Khmer Rouge leadership probably believed – and rightly – that Colombo was Hanoi's opening salvo in its bid to establish hegemony in the region. The ultra-nationalistic Khmer Rouge leadership had no intention of allowing Vietnam to dominate the Indo-China peninsula, let alone the entire Southeast Asia region.[8] Its opposition to Hanoi laid the ground for Vietnamese intervention in Cambodia two years later.

Shortly after the Colombo Summit, fighting between Khmer Rouge and Vietnamese forces erupted along their common border.[9] Conventional wisdom suggested that the Khmer Rouge was responsible for initiating the fighting by attacking villages inside southern Vietnam. Convinced that there would be no peace between the two countries unless and until the top Khmer Rouge leadership was removed, the Vietnamese leadership sponsored a coup by Khmer Rouge defectors to oust Pol Pot in the spring of 1978.[10] The coup failed. The consequence was the launch of a massive purge within the Khmer Rouge to weed out those whom Pol Pot suspected to be Vietnamese spies or sympathizers.[11] Failing to oust Pol Pot through a coup, Hanoi decided that the only way to remove him was to invade Cambodia. This was launched on Christmas eve of 1978. Within two weeks the Khmer Rouge government was driven out of Phnom Penh and into the mountains. A pro-Hanoi regime took its place.

As an added insurance, the Vietnamese leadership decided to align itself with Moscow in order to obtain protection against China. This was the underlying aim for the Vietnamese in signing the Soviet-Vietnamese Treaty of Friendship and Co-operation in 1978. Hanoi's relations with China had been cooling since the early 1970s. Nixon's 1972 visit to Beijing appears to have seen a deal struck whereby Chinese support of North Vietnam was reduced in return for US support for China in the various Sino-Soviet disputes. By the time Saigon fell, Moscow had replaced Beijing as Vietnam's main patron, though Hanoi was not yet fully in the Soviet camp, as its refusal to allow Soviet warships access to Cam Ranh Bay demonstrated. By the time of the invasion of Cambodia, Vietnam's relations with Beijing had worsened considerably: in 1978 China had terminated all aid to Vietnam, including the withdrawal of technicians; while Hanoi had begun a crack-down on ethnic Chinese in Vietnam, particularly those in the South, leading many to flee the country. The final, albeit somewhat belated, legacy of the Vietnam War therefore was Chinese-Vietnamese antipathy, and increased Soviet involvement in the area extending the Sino-Soviet split to Southeast Asia.

## The Cambodian Conflict and Regional Security

The invasion of Cambodia united three parties – China, the United States and ASEAN – against Vietnam and the Soviet Union. Each of the three parties was pursuing different agendas, but they shared the same strategic goal – to contain and reverse Vietnamese and Soviet aggression and influence in the region. China's role prior to Vietnam's invasion of Cambodia remains unclear: whether Beijing manoeuvred the Khmer Rouge into confrontation with Hanoi, or whether Chinese backing for Pol Pot was forthcoming only after Hanoi aligned itself with Moscow is still uncertain. Whichever was the case, China was clearly unhappy over developments in Soviet-Vietnamese relations, of which the Vietnamese invasion of Cambodia was part.

Similarly, the United States sought to 'punish' the Vietnamese government over Cambodia because of the humiliation it had suffered in losing the Vietnam War. This sentiment is vividly captured by a US State Department official who, when referring to the economic haemorrhage Vietnam was suffering as a result of its intervention in Cambodia, commented: 'Let them stew in their Soviet juice'.[12] Although the Reagan administration was committed to rolling-back communism world-wide, it was careful not to be seen to be involved in another conflict in mainland Southeast Asia. To avoid this problem, the Reagan administration invoked a strategy concocted by its Republican predecessor, Richard Nixon, in 1969, concerning fighting communist aggression in Asia. In essence, the strategy stipulated that the United States should let its Asian friends and allies fight communist aggression, and America's role should be to assist them by supplying them with military aid. The main beneficiaries of this strategy in Cambodia were the two non-communist resistance groups – Sihanouk's FUNCINPEC and Son Sann's KPNLF.[13]

As a result a situation emerged whereby China supplied arms to the Cambodian resistance groups; the United States, its Western partners and Japan imposed sanctions against Vietnam and the new regime in Phnom Penh; and ASEAN used its diplomatic influence to isolate the two governments within the region. But whereas China and the United States sought to punish Vietnam (both for its invasion of Cambodia, but more to settle old scores), ASEAN was motivated by somewhat different concerns. Although it was critical of Vietnam's actions on grounds of principle, particularly those of sovereignty and non-intervention, its concerns were more forward-looking than US and Chinese policy, which appeared to be motivated by a large dose of revenge for past Vietnamese actions. In particular ASEAN was concerned over future Vietnamese ambitions in the region. From ASEAN's perspective, there was a clear requirement to cut Hanoi down to size and to rob it of the belief that its army was invincible.[14] ASEAN feared that if this was not done then Vietnam would continue to be a dangerous and destabilizing force in the region. Of the six ASEAN members, Thailand and Singapore were probably the strongest supporters of this view, while in the early years of the conflict Indonesia and Malaysia continued to hope that Vietnam might prove a bulwark against China and therefore should not be weakened.

In spite of its military superiority, the Vietnamese army failed to destroy the Khmer Rouge and the two non-communist resistance groups despite nearly thirteen years of fighting. Reports of desertions and defections from the army fighting in Cambodia were matched by a lack of popular support for the war in Vietnam itself (as witnessed by the increased number of economic refugees fleeing from the North). The Cambodian conflict therefore served to limit Vietnam's regional ambitions and to destroy its army's image of invincibility. The conflict also allowed China to extend its influence in the area: with growing Soviet involvement and US reluctance to become embroiled in another land war in Southeast Asia, the Chinese were left to counter the Soviet-Vietnamese threat to the region. In particular Thailand was forced to seek protection from the Chinese, which allowed Beijing to develop its relationship with ASEAN. Finally the Cambodian conflict enabled ASEAN to develop as a political force in the region. Rather than following its traditional practice of relying on Western powers to provide peace and stability in the region, ASEAN took the lead in helping to restore peace in Cambodia and contain the Soviet-Vietnamese threat. Its high profile on Cambodia, particularly at the UN, not only demonstrated its ability to act in concert on the international scene, but led to increased international awareness and respect for its role in regional affairs.

**Vietnam after Cambodia**

The conflict in Cambodia therefore played a major role in setting the security agenda for Southeast Asia during the 1980s. The end of the Cold War, however, has enforced a number of changes. With the loss of Soviet military protection, Vietnam was compelled to accept the Cambodian peace agreement, make peace with China and cultivate new friendships with the member countries of ASEAN. Like other countries in the region, Vietnam also had to revise its thinking on what constituted a threat to its national security. While China continues to be a menace, the immediate danger to Vietnam's national integrity is internally generated, namely the possibility of the former South Vietnam breaking away because of social and economic disparities between the two sides.[15]

Having fought for nearly 30 years to unify the country, the Hanoi leadership will be unlikely to let the South break away again, either because of a rebellious leadership in Ho Chi Minh City or through an external attack on the South. Indeed, when Khmer Rouge forces attacked villages in the South in 1977 – to reclaim territories that formally belonged to the Khmer empire – the Vietnamese government responded with great force, even though the Vietnamese army was much superior. A more important reason is that the North is today relying totally on South Vietnam with its rich paddy fields in the Mekong delta to feed the rapidly expanding Vietnamese population. Thanks to good weather, rice export has become Vietnam's main means to obtain hard currency. Economically therefore, Hanoi cannot afford to lose the South. Force, however, is not the answer to keeping the South in line. Indeed, with the people in the North also restless, the Vietnamese leadership must find a better means of defusing the time bomb that is ticking away. One way is to narrow the social and economic gap between the North and the South, but without having to slow down the latter's rate of development.

Apart from domestic factors, the other reason that has prompted the Vietnamese leadership to pursue rapid economic development is that China is becoming economically stronger. Alliance with the Soviet Union was perhaps a strategic error, for while Vietnam might have been able to sustain its military superiority *vis-à-vis* its neighbours, the Vietnamese economy slipped even further behind these countries (either because Moscow never emphasized economic development sufficiently in its relations with its allies, or because of the misuse of Soviet aid in Vietnam). Thus, when Soviet economic assistance was drastically reduced in 1991 Vietnam found itself at the brink of an economic disaster. Under such circumstances, Hanoi had no choice but to make peace with China and accept the Cambodia peace agreement hammered out by the five permanent members of the UN Security Council.[16]

If Vietnam failed to pursue economic reform, it would not need a Chinese military attack to bring Hanoi to its knees; and even if its economic reform succeeds, it is not certain that Vietnam can avoid being drawn into the Chinese economic orbit. However, it is not Chinese economic preponderance that is worrying governments in the region, but what it would bring, namely the spread of Chinese political and military influence. For this reason, Vietnam will probably be seeking comfort and protection within ASEAN. There is, however, the danger that Vietnam may drag the grouping into a confrontation with China. Although

the two countries have normalized relations, Beijing and Hanoi will continue to be suspicious of one another. A China that is economically
vibrant and militarily strong may seek to put Vietnam in its place. How
effective an enlarged ASEAN can be in containing a China that is bent
on flexing its political muscles remains to be seen.

### 'New Thinking' in Vietnamese Foreign Policy

The collapse of the Soviet Union and the Cambodian peace agreement
have also led to what may be termed 'new thinking' in Vietnamese
foreign policy. Three key elements of this can be identified. First, Vietnam has made clear that it will avoid being dependent on any one
particular country for economic and military aid. This has been one of
the painful lessons it has learnt from aligning itself with the Soviet
Union in 1978: when the Soviet Union disintegrated in December 1991,
Vietnam found itself without security protection and an economic life-
line. It was forced to make peace with China, on the latter's terms. The
Vietnamese leadership wants to avoid being caught in a similar situation
again.[17] Indeed, the Chinese succeeded in extracting from Hanoi an
acceptance of the UN peace agreement in full. Even so, Vietnam was
not humiliated by accepting the peace agreement, except that its twelve-
year occupation of Cambodia had been in vain as the regime that it had
installed in Phnom Penh in January 1979 would now have to fight for its
own political survival.

   The second feature of Vietnam's foreign policy has been to cultivate
as many friends as it possibly can, regardless of ideology, but that it will
not allow itself to be dominated by any economic power. Indeed, the
Vietnamese government is trying to diversify its economic partners, as
indicated by the number of economic agreements it has signed with
foreign countries since October 1991. Japan and France are likely to be
big investors in Vietnam. The Vietnamese government has also been
courting the ASEAN states, which have responded enthusiastically to
Hanoi's overtures for increased economic co-operation. Equally, the
Vietnamese government has sought to improve its relationship with
Washington by providing the United States with assistance in ascertain-
ing the whereabouts of the remains of American servicemen still listed
as missing in action (MIA). The United States has responded by
announcing in 1993 that it would stop blocking loans to Vietnam by the
World Bank and the Asian Development Bank and, in February 1994,
by lifting the trade embargo. However, in order to benefit fully from a
bilateral relationship with the United States, and thus further its economic development, Vietnam still wants the restoration of full

diplomatic ties and to be granted the most-favoured-nation (MFN) trading status that is contingent on such a move.[18]

The third feature of Vietnamese new thinking has been to promote its security through diplomatic means. In this regard, Hanoi sees ASEAN as a weapon to wield against potential aggressors, particularly China. ASEAN's value is its political and diplomatic clout in the international community, especially at the United Nations. Ironically, ASEAN acquired this clout through its strong opposition to Vietnam's occupation of Cambodia. Having indirectly contributed to ASEAN's strength, Vietnam wants to exploit it to serve its own security needs. As with ASEAN's accomplishment on the Cambodia question, Hanoi no doubt hopes that the Association could be persuaded to mobilize the international community to restrain China in the event of a conflict with the latter. It is indeed an irony that in the past some ASEAN members have considered Vietnam a bulwark against an aggressive China, and now Hanoi views ASEAN as a potential protector against a China which is intimidating Vietnam at will.

Vietnam also hopes that China will listen to ASEAN since they have developed good relations over the past thirteen years. Indonesia reestablished diplomatic relations with China in September 1991, followed by Sinapore and Brunei. Hanoi is also aware that some ASEAN members, Malaysia and Indonesia in particular, are still concerned about the threat posed by China, even though communism has lost its appeal. However, the Vietnamese are careful in not playing up the Chinese threat as they had tried to do prior to the invasion of Cambodia in December 1978. The recent Chinese assertiveness in the South China Sea and reports of Beijing buying sophisticated armaments from Russia have once again aroused the concerns of some ASEAN members about Chinese intentions.

Hanoi has registered its first success in drawing on ASEAN's strength in restraining China. At their annual meeting in Manila in July 1992, the ASEAN foreign ministers issued a declaration calling on all the parties to resolve the issue of ownership of the Spratly Islands through negotiations.[19] Chinese Foreign Minister Qian Qichen, who, like his Vietnamese counterpart Nguyen Manh Cam, attended the meeting as an invited guest, accepted the declaration reluctantly. Three members of ASEAN – Brunei, Malaysia and the Philippines – also lay claim to the Spratly Islands. Like Hanoi, they too would like to see the dispute settled through negotiations.[20] Although the declaration might have reflected their views on the Spratly Islands, it has also served Vietnam's interest, namely in restraining China. Indeed, in renewing its claim to the Spratlys in February 1992, the Chinese government also stated that it was ready to use military means to enforce its claim.

Vietnam has come to the conclusion that its security interests are best protected and promoted by being a member of ASEAN rather than being allied to an external power. Until it becomes one, it will – as seen in the Spratly issue – try to modify its views according to those of ASEAN, in order to ride on the grouping's influence and clout. Meanwhile, Hanoi can also be expected to cultivate one or two 'close friends' among the ASEAN members in order to influence the thinking of the group in such a way that ASEAN would be sympathetic to Vietnam's interests.

While Hanoi's first priority is economic development, the underlying reason for this is clearly security. The leadership has realized that the longer it takes to transform itself into an economically vibrant country, the greater is the danger of it being bullied by China now that it has no military guarantor. Having lost the Soviet Union as a military guarantor, Vietnam lacks the resources to sustain a strong army. Vietnam's security concern is still China which has recently stepped up its own economic drive, no doubt in part because of the competition emanating from Vietnam. While it is waiting for the day when it has the resources to build up strong armed forces, the Vietnamese leadership has to rely on diplomacy to keep China at bay. To this end, it has thus far not done too badly.

Although Vietnam has retreated from Cambodia and Laos, it is doubtful that Hanoi has given up its ambition of dominating the two countries. The form of Vietnamese domination will, however, be different in the near future. If its economy begins to take off, Vietnam may use its newly-acquired economic might to dominate these two countries. But the Vietnamese will have to contend with Thailand, which will not allow them to have its way. Cambodia and Laos will, however, be a sideshow, as the Vietnamese main preoccupation will be the threat looming on the horizon – China.

**Cambodia and the 1993 Election**

For Cambodia the climax of the peace process was the UN-monitored elections in May 1993. Although the Khmer Rouge boycotted the elections and stated beforehand that it would not accept the results, some sixteen other parties contested the election. Most of those parties contesting the election were newly formed groupings based around emigrés living in the West and lacked a sufficient basis of support within Cambodia to mount an effective challenge for power. This left the existing Vietnamese-created Phnom Penh regime and the former resistance groups as the main contenders. The result, as expected, was no overall majority for any one party, and consequently a coalition government was formed between FUNCINPEC (led by Prince Sihanouk's son, Ranariddh), and the Cambodian People's Party (CPP), whose leader Hun Sen had been the former Vietnamese-backed government's prime minister.

The success of the CPP in the May 1993 elections was not surprising; nor was the Khmer Rouge reaction. Viewing the CPP as a creation of the Vietnamese intended at the very least to protect, if not actively promote, Hanoi's interests, the Khmer Rouge began a guerrilla campaign against the new government. The Khmer Rouge's immediate aim was not merely to extend its influence over Cambodian territory (some 20 per cent of which was already under its control) but to discourage foreign investment in Cambodia, which would be the key to economic growth and political stability. Its ultimate aim was to overthrow the new government and seize power for itself, if possible, but more realistically, to force it to be included in the new political framework in some way. A low intensity guerrilla war offered the Khmer Rouge three main advantages over the alternative, a full-scale war against the new government. First, a low intensity guerrilla war would not provoke the UN Security Council into re-intervening in Cambodia to 'save' the new government, which would have been recognized by the United Nations. The most the Council could be expected to do would be to tighten economic and other sanctions against the Khmer Rouge. Second, a low intensity guerrilla war would not automatically force the coalition government to seek substantial military assistance from outside powers. As the legitimate government of Cambodia it does, of course, have the sovereign right to call for such assistance. However, it is unlikely to want to do so immediately as it may threaten its search for legitimacy in the eyes of the Cambodian people. Third, a low intensity guerrilla war would discourage foreign investors from making long-term investments in Cambodia, but would not deter daring foreigners from putting money in areas that have quick returns, such as gem-mining and logging, which are largely under Khmer Rouge control. Revenue from these sources would enable the Khmer Rouge to purchase arms from the international black market, notwithstanding the UN-imposed arms embargo.

The Khmer Rouge's success has so far been limited. Morale appears to be low, with a large number of defections (some even returning to fight against former comrades). In January 1994 the government in Phnom Penh began a major offensive against the Khmer Rouge after it refused to respond to overtures to participate in peace talks. The Khmer Rouge also appears to have failed to deter foreign investors. Not only are businesses in many of the ASEAN states (especially Singapore) seeking to invest funds there, but the new government received substantial development assistance from the International Conference on Reconstruction of Cambodia which met in March 1994.[21] Indeed, the reaction of external powers to the new Cambodian government appears to be very favourable, with the Khmer Rouge being increasingly isolated (except by elements of the Thai military). However, Cambodia's relations with its neighbours Thailand and Vietnam may remain problematic, as a legacy of their past involvement in Cambodia. The new government has asked both states to return territory which it alleges they annexed during the 1980s.

Though the end of the Cold War has brought peace to Cambodia, and the threat of foreign occupation has receded, the danger of Cambodia being dominated by its immediate neighbours, Vietnam and Thailand, continues to occupy the minds of Cambodian leaders. The threat of foreign domination, however, takes a different form. While in the past Thailand and Vietnam have tried to dominate Cambodia through military means, these two countries now seem likely to try to assert influence in Cambodia in particular and the Indo-China peninsula in general through economic means. Indeed, as Thailand becomes an NIE (newly industrializing economy) and as the Vietnamese economy begins to take off, Thai-Vietnam competition in Cambodia and on the peninsula will grow.

Cambodia's independence can be protected in at least two ways. First, apart from arming itself it could (and probably will) embark on a rapid economic modernization programme. But even if it is successful in rebuilding the country, Cambodia, which is sandwiched between Thailand in the west and Vietnam in the east, will find it difficult to escape the influence of these two countries. Vietnam, with its hardworking people, is likely to surpass Thailand economically in the near future. Hence, Vietnamese economic influence (and therefore political influence) in Cambodia as well as on the entire Indo-China peninsula will be a new threat in that corner of Southeast Asia. The other way in which Cambodia could preserve its independence would be to join ASEAN, even though King Sihanouk had dismissed this idea in the wake of the successful UN-supervised election. If Cambodia and Vietnam become members of ASEAN, this will deter the latter from attacking and occupying Cambodia. To prevent a larger country from invading a smaller neighbour is ASEAN's *raison d'être*. This is in fact the single most important achievement of ASEAN. Indeed, in the organization's twenty-seven years of existence, none of the ASEAN members has gone to war with one another, even though there are many outstanding historical problems (including territorial disputes) between the member states. Cambodia's worst enemy, however, may not be the Vietnamese or the Thais, but the Cambodian people themselves. Although the UN-supervised general elections have turned out better than expected, the current coalition government is still very fragile, while the Khmer Rouge remain a serious danger. Indeed, if the present government is more interested in enriching itself than in rebuilding the country, support for the Khmer Rouge may grow from disaffected Cambodians, especially those living in the rural areas, who will inevitably lose out, as can be seen in other peasant-based countries in Southeast Asia. If civil war breaks out in Cambodia, with the danger of the ultra-nationalistic Khmer Rouge coming back to power, Vietnam would be tempted to intervene once again in Cambodia. History may yet repeat itself in Cambodia.

**Conclusion**

Vietnam and Cambodia dominated Southeast Asian security for the best part of three decades, from the early 1960s to the early 1990s. Their impact upon post-Cold War security, however, appears to be much more limited. Vietnam's ambitions have been severely curtailed, and the country's main security concerns appear to be internal and economic rather than external and military. Although China remains a major concern, Vietnam is seeking a *rapprochement* with ASEAN and is attempting to build new bridges further afield (most notably in normalizing relations with the United States). For Cambodia, although the 1993 elections failed to produce a universally recognized government able to unite the country, and although the Khmer Rouge remain a substantial thorn in the side of the government, the threat posed by the Khmer Rouge does not appear to jeopardize the new government's existence in the long term. As with Vietnam, the main security concern is internal and economic. This understandable preoccupation with its internal affairs has led to a very low-key approach to foreign affairs (with the exception of the desire for a return of its territory), demonstrated by the government's decision not to seek membership of ASEAN in the short term. However, given the prevailing trend towards regionalism (in respect of both security and economies) in Southeast Asia, it is difficult to foresee Cambodia remaining outside regional structures indefinitely.

NOTES

The guerrilla movement in South Vietnam began sometime in 1960. While America's involvement started in the early 1960s with the despatch of military advisers, it was not until the landing of US marines in Da Nang in 1965 that the United States became fully engaged in the ground war in Vietnam. For a well-documented account of the genesis of US intervention in Vietnam, see George McT. Kahin, *Intervention: How America Became Involved in Vietnam* (New York: Alfred A. Knopf, 1986).

2. See, for example, Nayan Chanda, *Brother Enemy: The War after the War* (New York: Harcourt Brace Jovanovich, 1986).

3. By the mid-1970s, the Soviet Union saw opportunities opening up in Asia (as a result of communist victories in South Vietnam, Cambodia and Laos) that would allow it to extend its reach and influence into a region hitherto closed to Moscow. But the Soviet Union would have to contend with Beijing, which considered the region a traditional Chinese area of influence and would never countenance a Soviet military presence in a region.

4. In essence, the domino theory maintained that once South Vietnam fell to North Vietnam, the rest of Southeast Asia would country-by-country fall prey to communism. The domino theory was repudiated by anti-war activists, who maintained that although China and the Soviet Union were backing Hanoi, the North Vietnamese were nationalists and their sole objective was to liberate South Vietnam from foreign powers. Subsequent events, specifically the outflow of boat refugees and Vietnam's invasion of Cambodia, vindicated the contention of former officials of the Kennedy and Johnson administrations that the leadership in Hanoi was interested in more than just 'liberating' the South. Hanoi, they argued, was bent on exporting people's revolution to the rest of Southeast Asia, especially Thailand which had backed the US war effort. By the early 1970s Hanoi had concluded that, given the changed domestic situation in these countries, communist parties in these countries were unlikely to succeed in overthrowing those governments. In a change of strategy, Hanoi decided to support 'progressive' elements in these societies, such as the Thai student movement which succeeded in overthrowing the military-backed Thanom regime in October 1973 through a popular uprising. For a discussion of the change in Hanoi's strategy, see Gareth Porter, 'Vietnam-ASEAN Relations: A Decade of Evolution', *Indo-China Report*, (April-June 1985).

5. See Truong Nhu Tang, *A Vietcong Memoir: An Inside Account of the Vietnam War and Its Aftermath* (New York: Harcourt Brace Jovanovich, 1985).

6. The Nixon administration argued that the bombing of Cambodia was necessary because the Vietcong were using sanctuaries in Cambodia to launch attacks against US forces. See William Shawcross, *Sideshow: Kissinger, Nixon and the Destruction of Cambodia* (New York: Pocket Books, 1979).

7. In exchange for President Nguyen Van Thieu's acceptance of the Paris peace agreement, Nixon pledged to provide military aid as well as air support to his government if North Vietnam resumed the war in the South. In 1974 the White House requested increased military aid for the South in response to North Vietnam stepping up its attacks. In seeking aid for the Thieu regime, President Nixon was honouring his part of the bargain. Congress would have none of it, and rejected the aid request.

8. One theory has it that Cambodia's opposition to Vietnam is a manifestation of the psychology of the Khmer Rouge leadership. According to this theory, Pol Pot and his top lieutenants were motivated by the desire to prove that they were better Marxists than the Vietnamese. Thus, by launching a radical agrarian programme Pol Pot sought to transform Cambodia into a communist state, ahead of Vietnam. The French colonial authorities probably contributed to this state of affairs, as during the French occupation of Cambodia ethnic Vietnamese rather than Khmers were employed to work in the French offices. It was a classic divide-and-rule game played by the colonial authorities to keep the colonized people subdued. For more details on this theory, see David P. Chandler, *Brother Number One: A Political Biography of Pol Pot* (Boulder, Colorado: Westview Press, 1992).

While Khmer Rouge units were attacking villages in South Vietnam in 1977, similar attacks were also taking place inside Thailand which, like Vietnam, had annexed land belonging to the Khmer kingdom since the fifteenth century. For a debate on which side launched the aggression first, see Anthony Barnett, 'Inter-Communist Conflicts and Vietnam', *Bulletin of Concerned Asian Scholars*, Vol.11, No.4 (1979), pp.2–9, and Laura Summers, 'In matters of war and socialism, Anthony Barnett would shame and honour Kampuchea too much', ibid., pp.10–18.

10. The coup was led by Khmer Rouge commanders who were disenchanted with Pol Pot's policies. Remnants of this group, who fled into Vietnam after the failure of the coup, formed the backbone of the government installed by Vietnamese forces in January 1979.

11. For a review of the arguments relating to the Vietnam-Cambodia conflict, see Paul Kelemen, 'Review Essay: How Pol Pot Came to Power', *Bulletin of Concerned Asian Scholars*, Vol.20, No.4 (1988), pp.62–71.

12. See K. U. Menon, 'The Paralysis of Power: The United States and Cambodia', *Contemporary Southeast Asia*, Vol.7, No.4 (1986), p.274.

13. See Kenton J. Clymer, 'American Assistance ot the Cambodian Resistance Forces', *Indo-China Issues* (April 1990), p.2. FUNCINPEC is a French acronym for the United Front for an Independent, Neutral and Peaceful Cambodia, and the KPNLF stands for the Khmer People's National Liberation Front.

14. One scholar contended that one of Deng Xiaoping's objectives in launching the attack on Vietnam in February 1979 was to 'explode the myth' of Vietnamese military invincibility. Scholars, however, could not agree on whether Deng succeeded in achieving his objective, as the Chinese forces took a heavy beating in that war. See Harlan W Jencks, 'China's "Punitive" War on Vietnam: A Military Assessment', *Asian Survey*, Vol.19, No.8 (1979), p.814.

15. See *Far Eastern Economic Review*, 15 Oct. 1992, pp.46–51.

16. For details of the peace agreement, see Frank Frost, 'The Cambodia Conflict: The Path Towards Peace', *Contemporary Southeast Asia*, Vol.13, No.2, Sept. 1991, pp.143–6.

17. See Henry Kamm, 'Vietnam, On Its Own at Last, Jostles for Place in New Asia', *International Herald Tribune*, 20–21 June 1992, p.1.

18. *Far Eastern Economic Review*, 17 Feb. 1994, p.14.

19. The Spratly Islands are claimed wholly or partially by Brunei, China, Malaysia, the Philippines, Taiwan and Vietnam. See *Straits Times*, 23 July 1992, p.15.

20. While most of the ASEAN governments have normalized relations with Vietnam after the signing of the Cambodia peace agreement in October 1991 and have urged their businessmen to do business with Vietnam, Malaysia appears to be the most active among them in promoting ties with Hanoi. The two governments have agreed to explore for oil jointly in those areas of the Spratly Islands where they have overlapping claims. As China claims the whole of the Spratlys, it means Malaysia and Vietnam would both have to deal with Beijing. For the first time, a Malaysian minister, Defence Minister Najib Tun Razak, openly called on the United States to maintain its military presence in the region, citing the possibility of fighting in the South China Sea. See Mike Yeong, 'China's New Assertiveness', *ISEAS Trends*, *Supplement in Business Times*, 27 Aug. 1992.

21. *Far Eastern Economic Review*, 24 Feb. 1994, p.32.

# Thailand's Post-Cold War Security Policy and Defence Programme

## MARK G. ROLLS

Like many other Southeast Asian states, Thailand has traditionally pursued a complex security policy which has had both an internal and external orientation and encompassed a number of issues (military, political, social and economic). In the 1970s, after the communist victories in Indo-China, the prevailing communist insurgency combined with a high degree of political instability led to Thai security policy (broadly defined) being primarily internally oriented. The Vietnamese invasion of Kampuchea (Cambodia) in 1978, and the subsequent occupation during the 1980s, represented a very pressing threat to Thai security and led to a reorientation away from an internal towards an external focus: an adjustment which was also influenced by the gradual decline in the threat posed by the Communist Party of Thailand and an increase in the degree of political stability under the prime ministership of General Prem. The external orientation of Thai security policy emphasized, in common with traditional Thai conceptions of external threats, political-military issues.[1]

Whilst post-Cold War Thai security policy will continue to have an internal dimension – Thailand is still, to some extent, a 'weak' state – its importance could well continue to decline. The communist insurgency has ended and there is a relatively high degree of political stability under Prime Minister Chuan's civilian administration, the apparent outbreak of Muslim 'separatist' violence in the South in 1993 notwithstanding.[2] Moreover, an increasing stress on the external orientation of security policy will be necessitated by the changing regional environment, particularly as it involves and affects those states and organizations with which Thailand is more or less continuously concerned. There will, however, be some changes in the issue emphasis of Thai security policy as the priorities in the region change.

No state's defence programme will, of course, solely reflect, or be determined by, its prevailing security policy (even its political-military aspects). Indeed, a host of other contributory factors revolving around, for example, bureaucratic politics and available resources will also come into play. Thailand is certainly no exception to this, with some decisions in recent years (especially with regard to procurement) subject to the prevailing power of the military in the political system. It has even been contended that weapons procurement decisions have often been determined on the basis of the 'commissions' paid by the arms suppliers to the officers awarding the contracts.[3] Current defence programmes are also often influenced by more long-term trends, the external aspects of which may have preceded any major change in the strategic environment. In Thailand's case, in common with many of its ASEAN colleagues, there was a clear shift during the 1980s away from a focus on counter-insurgency capabilities towards the enhancement of those for conventional warfare. This shift was brought about by a number of factors including the declining threat posed by communist insurgency, the geo-political changes in Indo-China, and an increasing concern about aspects of maritime security. Thailand's post-Cold War defence programme will continue to be determined by a range of domestic and external factors (some long-standing). Elements of this programme, however, will also be closely related to specific changes in externally-oriented security policy, some of which have resulted from the changed strategic environment.

Before the various aspects of continuity and change with regard to the external orientation and issue emphasis of Thai security policy can be considered, it is necessary to provide the historical context within which this consideration can occur. This includes an analysis of the primary conceptual aspect of Thai foreign relations and security thinking, the 'balance of power', which has influenced the overall direction of Thai security policy towards its neighbours and external powers, and still has an important bearing on the post-Cold War environment. It is also necessary to include the role of the Thai military in the determination of security policy. This role, despite the reduced involvement of the military in domestic politics and the related emphasis on 'professionalism', is still important in some cases.[4]

## The Historical Context

Historically, Thai security policy has focused on Indo-China and has thus been concerned about the political make-up of, and relations with, Cambodia, Laos and Vietnam. For reasons also resulting from its close proximity, Myanmar (Burma) too has been an area of concern. Cambodia and Laos have long been regarded as 'buffers' against the perceived threat of Vietnamese hegemony in Indo-China, a hegemony which would threaten the security of Thailand's external environment and challenge Thailand's own regional ambitions. At the heart of Thai security thinking, therefore, was the desire to ensure a favourable 'distribution of power', both on mainland Southeast Asia and – often inter-linked – in terms of external power involvement.[5] Thai security thinking has thus emphasized the 'attainment of a secure environment through balance of power arrangements in which preponderant power was organized on the side of Thailand' throughout the myriad changes in power alignments which occurred.[6]

This primary desire to preserve, or recreate, a favourable 'balance of power' has accordingly influenced Thai foreign relations and security thinking towards the role of extra-regional powers and the wider global confrontation of the Cold War. Thus, throughout the various developments in the post-1945 period (notably the US failure in the second Indo-China war, the communist victories in Indo-China and the Vietnamese invasion of Cambodia) Thai thinking has focused on the 'distribution of power that can be brought to bear on mainland Southeast Asia'.[7] Consequently, Thai foreign and security policy has eschewed rigidity and has been highly flexible and pragmatic.[8] For example, when the US failure in Vietnam and the communist victories in Indo-China threatened to upset the prevailing power alignments and portended Vietnamese dominance, Thailand sought to transform its relationship with China from one of enmity to friendship. With the Vietnamese invasion of Cambodia in 1978, this developed, in effect, into a military alliance between the two.

The need for flexibility and pragmatism has, of course, been influenced by the fact that for much of the post-1945 period Thailand has been a 'frontline' state, irrespective of whether the threat to it was 'actual', or just 'perceived'. Thai security policy-makers have thus been anxious to ensure the maintenance of national security by whatever means necessary. Hence, during the period of confrontation with the Vietnamese-backed regime in Phnom Penh, the Thai government was prepared to support the communist Khmer Rouge despite simultaneously being involved in a lingering campaign against the Communist Party of Thailand. This pragmatic approach has also led the Thai government to respond rapidly to any perceived changes in the regional environment in order to further Thai security, in spite of the wider diplomatic consequences. This occurred notably with the Chatichai administration's opening to Vietnam and the Phnom Penh regime in 1988, which was in complete contrast to the then policy of ASEAN and consequently undermined the Association's solidarity.

A final historic characteristic of Thai security policy has been what has been termed 'double-track diplomacy' – that competing groups within the foreign and security policy-making circles have different approaches to the maintenance of national security.[9] Differences of policy were evident, for example, between the foreign policy elite and the military over

Thailand's attempt to improve relations with China in the mid-1970s; and between Prime Minister Chatichai and many military officials over his 'battlefield into marketplace' initiative in 1988–89. Although it has been noted that this characteristic can provide 'flexibility' in meeting threats to national security, it can also make security policy highly un-predictable, particularly in view of the frequent changes in administration, and its civilian or military composition, which have occurred.[10]

The military has had an important role in the determination of security policy not only by virtue of its long-term involvement in govern-ment and politics, but also because it has been given a primary role in the preservation of national security beyond its purely military aspect. This role has been exercised through its involvement in all aspects of the maintenance of national security, and the creation of national 're-silience', under Prime Ministerial Orders 66/2523 (1980) and 65/2525 (1982),[11] and through agencies such as the Internal Security Operations Command and increasingly the National Security Council as the threat from the Communist Party of Thailand declined.[12] In addition, the mili-tary's widespread business and commerical interests have 'bolstered' and enabled it, to some extent, to act as an 'independent force'.[13] These interests have also significantly influenced the military's attitudes towards certain areas of Thai security policy.

### Indo-China

The Indo-China region has been pre-eminent in Thai security policy around the end of the Cold War and will continue to be so in the post-Cold War period despite important developments in the competition for maritime resources. The changed geopolitics in this region, and in Southeast Asia as a whole, are increasingly revolving around aspects of states' economic security (that is, the maintenance of a state's economic development through securing access to resources, capital and markets) which encompass both regional economic competition and co-operation.[14] The changed geopolitics have thus led to a general shift in the issue-emphasis of Thai security policy in Indo-China away from the military and towards the economic component. The main concern is no longer the overwhelming military threat posed by a Vietnam seeking hegemony, and the consequent need to establish 'buffers', but, instead, the promotion of Thai economic interests in the region and the pros-pects for trade and co-operation with the Indo-Chinese states. The exception to this economic-oriented focus will, to some extent, be pro-vided by Cambodia. There will still be an important political-military element in Thai security policy towards Cambodia because of the prevailing situation there and the nature of Thai relations with the Cambodian government and the Khmer Rouge.

The basis for Thailand's post-Cold War security policy towards Indo-China, with its emphasis on the economic issue, was laid down by Prime Minister Chatichai's 'New Look Diplomacy'. The impetus for this 'New Look' was provided by the stalled Cambodian peace process with the rationale being that the changed regional environment meant Thailand had achieved a degree of security from external threats and that it was important to focus on economies and trade in order to strengthen Thailand's economic position. Thailand's economic strength was regarded as an increasingly important factor in the maintenance of national security in the long term.[15] Indeed, it has been recognized that Thailand faces many economic challenges as an NIE (Newly Industrializing Economy) including competition for foreign investment and markets and access to resources (particularly maritime ones).[16]

The essence of the new security initiative was to create favourable political relationships with the Indo-Chinese states, in order that Thai economic interests could be furthered and economic co-operation fostered.[17] Significantly, in view of the propensity for 'double-track' diplomacy in the determination of Thai security policy, there was a high degree of convergence between the administration and the military. This was no doubt partly due to the fact that the enhancement of security through furthering economic interests would fit in with the historic hegemonic vision held by the military (*Suwannaphum*), a vision which would see Thailand employ the resources of its neighbours to become a 'regional power centre', and was given substance by Thailand's considerable economic strength in comparison with its neighbours.[18]

In practical terms, Thailand has sought simultaneously to enhance political relationships and further its economic interests, thereby enhancing its security. With regard to furthering its economic interests, Thailand has attempted to do this by both acting as a facilitator for general economic growth in the region (based on the idea of it being a 'strategic window')[19] and through the provision of aid and promotion of specific development projects. In Laos, for example, Thailand established a 200m baht (US $7.9m) aid fund in 1991, and in early 1993 the two countries began talks aimed at resolving a long-standing border dispute.[20] Last year also saw the signing of a Memorandum of Understanding between them which focused on co-operation in the development of hydro-electric power schemes in Laos which will provide a vital source of energy for Thailand's north-eastern provinces.[21]

The attempt to establish a favourable political relationship with Vietnam is, as in the past, rather more problematic, with the furthering of Thai economic interests there holding out the prospect of both opportunities and challenges for Thai security. Thailand's willingness and ability to promote development in Indo-China as a whole (the proposed road link from Northeast Thailand, through Laos, to the port of Da Nang in Vietnam, for example), and further economic links with Vietnam, have been generated by the end of the military threat posed by Vietnam. Indeed, Vietnam is now regarded as having 'no potential' to threaten Thailand or its neighbours militarily.[22] However, although it has been suggested that a crucial element of Thailand's security policy in Indo-China will be the need to establish some form of 'political co-existence',[23] this co-existence will require more than the absence of a sense of military threat on Thailand's part. There is a need to resolve some of the often deep-seated problems which have afflicted Thai-Vietnamese relations. Such problems include the issue of the citizenship of Thailand's Thai-Vietnamese population, and the problem of overlapping territorial claims in the Gulf of Thailand. This latter issue has been a persistent source of confrontation leading, for example, to the arrests of both countries' fishermen for apparently encroaching into the respective territorial waters.

Thailand and Vietnam have begun the process of seeking to reduce the conflict potential of such disputes by agreeing to the joint exploitation of resources in the disputed zones[24] and, more recently, by reaching an agreement on the principles which will govern the resolution of territorial disputes (both land and maritime).[25] This process will not be particularly easy, however, in view of the proclivity of states to feel that they may be disadvantaged by any proposed arrangements, a factor which could be exacerbated because the maritime area under dispute has gained in importance owing to the discovery 'of offshore oil and gas deposits . . . along with mineral deposits on the continental shelves'.[26] Current trends in Southeast Asia as a whole are seeing an increased willingness by states to raise the issue of territorial claims as states seek to acquire access to vital maritime resources, and are increasingly using the declaration of Exclusive Economic Zones to do so.[27]

The long-term prospects for future competition between Thailand and Vietnam may, paradoxically, also be increased by Thailand's attempts to further its economic interests through assisting in Vietnam's economic development, both on a bilateral basis and through its participation in large-scale development projects aimed at Indo-China as a whole (notably the Mekong development plan).[28] Although Thailand will undoubtedly accrue significant economic benefits from its involvement in these projects, it has been argued that such a policy will bring

Vietnam out of isolation and foster its competitive strength, thus enabling it to compete with Thailand again for regional dominance.[29] The former Thai ambassador to Hanoi, Surapong Jayanama, has been reported as saying that Vietnam 'was seeking to assume economic leadership over the Indo-China region'.[30] Thailand may, therefore, find that its security can best be enhanced by seeking to tie Vietnam into the wider politico-economic framework in Southeast Asia by pushing for its eventual membership of ASEAN and its participation in the Free Trade Area.

The likelihood of renewed friction between Thailand and Vietnam over Cambodia seems more remote following the formation of a coalition government in September 1993 consisting of the royalist FUNCINPEC Party and the once Vietnamese-backed governing party, the Cambodian People's Party (CPP).[31] Cambodia, however, will continue to occupy a central place in Thai security policy by dint of its contiguous border, with the issue-emphasis still being primarily politico-military. The reasons for this continued politico-military emphasis, in contrast with the economic approach towards the other Indo-Chinese states, are a function of not only the formation of the new Cambodian government but also the legacy of Thai involvement in Cambodia (particularly that of the military).

Despite the formation of the coalition government in Cambodia, which has resulted in a greater degree of stability there, the situation remains volatile as the Khmer Rouge (who are thought to still control some 20 per cent of Cambodian territory and number around 10,000 fighters)[32] continue to remain outside the political structure and hostile to the new government. They have not responded to the government's overtures to engage in peace talks and the government has reacted by launching an offensive against Khmer Rouge controlled areas, many of which border Thai territory. Thailand, consequently, will remain concerned about the prospect of any fighting spilling over into its territory. Indeed, the Thai's had earlier recognized the need to respond to such a security problem during the factional fighting which occurred when Untac was in (nominal) control. The Thai government then announced contingency plans for border security problems and stated that its troops were ready to respond to any spillover of fighting.[33] More recently, immediately prior to the official institution of the new Cambodian government, Thailand warned that it would fire warning shots into Cambodia if fighting between the Khmer Rouge and government forces spilled over.[34] This threat provoked an angry reaction from the Cambodian leaders and has been indicative of increasing friction in the relationship between the two states. This friction revolves primarily around the Cambodian government's belief that Thailand is continuing to provide support for its opponents, the Khmer Rouge.[35] However, a new dimension has been added with the Cambodian government's desire for a return of the territory which it claims Thailand annexed during the 1980s (at the height of its involvement in supporting the anti-government guerrillas).[36] The Thai government and military leadership have sought to respond to the Cambodian government's allegations of continued support for the Khmer Rouge by announcing the disbandment of a special military unit (Unit 838) which had provided services for, and assistance to, the Khmer Rouge[37] and by removing military officers in the border area who had 'vested interests' in continued ties with the Khmer Rouge (revolving around business links over a lucrative cross-border trade in gems and timber).[38] Prime Minister Chuan has also visited Cambodia in an attempt to relieve the tension generated by this issue.[39]

Although the security policy being pursued by the Thai government and military leadership is aimed at establishing a good political relationship with Cambodia, no doubt as a precursor to seeking to promote its economic interests there (in line with its policy towards the other Indo-Chinese states), this will be difficult to achieve in the short term. In particular it appears that elements in the Thai military have the potential to disrupt this policy through their continued links with the Khmer Rouge. These links have been evinced by the recent discovery of a large cache of arms apparently destined for the Khmer Rouge and a Thai-built compound in Cambodia for them.[40] These continued links are a product of not only the shared business interests but also the long-standing military relationship between the Thai military and the Khmer Rouge, and continued distrust by elements of the Thai military of both the new government and Vietnamese intentions. The Thai government could also face hostility from Cambodia in respect of the promotion of Thai economic interests there. The Cambodian government is reported to be considering investigating all business deals with Thai companies signed before the May 1993 elections,[41] and there appears to be increasing resentment in Cambodia towards the promotion of Thai economic interests.

## Myanmar (Burma) and China

The current pattern of regional developments suggests that, in the future, Thai security policy towards Myanmar and China will increasingly be determined by the growing nexus between them. Traditionally, bilateral relations between Thailand and Myanmar have been based on mutual suspicion and enmity, fostered by a long and ill-defined border and the continued existence of various insurgencies in the border areas. Indeed, as part of its then security policy of maintaining 'buffers', Thailand provided sanctuary and indirect support to insurgent groups fighting against the military regime in Myanmar.[42] From 1989, however, as part of its economic-oriented security policy, Thailand sought to improve relations with Myanmar by developing areas of political and economic co-operation. To facilitate this co-operation, and because of the ASEAN principle of 'non-interference' in domestic politics based on mutual self-interest, Thailand (along with its other ASEAN colleagues) continued to pursue a policy of 'constructive engagement' towards the military regime in Yangon despite the latter's human rights abuses and the associated international criticism of such a relationship.[43] Thailand has tried to improve relations with the military regime (the State Law and Order Restoration Council or Slorc) by seeking to mediate in the latter's conflicts with various ethnic insurgents and, more recently, by putting pressure on the rebels still fighting to reach an agreement with the Slorc.[44] Part of the rationale behind this is no doubt an attempt to recover valuable logging concessions which Thai companies (including ones with military involvement) had in Myanmar. The Slorc had revoked these because of Thailand's support for the insurgents and has refused to grant more.[45]

Significantly for long-term Thai policy, Thailand and Myanmar agreed in January 1993 to form a joint commission to 'promote economic and trade co-operation', with the commission holding its inaugural meeting in September.[46] At the same time Thailand also indicated that it wanted Myanmar to become a member of ASEAN and has since invited the Myanmar foreign minister to attend the 1994 ASEAN Annual Ministerial Meeting (AMM) as an observer.[47]

Thailand is clearly attempting to pursue a similar security policy towards Myanmar as it is towards the Indo-Chinese states, although in the case of Myanmar it also has an important wider dimension to it: Thailand is anxious to enhance its relationship with the Slorc regime in order to retain some influence in the face of increasingly close Sino-Myanmar ties. These ties have been steadily improving since the signing of a major arms deal in 1989 and have led, through a series of development projects in Myanmar carried out by China, to a highly influential role in Myanmar for Beijing.[48] Of particular concern to Thailand is the reported Chinese assistance in the development of Myanmar's naval facilities (for example, on Hanggyi Island in the Cocos Islands and at Mergui near the Thai-Myanmar border). This could lead to the Chinese navy gaining access to these facilities, perhaps for refuelling, thus enabling Chinese warships to operate in the Andaman Sea and

Sea, particularly in view of the perception that the US Navy can no longer be relied upon to protect the Thais' 'blue water' interests.[69] Notable aspects of Thai naval expansion and modernization include: the restructuring of the naval command into three regional centres (two in the Gulf of Thailand and one in the Andaman Sea);[70] the establishment of a naval base in the Andaman Sea;[71] the deployment of four recently delivered Chinese-built frigates, with another two on order;[72] the purchase of six Sea Hawks and planned acquisition of Harrier jump-jets for the helicopter carrier due to be delivered in 1997;[73] and the proposed acquisition of a second helicopter carrier, and three submarines.[74] The navy may also develop a land-based air capability if the acquisition of 30 US A-7 aircraft goes ahead.[75] In tandem with this naval expansion, Thailand's capacity for air operations in support of maritime interests in the Gulf of Thailand and the Andaman Sea will be enhanced by the eventual acquisition of a second squadron of F-16s,[76] and three E2C Hawkeye early warning and control aircraft.[77]

Although not yet overtly acknowledged, part of the rationale behind the current naval (and air force) expansion may be Thailand's concern about the arms build-up in Southeast Asia, particularly by its ASEAN colleagues. It has already been suggested that Thailand's military strength should be reviewed in the light of its neighbours' arms purchases,[78] with the naval expansion being continued in order to ensure a 'balance of power' with the navies of Thailand's neighbours.[79] The long-term implications of this prevailing regional arms dynamic remain to be seen.

## Conclusion

Post-Cold War Thai security policy displays important aspects of continuity and change. Continuity is, above all, reflected in Thailand's concern with the creation and maintenance of a favourable regional environment, particularly with regard to Indo-China, but also with respect to the wider region, too. Although there has been an obvious shift in emphasis of much of Thailand's externally-oriented security policy (from the political-military aspect to the economic), the new issue emphasis is still influenced by and directed towards Thailand's security relationships with its neighbours. The old (political-military) and new (economic) concerns of Thai security policy are thus linked by virtue of the states which they include. Of course, in respect of Cambodia and, to a lesser extent, Myanmar, the issue emphasis of Thai policy is still on the political-military aspect.

Continuity is also demonstrated by Thailand's adherence to its long-standing security concept of seeking a 'distribution of power' conducive to the maintenance of its security. This is now illustrated by its desire to further ASEAN's development (political and economic) and enhance its bilateral relationships with the United States and Japan. These bilateral relationships are influenced by both political-military and economic security concerns. The 'interplay' among political-military and economic security issues is also evident with regard to Thailand's increasing concern with aspects of its maritime security. Indeed, this is perhaps how security should be perceived in any case, with no one issue being given 'primacy'.[80]

Clearly, the issue emphasis of Thai security policy is influenced by changes in the prevailing regional environment and in the priorities which exist there. Thus the increased priority given to aspects of economic security (especially maritime) in the region as a whole has been reflected in Thai security policy. The nature of these changed priorities may, in fact, be indicative of changes in parts of the wider international environment in which 'other [non-military] types of threat are rising in importance regardless of the decline in military concerns'.[81] Thailand, however, will continue to have an important political-military dimension to its security policy both because of the nature of its relations with some of the neighbouring states and of the Southeast Asian environment as a whole. The latter has a potential for instability which may be realized given the prevailing arms dynamic. Moreover, any changes in the Indo-China region, particularly in respect of the situation in Cambodia and the issue of Vietnamese actions and ambitions, could see a return to the earlier military-oriented policy. Any change in security policy necessitated by an alteration in the situation in Indo-China could also bring about a partial (Thailand is unlikely to abandon its maritime-oriented defence programme) reversal in Thailand's defence programme. This would see a renewed emphasis on the army and land-based threats.

Finally, there currently appears, with some exceptions,[82] to be a high degree of convergence between the civilian administration and the military over the direction of post-Cold War Thai security policy and the defence programme. Thus any return to military rule (remote as it seems) is unlikely to raise the possibility of a radically different approach to security policy being adopted. Renewed military rule, however, could affect the pace and scope of manpower reductions and lead to procurement decisions being determined less by the nature of security policy and more by bureaucratic politics and other such factors.

## NOTES

1. Muthiah Alagappa, *The National Security of Developing States: Lessons from Thailand* (Dover, Mass.: Auburn Publishing House, 1987), p.39.
2. This violence, which saw a series of attacks in the South, initially on schools, was thought to indicate a resurgence of activity by the Pattani United Liberation Organisation (PULO). However, in view of the low numbers of active insurgents and a degree of apparent Muslim contentment with the prevailing political and economic situation, the violence has been attributed to local officials and/or disaffected elements in the military. *Straits Times*, 6 Sept. 1993 and *Far Eastern Economic Review* (hereafter FEER), 16 Sept. 1993, p.12.
3. See FEER, 2 July 1992, p.13.
4. For a general discussion of the role of the military in Thailand since the September 1992 elections, which brought in a civilian government headed by Chuan Leekpai, see FEER, 20 May 1993, pp.18–20.
5. Alagappa, op.cit., pp.57–8.
6. Ibid., p.57.
7. Ibid.
8. For an historical analysis of various aspects of 'pragmatism' in Thai foreign and security policy see Surin Maisrikrod, 'Thailand's Policy Dilemmas towards Incho-China', *Contemporary Southeast Asia*, Vol.14, No.3 (1992), pp.287–96.
9. Alagappa, op.cit., p.58.
10. Ibid.
11. Ibid., p.36.
12. Chandran Jeshurun, 'The Military and National Security', in Sandhu, Siddique *et al.* (eds.), *The ASEAN Reader* (Singapore: Institute of Southeast Asian Studies, 1992), p.120.
13. Ibid.
14. For an analysis of the complex issues of economic security, at different levels, see Barry Buzan, *People, States and Fear* (Hemel Hempstead: Harvester Wheatsheaf, 2nd ed., 1991), pp.230–69.
15. Khatharya Um, 'Thailand and the Dynamics of Economic and Security Complex in Mainland Southeast Asia', *Contemporary Southeast Asia*, Vol.13, No.3 (1991), pp.245–6.
16. Ibid., pp.248–9.
17. Ibid., p.249.
18. Ibid., pp.246–7.
19. Ibid., p.247.
20. See FEER, 4 Nov. 1993, p.34 and *Sunday Times* (Singapore), 21 March 1993.
21. *Straits Times*, 7 June 1993.
22. The comment of Thai army commander, General Vimol Wongwanich, *Straits Times*, 3 June 1993.
23. Khatharya Um, op.cit., p.263.
24. See *Sunday Times* (Singapore), 9 June 1991 and *Straits Times*, 8 Jan. 1993.
25. FEER, 28 Oct. 1993, p.15.
26. Khatharya Um, op.cit., p.263.
27. See ibid., p.261.
28. For details of the proposed Mekong development plan and its effects, see FEER, 16 Sept. 1993, pp.68–72.
29. Khatharya Um, op.cit., p.261.
30. *Straits Times*, 8 Jan. 1993.
31. It is not altogether impossible, though, especially if the Vietnamese should feel compelled to intervene again in Cambodia in order to protect Vietnamese residents and immigrants there in the wake of renewed attacks upon them. There were a series of attacks upon them by many of the Cambodian factions during UNTAC's (United Nations Transitional Authority in Cambodia) involvement with the administration of

Cambodia. See FEER, 30 July 1992, pp.14–16. On the Cambodian elections, see the preceding essay by Mike Yeong.
32. *Asia 1994 Yearbook* (Hong Kong: Review Publishing Company, 1994), p.103.
33. *Sunday Times* (Singapore), 25 April 1993 and *Straits Times*, 3 May 1993.
34. *Straits Times*, 20 Sept. 1993.
35. Thailand had provided considerable support to the Khmer Rouge, in particular, during the guerrilla campaign against the Vietnam-backed regime in Phnom Penh.
36. FEER, 28 Oct. 1993, p.32.
37. *Straits Times*, 28 Sept. 1993.
38. FEER, 14 Oct. 1993, p.20.
39. FEER, 27 Jan. 1994, pp.19–20.
40. *Straits Times*, 20 Dec. 1993.
41. FEER, 28 Oct. 1993, p.32.
42. See FEER, 3 Dec. 1992, pp.22–23.
43. See FEER, 26 March 1992, p.27.
44. FEER, 27 Jan. 1994, p.20.
45. *Straits Times*, 30 June 1993.
46. *Straits Times*, 23 Jan. 1993.
47. FEER, 20 Jan. 1994, p.9.
48. See FEER, 11 Feb. 1993, p.28.
49. See *The Economist*, 23 Jan. 1993, pp.62–3, *Straits Times*, 15 Sept. 1992, and FEER, 16 Dec. 1993, p.26.
50. See *Straits Times*, 15 Sept. 1992.
51. See Khatharya Um, op.cit., p.264.
52. Yong Deng, 'Sino-Thai Relations: from Strategic Co-operation to Economic Diplomacy', *Contemporary Southeast Asia*, Vol.13, No.4 (1992), p.372.
53. Michael Leifer, *ASEAN and the Security of South-East Asia* (London: Routledge, 1989), p.91.
54. For an analysis of Thailand's place within the Association, see Michael Antolik, *ASEAN and the Diplomacy of Accommodation* (Armonk, New York: ME Sharpe, 1990).
55. Alagappa, op.cit., p.59.
56. The term used by Sarasin Viraphol, director-general of the Department of American and South Pacific Affairs in the Ministry of Foreign Affairs, FEER, 19 Nov. 1992, 'The Fifth Column', p.30.
57. Vietnam and Laos have already been accorded 'observer' status at the ASEAN AMM in July 1992 (when they also signed the Treaty of Amity and Co-operation). *Straits Times Weekly Overseas Edition*, 25 July 1992.
58. The original proposal for an ASEAN Free Trade Area was made by the Thai PM, Anand Panyarachun, in June 1991.
59. *Straits Times*, 24 Feb. 1993.
60. See *Straits Times*, 9 Jan. 1993, and *Sunday Times*, (Singapore) 22 Aug. 1993.
61. See Surin Maisrikrod, op.cit., pp.298–9.
62. *Straits Times*, 25 June 1993.
63. FEER, 18 Feb. 1993, p.12.
64. *Asia 1994 Yearbook*, op.cit., p.25.
65. *Straits Times*, 20 May 1993. Thailand, in fact, made a similar request as early as 1990.
66. FEER, 18 Feb. 1993.
67. See FEER, 21 Oct. 1993, pp.30–31.
68. These reductions will see army manpower reduced by a total of 25 per cent (c.80,000 troops) over the next ten years according to army commander General Vimol. *Straits Times*, 3 June 1993.
69. FEER, 21 Oct. 1993, pp.30–31.
70. *Straits Times*, 23 Nov. 1993.
71. This new naval base will be located in Krabi province. *Straits Times*, 11 Jan. 1993.
72. *Straits Times*, 25 Feb. 1993.

73. *Straits Times*, 9 Nov. 1993.
74. *Straits Times*, 12 June 1993.
75. FEER, 21 Oct. 1993, p.30.
76. See FEER, 18 Feb. 1993, p.13.
77. See FEER, 11 March 1993, p.9.
78. *Straits Times Weekly Edition*, 24 July 1993.
79. *Straits Times*, 27 Dec. 1993.
80. Buzan, op.cit., p.368.
81. Ibid., p.369.
82. Notably, elements of the military's attitude towards the Khmer Rouge and the military's opposition to government proposals for barter deals for arms (see *Straits Times*, 21 Feb. 1994).

# Dragon's Fire and Tiger's Claws: Arms Trade and Production in Far East Asia

## SUSAN WILLETT

Far East Asia is by far the most dynamic region of the global economy.[1] It is also a region undergoing a significant military build-up, giving cause for concern in some quarters. SIPRI estimates show that in the early 1980s regional defence expenditure rose by almost 4 per cent per annum in real terms. This trend was exceeded in the late 1980s. Regional economic development and rising military expenditures appear to be intrinsically linked, as many Far East Asian countries have pursued defence industrialization as an integral part of their broader industrialization and economic development strategies. Rapid rates of economic growth have enabled these countries to increase defence expenditure without incurring the economic costs experienced elsewhere in the Third World.[2] No formal arms reduction agreements exist in the region and as a reaction to increasing regional insecurity since the end of the Cold War, military expenditure has continued to soar. These trends have led a number of analysts to claim that Far East Asia is participating in a regional arms race which could have unfortunate consequences if it continues unchecked.[3]

Latent security issues in the region are fuelling the regional arms build-up and could have the potential to escalate into conflict in the absence of regional arms control initiatives.[4] These entail unresolved territorial disputes such as the controversy over ownership of the Spratly and Paracel Islands and China's claim on Taiwan.[5] In addition, the lingering feud between South and North Korea, the latter's nuclear programme, and Japan's dispute with Russia over the Kuril Islands contribute to the growing sense of regional insecurity. Two other major phenomena add to the sense of regional instability: the US withdrawal from the Subic Bay naval base in the Philippines, which has created something of a power vacuum; and the increasing nervousness about China's, and to a lesser extent Japan's, regional intentions. The fact that both of these countries are increasing their defence expenditure in absolute terms in order to modernize their forces has encouraged the smaller countries in the region to follow suit.

Force modernization has generated an increase in demand for both imported and indigenously manufactured weapon systems. The Pacific-

Asian states have raised their share of imports from 15 per cent to 34 per cent between 1982 to 1991.[6] As a consequence, the region has become one of the most dynamic arms markets in the world. Western suppliers jostle with the Russians at regional arms bazaars to capture lucrative market shares. But Far East Asia is not the Middle East – buyers in this market are not content simply with the supply of completed weapon systems, rather they want the technological know-how as well. Most deals now involve technology transfer which have allowed Far East Asian countries to build relatively sophisticated indigenous arms industries.

Pressures on both the supply and demand side of the international arms market are forcing a major structural adjustment of the defence producing sector. It is undergoing a rapid process of international restructuring and globalization of production.[7] The forms that globalization are taking (that is, cross-border restructuring of ownership, international co-production schemes between companies, foreign investment, international sub-contracting, international licensing and international joint ventures) bear many similarities to the transnationalization of commercial production which occurred from the 1960s onwards.[8] As a region, Far East Asia captured many benefits from the transnationalization of commercial production; the question now is are they now about to make similar strides in the defence production sphere? If so, the balance of power within the arms market, which was dominated by the Permanent Five throughout the Cold War period, may be challenged in the not so distant future. This could have serious consequences for the structure of the international arms industry, weapons proliferation and thus international security.

This paper examines the dynamics of the relationship between the arms trade and defence production in Far East Asia. In the first instance, it explores the supply side trends which are leading to the globalization of the defence sector in which Far East Asian countries are becoming small but significant players. The second section looks at the demand side by examining the changing nature of the regional arms market. The third part analyses the process of defence industrialization in Far East Asia. The final section examines the implications of these trends for the international arms industry and arms control.

**Supply Side Dynamics**

The structure of the international arms market has changed profoundly in the last five years. The diminished threat of a superpower confrontation has led to a dramatic decline in global military expenditure and a significant drop in the international demand for weapon systems. In the United States military expenditure declined by 29 per cent between 1985 and 1993 and is projected to drop a further 17 per cent between 1993 and 1997. Between 1985 and 1996 defence expenditure in the United Kingdom will have fallen by 21.5 per cent, and in Germany by nearly 30 per cent. With Western defence budgets declining and fewer military development programmes in the offing, many West European and American defence firms are seeking export markets. Defence export promotion is being actively encouraged by governments as a means of subsidising domestic procurement. It is argued that foreign sales lower unit costs of production and increase the returns on research and development. Companies also maintain that they benefit from foreign government subsidies and that sharing risks for new developments may be increasingly necessary because of the escalating costs of major new weapon systems.

In the past Western states have considered the unilateral command of military high technology as a crucial strategic asset. However, as Krause's history of the diffusion of military technology demonstrates, a leading edge has never been maintained for long periods and historically the arms trade has been instrumental in the proliferation of military technology. Periods of qualitative innovation have always been followed by export driven technological proliferation.[9] In the last few years, as domestic budgetary pressures have built up, the economic incentives to export state-of-the art defence technology has grown. Global overcapacity has reinforced buyers' power in the market, leading recipients increasingly to insist on the export of production technology. Thus the supply of components, sub-systems and technology know-how has been on the increase in recent years, while exports of completed weapon systems are decreasing.[10] Western suppliers have accepted technology transfer in its various forms because it is often the only way to sell to nations with sophisticated defence requirements. This situation has resulted in considerable concern over the strategic implications of the loss of control over technology. The current situation bears all the hallmarks of a new age of export driven proliferation, for despite urgent calls to control the trade in conventional weapons in the aftermath of the Gulf War, the West through intensive competition in the arms market has actively engaged in a qualitative escalation in arms transfers.

The changes in the international defence market are accompanied by a fundamental restructuring and reorientation of the global defence industry.[11] A significant feature of this restructuring process is the rapid internationalization of defence production as sellers seek competitive advantages through joint ventures with countries offering cheap factor inputs particularly in the form of skilled labour. Internationalization takes a number of forms, including licensed production, sub-contracting, full-scale collaboration (including R&D co-operation) and cross border mergers and take-overs. International restructuring of ownership, such as mergers, acquisition and joint ventures, is a rela-tively new phenomenon in the defence sector as defence companies previously enjoyed highly protectected domestic markets. However, budgetary constraints and the ever increasing costs of sophisticated weapon systems has reduced the ability of individual states to subsidize across the board national capabilities in defence production. The re-moval of state protection has exposed the national defence sectors to greater commercial pressures forcing them to operate more like any other industrial sector. The inducement to internationalize is particu-larly strong in those defence companies operating in advanced technology markets with high R&D costs and short production runs. The new patterns of corporate linkages established around complex international networks of research, production and information (a form of 'technology networking') has become known as 'techno-globalism'.

Unlike civil markets, cross-border mergers and international take-overs in the defence industry emerged as a discernable trend in the late 1980s, accelerating from 1990 onwards. The main producers of engines, military electronics, missiles and helicopters are in the process of form-ing joint companies at a European and trans-Atlantic level.[12] In addition to mergers and take-overs, large defence companies have been involved in cross share ownership and the formation of brand new companies as they seek more formal integration of production and research and de-velopment. The most recent phenomenon to appear in the early 1990s has been 'offshore' arms production. This is where firms relocate pro-duction to capture advantages in factor markets. The principal recipients of 'offshoring' have been the more industrially advanced Third World countries, particularly those in Far East Asia such as Tai-wan, Singapore, Indonesia and South Korea, who offer highly skilled but relatively cheap labour along with considerable expertise in high technology capabilities, particularly in electronics. For instance, it has been estimated that Singapore's wage costs are half those of Europe and the United States, resulting in production savings of between 25 to 40 per cent for some companies.[13] Induced by such comparative advantages companies such as Pratt & Whitney, Hawker Pacific, TRW, General Electric and Garret and Westinghouse have made direct investments in component manufacture, assembly and repair service work in Singa-pore.

At the centre of the current phase of internationalization is the im-portance of technology as a factor in defence industrial competitiveness and the emergence of civil innovation as the driver of technological change. In the 1950s and 1960s the development of fundamental new technologies in semi-conductors, computing and in many other fields occurred substantially in response to spending on defence R&D, and to military consumption, which enabled producers to make the first moves down the production learning curve. During the 1970s and 1980s, however, the direction of dependence gradually began to change; technological advances have been driven from commercial rather than military applications, and innovations are diffusing from civilian into defence rather than vice versa, a trajectory characterized by spin-on rather than spin-off. This phenomenon is most apparent in Japan, where an increasing range of commercially developed technologies, particularly electronic components, are finding their way directly into advanced military systems. Military artifacts are increasingly coming to rely on the pool of technology deriving from civil innovation. If defence markets shrink while civil markets continue to expand, the costs of autonomy for defence production can only rise. Thus, the ability to integrate systems, to absorb civil technology and adapt it to military ends will be at a premium.

Another consequence of the shift in the technology balance between civil and military production is that, as military production becomes a much smaller part of the high technology market, defence firms are having to change the ways in which they organize R&D and production, and the way in which they manage relations between their civil and military divisions. The hazard they face is that companies at the leading edge of civil technologies will move horizontally into defence markets. To a degree this is already happening. Japan's success in electronic componentry makes it a latent but formidable force within the international defence industry. In the United States for instance, almost all of its weapon systems contain component parts from foreign sources, predominantly incorporating dual use technologies with both military and civilian applications, such as microelectronic chips, composite materials, and flat-panel displays.[14] Internationally, the implication is that countries and firms which are the leaders in civil technology will ultimately gain a competitive advantage in defence technology.

For the traditional arms producers globalization means not only increasing dependence on foreign sources of supply for components and parts but also for manufactured products. The growing dependence of the Western defence sector on the supply of crucial inputs by nations such as Japan, South Korea and Singapore, whose political interests may diverge from those of the West, could present a real security risk in the future. If present developments go unchecked, it is possible that technologies only obtainable from abroad will be sufficiently critical to provide economic leverage on Western foreign and security policies. Questions about who commands the generic high technology base, and in which countries they locate which R&D and production, may become increasingly pertinent to defence procurement and arms control in the years ahead.

## The Demand Side: The Far East Asia Market

### Military Expenditure Trends

The growth in demand for weapon systems in Far East Asia has been dependent on significant increases in military expenditure (see Figure 1). The available data on military expenditure suggest a military build up in the region, though the regional data on defence expenditure are notoriously unreliable and there are problems with comparability. With such caveats in mind the graph should be regarded only as a measure of trends rather than an absolute. According to the data Far East Asian defence expenditure increased by 25 per cent over the ten year period 1982–91.[15] The continuing increase in regional defence expenditures stands in marked contrast to trends elsewhere, global defence spending having declined by over 20 per cent since its peak in 1987. The rise in defence spending has not been uniform for all the Far East Asian countries during this period. For example, the SIPRI figures show a decline for Malaysia and the Philippines, while Japan, China and South Korea have made significant increases to their military budgets despite the end of the Cold War. Although Japan's defence expenditure remains around a self-imposed limit of 1 per cent of GDP – representing a low economic burden – the rapid rate of economic growth in Japan disguises the absolute increase in defence expenditure over the last decade. Japan's defence budget has increased in constant 1988 dollars from $21.3bn in 1982 to $31bn in 1991, an increase of about 30 per cent in ten years (see Figure 2). Japan's defence expenditure is now five times greater than that of Australia, three times that of North and South Korea combined, four times greater than ASEAN's total, and is also about 20 per cent greater than China's. While its defence expenditure increases have slowed down from the 6 per cent annual rise of the early 1980s, the current annual increases of 2–3 per cent represent a rate that exceeds any other OECD country. Equipment expenditures have risen from 26 per cent to 28 per cent of the defence budget during the same period. The research and development activities of the Japanese Defence Agency enjoyed the sharpest increase in the fiscal year 1988 with a budget increase of almost 12 per cent. Japan now has the sixth

FIGURE 1

TOTAL MILITARY EXPENDITURE FOR FAR EAST ASIA 1982–91
CONSTANT US$M 1988 PRICES

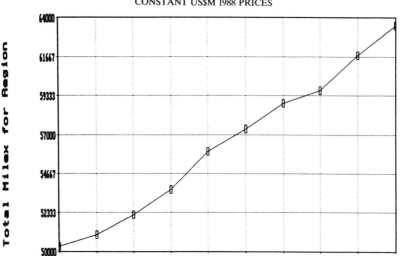

*Source: SIPRI Yearbook 1992.*[15]

largest defence budget in the world, though to put this into perspective it still amounts to only 10 per cent of the US defence budget.

Over the past thirty years Japan's defence policy has been directed towards the potential threat posed by the Soviet Union and other communist powers in the region. Now that the Cold War has ended there are strong internal and external political pressures on Japan to reduce defence expenditure. Not least, the emergence of Japan as one of the largest defence spenders in the world has raised the nascent fear of Japanese militarization, over which China has already openly voiced its concern. However, many officials in the Japanese Defence Agency believe that greater uncertainties in the region demand an increase in defence capabilities. It may also be misplaced to equate military expenditure with militarization *per se*. The rapid growth of the former is neither a necessary nor sufficient condition for the latter. There is still a very strong pacifist commitment in Japanese society which has so far ensured that Japanese security policy is narrowly committed to a doctrine of self-defence, and hotly opposed to overseas military activities.

Japan's largest regional rival is China, which has substantially increased its spending on defence. Official statistics on defence spending are highly unreliable and inaccurate, and what is provided is widely

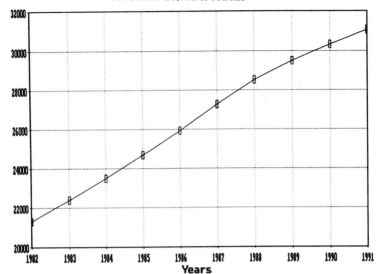

## FIGURE 2
### JAPANESE MILITARY EXPENDITURE 1982–91
#### CONSTANT US$M 1988 PRICES

*Source: SIPRI Yearbook 1993.*

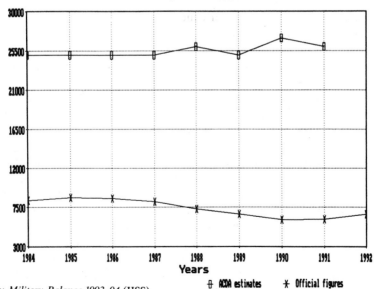

## FIGURE 3
### CHINA'S MILITARY EXPENDITURE
#### CONSTANT US$M 1991 PRICES

⊟ ACDA estimates   ✶ Official figures

*Source: Military Balance 1993–94* (IISS).

believed to be only a fraction of total military spending, the rest coming under different budgetary accounts or from revenues raised by the People's Liberation Army (PLA). This type of secrecy leads to contradictory evaluations of China's military capabilities, which are often portrayed as being formidable but obsolete. At the official figure of $7.4bn in 1993 China's defence spending is only about one-tenth of Japan's. In reality the defence budget may be three to four times higher than the official figures, as the army has considerable income from investments and arms exports which do not appear in the official statistics. But even at four times the size of the official defence budget China's expenditure remains lower than that of Japan. If one compares annual per capita allocations of defence expenditure the differences are even more marked. Using IISS figures, China's was $19 in 1992 while Japan's was $136 (1985 prices).[17] (The highest per capita allocation for defence expenditure in the region was in fact Singapore with $590 per annum.) The cyclical swings in China's military expenditure are not common to the rest of the world. During the 1980s, when global expenditure was on the rise, China was consciously reducing its military burden and converting its defence industries to civil production.[18] In the 1990s, when the rest of the major military powers began to cut their defence budgets, China found itself armed with obsolete weaponry and consequently began a programme of equipment modernization creating upward pressure on its defence budget.[19] The changes are partly related to a structural transformation in military doctrine and strategy that followed the abandonment of the Moaist concept of 'people's war'. The new theory, 'people's war under modern conditions', places emphasis on weapon modernization, professional armed forces, forward defence and limited aggression where necessary. China has recently formed rapid deployment forces and purchased a considerable amount of modern military equipment from Russia, giving rise to the suspicions about China's regional intentions. Although the import of modern weapons from Russia has become a potent symbol of China's military build-up, this conception may be misleading.[20] The pace of modernization in China has in fact been much slower than that of Taiwan and South Korea, curtailed as it is by China's lack of hard currency and poor production technology. Its trade deficit is such that to purchase new Su-27s from the Russians it paid in part by bartering canned meat.

Of the other countries in the region, both Taiwan and Singapore have increased their military expenditure rapidly. In 1991 Singapore's increase was an astounding 21 per cent, modernizing its forces to provide adequate cover for the important sea routes which pass through its territorial waters. Both countries are dedicated to increasing their

FIGURE 4

SINGAPORE MILITARY EXPENDITURE 1982–91
CONSTANT US$M 1988 PRICES

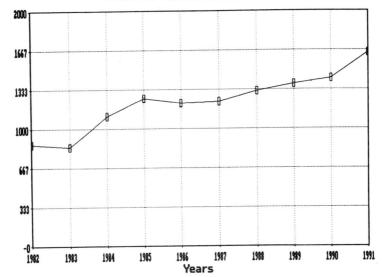

*Source: SIPRI Yearbook 1993.*

FIGURE 5

TAIWAN MILITARY EXPENDITURE 1981–92
CONSTANT US$ 1988 PRICES

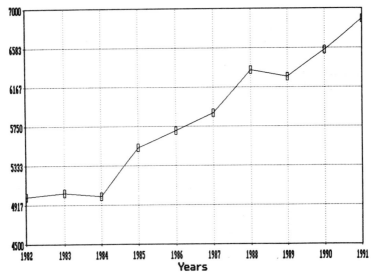

*Source: SIPRI Yearbook 1993.*

TABLE 1

TRADE IN MAJOR CONVENTIONAL WEAPONS TO FAR EAST ASIA 1988–92
(US$M 1990 PRICES)

| Recipient | Sellers | | | | | | | |
|---|---|---|---|---|---|---|---|---|
| | USA | USSR/ Russia | FRG | France | China | UK | Others | Total US$m |
| China | 84 | 1,286 | – | 130 | – | – | 19 | 1,519 |
| Japan | 9,017 | – | – | 50 | - | 157 | - | 9,224 |
| Indonesia | 390 | - | 156 | 43 | - | 201 | 384 | 1,174 |
| Korea N. | - | 2,816 | - | - | 307 | - | - | 3,123 |
| Korea S. | 3,238 | - | 96 | 53 | - | 106 | 31 | 3,524 |
| Malaysia | - | - | - | 11 | - | 78 | 42 | 131 |
| Myanmar | - | - | - | - | 407 | - | 102 | 509 |
| Philippines | 75 | - | 5 | - | - | 3 | 43 | 126 |
| Singapore | 856 | - | 376 | 55 | - | - | 29 | 1,316 |
| Taiwan | 1,473 | - | 217 | - | - | - | 544 | 2,234 |
| Thailand | 1,409 | - | 36 | 80 | 1,482 | 167 | 97 | 3,271 |
| Totals | 16,542 | 4,102 | 886 | 422 | 2,196 | 712 | 1,291 | 26,151 |

*Source: SIPRI Yearbook 1993.*

self-sufficiency in weapon systems production in order to reduce their dependency on foreign sources of supply. Taiwan, ever fearful of China and increasingly isolated by the international community in the early 1980s, rapidly increased its defence expenditure in order to achieve self-reliance in national defence. During this period its defence spending grew at an average of 25 per cent per annum. More recent expenditure increases are linked to the programme of augmenting its firepower which is being pursued through a combination of overseas purchases and the 'vigorous development' of defence related science and technology.[21]

*The Arms Trade*

The perception of a regional arms race is being fuelled by the scale of arms exports to the region, which has rapidly expanded since the end of the Cold War. Based on the figures in Table 1, the Far East Asian arms market for conventional weaponry averages out at $5.23bn per annum. Japan is the largest market with South Korea in second place. High rates of economic growth have enabled countries in the region to spend large amounts on weapon systems. Based on SIPRI estimates of the global arms trade, Far East Asian countries generated 34 per cent of global demand for weapon systems. Major equipment purchases include: two guided missile frigates by Malaysia off the United Kingdom; a Thai order for six Chinese-built frigates and three British-built anti-submarine warfare corvettes; the Indonesian 1993 purchase of one-third of the former East German navy; and Indonesia, Thailand, Brunei,

Malaysia, Taiwan, the Philippines and Singapore have all announced or are considering major aircraft purchases. Although most of the weapons suppliers are Western (particularly the United States and Britain), Russia has also been exploring this buoyant regional market. Malaysia is the first ASEAN country to place a major order with the Russians, agreeing in July 1993 to purchase 18 MiG-29 aircraft. Six of the MiGs will be the fly-by-wire variant which are not even operational with the Russian air force, and a range of offset benefit programmes and technology transfers are also included in the deal.

*Transfer of Production Know-How*

During the 1970s rapid economic growth encouraged many Far East Asian countries to arm and manufacture their own weaponry in an attempt to reduce their dependence on the major suppliers. Over-capacity in the West, particularly amongst European producers, encouraged arms exports to provide recipient countries with the market leverage to extract the transfer of military technological know-how. By the 1980s the defence trade in the region increasingly combined sales of finished systems with the transfer of production technologies and industrial infrastructure necessary for indigenous production. By the late 1980s the United States and Europe routinely transferred a great deal of advanced defence technology to the region. In fiscal year 1992 the total value of US commercial licences/approvals was $15,997 bn; Far East Asia accounted for just under 30 per cent of this business. As a consequence of this transfer of production know-how, several countries in the region have attained significant defence industrial capacity and have themselves entered the international arms market. South Korea and Japan supply a range of specialist components and parts for Western defence systems, and even ASEAN nations such as Indonesia and Singapore have begun to penetrate the international arms market. The Japanese government is committed to maintaining a maximum level of indigenous production and development, therefore foreign firms are being forced to make Japanese firms generous technology licensing deals in order to secure sales. The bilateral security arrangement with the United States for example, has resulted in large scale US collaboration in military technology with Japan and massive technology transfers (see Table 3). Licensed production of a variety of types of US military aircraft has contributed to the development of a core of Japanese companies skilled in diverse aspects of aerospace production.[22] These programmes have also helped to establish critical industries such as defence electronics and advanced materials. Co-operative defence production programmes have therefore enabled the

TABLE 2

US COMMERCIAL ARMS LICENCES IN FY 1992
(IN US$M)

| | |
|---|---|
| Indonesia | 100.4 |
| Japan | 2,099.9 |
| South Korea | 904.0 |
| Malaysia | 360.5 |
| Singapore | 184.3 |
| Taiwan | 101.8 |
| Thailand | 376.1 |
| Total | 4,127.0 |

Source: Arms Trade News, May 1993.

TABLE 3

RECENT US-JAPAN CO-PRODUCTION TRANSFERS
(IN US$M)

F-15J Eagle Fighter Aircraft
FSX Fighter Aircraft
CH-47 D Chinook helicopter
KV-107/2A helicopter
Model 205 UH-IH Huey helicopter
Model 209 AH-IS Cobra helicopter
UH-60J helicopter
EP-3C Orion electronic intelligence aircraft
M-110A2 self-propelled howitzer
Patriot missile battery
MIM-104 Patriot mobile surface -to-air-missile
MIM-23 Hawk mobile surface-to-air missile
AIM-7F Sparrow air-to-air missile
AIM-9L Sidewinder air-to-air missile
BGM-71C i-TOW anti-tank missile

Source: SIPRI Yearbooks 1970 to 1990.

Japanese to develop a high degree of self-sufficiency in defence production.

In recent years the regional market has become increasingly competitive. Not only are traditional US suppliers facing fierce competition from Western European equipment suppliers and indigenous producers, but countries on the fringe of the region, such as Australia and India, are also becoming competitive. The most notable change in the regional market is the realignment of arms sourcing. Countries such as Taiwan and South Korea are moving away from the United States as their traditional source of supply because of its reluctance to transfer sophisticated technology for local production and its stringent restrictions on third country exports. This shift away from the United States has been to the advantage of European suppliers. Western European arms manufacturers who have lost traditional markets elsewhere have turned their attention to Far East Asia with a vengeance, while a number of Far East Asian countries view Russia as a possible source of sophisticated military technology transfer. The Treaty on Basic Relations between Seoul and Moscow for example, and the signing of a Memorandum of Understanding to promote exchanges and co-operation between the respective defence ministries have been seen as a first step towards possible military technology transfers between the two states.[23]

Some countries in the region are arms exporters in their own right and intra-regional trade appears to be on the increase. A notable instance of this was the South Korean sale of of 42 Korean Infantry Fighting Vehicles worth $25.2m to Malaysia.[24] South Korea has been exporting military equipment since the late 1970s, and during the 1980s annual exports ran at about $100m per annum, comprising mainly munitions and light naval vessels.[25] Most of its exports are indigenously designed without foreign collaboration. South Korea's largest markets are the Middle East, Latin America and Southeast Asia. South Korean firms have even been able to penetrate Western markets with competitively priced and high quality components. Export sales fell from $90.97m in 1991 to $21.25m in 1992. Unperturbed by this dramatic decline, the government remains committed to export promotion as a means of maintaining a profitable domestic defence industry. In the 1980s China was the fifth largest exporter of arms in the world, supplying to many pariah states shunned by the Western world, including both sides in the Iran–Iraq War. China has transferred missile technology, nuclear reactors and nuclear materials to states such as Iran, Iraq, Algeria, Syria and Pakistan, and has subsequently been accused of lacking great power responsibility. Within the region China is a supplier to North Korea, Myanmar and Thailand. North Korea is one of the most insular and militaristic regimes in the world, and as part of its policy of self-sufficiency has developed significant defence industrial capacity. Ingenuity in reverse engineering has enabled the North Koreans to gain access to lethal military technologies such as ballistic missiles and chemical weapons. For some time there have been strong suspicions that it has attempted to develop nuclear weapons. Its 1993 indecision to bar an IAEA inspection of its nuclear facilities at Yangbyon has exacerbated such concern. It has achieved the status of the seventh largest arms exporter in the world, demonstrating little constraint in supplying its lethal technologies. Finally, although Japan continues to prohibit the export of complete weapon systems, it is likely that Japanese firms will exert increasing pressure on the government to relax this, while component exports are not subject to the same restrictions. Japan has become a significant supplier of critical dual-use technologies to the West in the form of microprocessors and new materials, to the extent that there is growing concern in the West, and particularly the United States, about military dependence on Japanese dual-use technologies. Should the export ban be lifted, the Japanese defence sector is uniquely placed to profit from the future economic and security environment.

Although Far East Asian countries cannot compete against the major suppliers in leading edge military equipment, they have identified market niches through which they have been able to gradually increase their military technology transfers. It would appear that a world-wide division of labour is emerging in the international arms market with Western countries supplying high-tech, high value-added weapon systems and Far East Asian suppliers providing competitive technologies at a lower end of the defence technology spectrum.

## Defence Industrialization in Far East Asia

The desire to establish indigenous defence industries stems from an amalgam of strategic, political and economic motivations. Strategic considerations involve the desire for self-sufficiency, ensured security of supply, regional power aspirations and local and regional arms races. The political incentives to establish a defence industrial base often relate to the central political role of the military in countries such as South Korea and Indonesia. Finally, economic incentives have played an important role in motivating the newly industrializing nations to establish indigenous arms production. Domestic arms production can lead to procurement cost reductions and potential foreign exchange earnings through exports. Furthermore, defence production is believed to contribute to the civilian economy indirectly by providing spin-offs to other industrial sectors and by upgrading the skills and productivity of the industrial labour force. During the period 1970–90 South Korea, Taiwan, Singapore and Indonesia achieved remarkable growth in their indigenous defence production capabilities. The maturation of their defence sectors is signified by the growing sophistication of their military products – fighter aircraft, tanks, armoured personnel carriers, missiles and naval craft. For countries such as South Korea, Singapore and Indonesia, indigenous defence industrialization has been adopted as an integral part of import substitution strategies for late-comer industrialization. Import substitution has not, however, enabled these countries to reduce their technological dependence on the advanced industrial countries completely.[26] Most Third World defence products continue to incorporate foreign components. In effect indigenous defence production has created other dependencies, shifting the nature of their requirements from the need for finished weapon systems to the need for the technologies to manufacture those systems, altering the nature of their dependency rather than reducing it. But, as Ross has argued, more has happened than simply a change in the form of dependency. The nature of dependence has undergone a subtle but profound transformation, notably a move from a static form of dependency to a more dynamic relationship.[27] As one observer noted, 'The release of technology is an irreversible decision. Once released it can never be taken back or controlled. The receiver of know-how gains a competence which serves as a base for many subsequent gains.'[28]

A number of factors re-configured the international arms market in the 1980s which reinforced the defence industrialization strategies of Far East Asian countries. The most important shift was the erosion of US and Soviet market shares in the international market in the face of growing competition from West European suppliers. The emergence of a buyer's market and the enhanced technological capabilities of developing arms producers provided the latter with the additional leverage to secure licensed production and offset agreements. Moreover, transfers increasingly consisted of military technology, not simply the supply of completed weapon systems. There is a pattern of defence industrialization which is common to the region. It has been summarized as a progression of four integral strategies:[29]

1. initial import of arms from foreign suppliers;
2. gradual creation of maintenance and servicing capabilities including the manufacture of spare parts, made possible by the provision of equipment, data, training and supervision from foreign sources;
3. assembly and production of major weapons under license, to include varying levels of technical participation by the host country; and
4. indigenous design, development and production of systems.

Nevertheless, within this framework the patterns of defence industrialization have not been uniform: financial and technological limitations have led Singapore and Malaysia to concentrate their defence production activities on overhaul, modernization and subcontracting mainly in the aerospace sector, while in Korea and Taiwan production has been made possible through US-licensed production agreements and military assistance programmes. Nor has progress from stage to stage proceeded in sequence, and at present elements of all four stages operate simultaneously in countries such as Taiwan and South Korea. Even the most successful indigenous development programmes require the importation of foreign sourced components and parts.

The ability of these states to establish defence industrial capabilities has been founded upon several factors:

1. The availability of large amounts of capital to invest in manufacturing facilities, create R&D centres, pay for imports and train skilled technicians and engineers. In addition, a sizeable domestic defence procurement budget is a prerequisite of generating a significant domestic market for firms to be viable.
2. Defence production requires a diversified industrial base, especially in aerospace which demands extensive industrial inputs from sectors such as steel, metallurgy, machinery and electronics. The recent increase in defence manufacturing activities in countries such as Singapore and Indonesia can be explained in large part by their growing manufacturing capabilities.
3. The status of scientific and educational facilities in these countries. The arms industries of Singapore, Taiwan and South Korea have created the need for the establishment of institutions for scientific research and applied technology.
4. Strong state involvement through the direct ownership of defence industries and various fiscal and trade incentives are necessary to help both domestic and foreign companies to reduce their costs.
5. Access to export markets primarily in the developing world. The ability of these countries to tailor defence products to external demand and to compete aggressively in the international arms market is the most important condition for long-term survival.

The complexity of defence programmes varies not only with the technical proficiency of the recipients but also with the terms of the licensing agreements the suppliers have been willing to provide. Licensing agreements include:

1. provision of data for the production of simple components;
2. technical assistance to create a production facility for components or entire systems with foreign assistance and supervision;
3. final assembly and testing of systems, components for which are provided by the supplier; and

4. manufacture of systems in a supplier country facility with the percentage of locally built components gradually increasing over time.

Licensed production arrangements have been highly favoured by most developing arms producers. In return for the production of proven weapon systems, governments can conserve foreign exchange and elevate their countries' technological bases. Licensing is also attractive because it is intrinsically flexible. Agreements can be secured which allow for a broad range of manufacturing activities including components, sub-assemblies, or the production of a complete weapon system and its components.[30] Japan, South Korea, Taiwan, Singapore and Indonesia have relied extensively on licensed production from foreign companies as a means of acquiring and expanding their defence industrial capabilities. A second though less frequent means of acquiring defence-related technologies is through joint venture agreements and company-to-company teaming with both Western and other developing defence industrial nations. The economic advantages of collaborative agreements are threefold:

1. risk sharing (and risk reduction) of technical and commercial processes inherent in the development of new weapon systems;
2. access to partners' technology and capital resources; and
3. marketing and market penetration benefits.

In the last five years defence collaboration has moved into the early research and pre-development stages with companies co-operating on design, fabrication and application of advanced technologies. A final means by which Far East Asian countries have accessed advanced military technology is through subcontracting to large foreign defence contractors. Many US and European companies have established production lines in countries belonging to the ASEAN members to capture the advantages of low wages and skilled labour. The development of arms production in Singapore and Indonesia, for example, has been greatly aided by the inward investment of such companies as United Scientific Holding of the United Kingdom and General Dynamics of the United States. Foreign companies are also attracted to these countries because of easy access to the regional market.

The defence industrialization programmes being pursued by many Far East Asian countries were actively encouraged by the United States as a matter of deliberate policy derived, in part, from a desire to extricate its own forces and lower the level of its commitments in the region. In so doing the United States believed that it could maintain control over the disposition of defence resources and the nature of both production and deployment. In addition it assumed that these programmes would continue to be used to strengthen the countries' deterrent capabilities and not pursue solutions independently or aggressively. The defence production programmes which the United States supported were essentially defensive and did not digress in any significant way from the force planning objectives which were adopted when the countries imported technology. As such, additional capabilities did not present a threat to regional stability any greater than that posed by these countries' forces. However, the recent decisions by Taiwan and South Korea, to concentrate resources on developing new, more offensive technologies independent of US leverage could have the effect of raising regional tension and, in the long run, of antagonizing bilateral relations with the United States.

**Implications**

For the traditional Western suppliers, military technology transfers may increase profits for individual companies in the short run but the long-term benefits are not so clear cut. International defence industrial collaboration creates competition and in the future it is likely that highly capable defence firms in the Far East will seek strategic business alliances and sub-contracting relationships with major suppliers as a means of penetrating Western markets. Already Far East Asian countries are capturing niche markets and growing parts of the international market. For instance, Indonesia has emerged as a competitive overhauler and aircraft parts manufacturer including component production for the Fokker-100 and the F-16 aircraft.[31] Singapore has been building up its retro-fitting capabilities based on its strengths in electronics, with engine overhaul for Pratt & Whitney, General Electric and Grumman and the manufacture of sub-components for General Dymanics and Northrop. The Singapore Technology Corporation (STC) has also recently begun to invest in foreign companies, with a 2 per cent stake in Pratt & Whitney's PW4000 engine project and the 1988 joint venture with British Aerospace for the manufacture, repair and integration of BAe components in return for marketing services. France uses STC for repair and overhaul work on its fleets operating in the Indian and Pacific Oceans, and in Taiwan the China Shipbuilding Corporation is involved in extensive retro-fitting for US destroyers and frigates.

The level of technological competence within indigenous defence industries has resulted in the potential for co-production between countries within the region. In 1992 Singapore entered talks with Taiwan over the possibility of a joint combat aircraft venture. This move towards regional co-operation is part of the general attempt to reduce dependence on the major suppliers. Malaysia has been actively pursuing a diversification strategy and in 1992 signed MoUs with Brunei, France, India and Italy, while the recent signing of a defence related MoU between Malaysia and Chile is an attempt to promote South/South contacts.[32] The bid for maturation is nowhere more pronounced than in South Korea. In 1992 the government adopted a new defence industrial strategy which places emphasis on dual use technologies which will be beneficial to both civil and military industries. This is part of an attempt to produce more sophisticated military equipment in the future such as missiles, aircraft, telecommunications equipment and defence electronics. The Koreans have outlined a broad set of objectives for developing an aircraft industry, reaching parity with the developed countries in the manufacture of airframes and engines by the early part of the next century and reaching parity some time after in avionics and other specialized systems. South Korea appears to have adopted a similar defence industrial strategy to that of Japan; the difference is that South Korea does not have a self imposed restrictive export policy like Japan. The distinguishing feature of the Japanese military industrial complex is the dual use nature of basic research and technological development. The Japanese government has targeted certain technologies that are viewed as key to both commercial and military enterprises, particularly those associated with aerospace, artificial intelligence, advanced materials, and superconductivity. As a result, Japanese firms are now important suppliers of high technologies for Western military hardware. For example, the modular technology used in ship retro-fitting is borrowed from Japan and the bulk of commodity microprocessors are now produced by Japanese enterprises. Over the past thirty years Japan has built up its aerospace capabilities on the basis of collaborative projects with the United States. Mitsubishi Heavy Industries undertook the co-production of two fighters in the 1970s, the F-4J and the F-15J, and in the late 1980s signed an agreement with General Dynamics for the co-development and co-production of a new combat aircraft, the Fighter Support Experimental (FSX). This last project has generated substantial controversy in the United States over the costs and benefits of technology transfer with a leading competitor. This concern has been expressed most vociferously in the 101st Congress of the United States. The principal apprehension is that the FSX project might ultimately help Japan become more competitive in aviation markets. US awareness of the threat to their technological sovereignty, and of the implications for the defence market, is very much in evidence.[33] Concern about interdependence and the relative decline of the domestic defence technology base led US Congress to instruct the Department of Commerce to identify those civil technologies critical to defence needs in the future. According to the US Department of Defense, of the critical technologies it has identified at least fifteen are dual-use and Japan is at present leader in five of them.

Although Japan has a strict ban on arms exports which is unlikely to be revoked in the near future, its strength in many dual use technologies makes it a latent force in the global arms industry. The Japanese government is actively promoting R&D activities in advanced technologies in aerospace, advanced materials, superconductivity and artificial intelligence. These are regarded as key technologies for maintaining Japan's competitive edge in the future. In assessing the potential global power that these technological strengths may bestow on Japan, Vogal has identified three possible outcomes: firstly, it could enable Japan to gain political leverage in international relations; secondly, it could give Japan the ability to play a pivotal role in the global race for superiority in military technology; and thirdly, Japan's advances in commercial technology give it the ability to become a major military power in its own right by the early twenty-first century.[34] The fear is that if countries like Japan, South Korea and Singapore begin to apply their innovative ingenuity to defence production processes in the way they have to civil manufacturing, then it is possible that the United States and other Western suppliers will lose control of the weapons technology and the industry necessary to produce and support weapon systems.

## Conclusions

During the Cold War the transfer of completed weapon systems by the major powers served to maintain regional balances of power, and were used in part for political leverage in foreign policy. The recent transfer of production technologies and the growth of relatively sophisticated indigenous defence industries in economically dynamic countries will subvert the ability of major powers to use arms transfers in this way in the future. It is therefore of no surprise to find that in the post-Cold War era the control of high technology has become a new dimension in international relations, intimately linking economic leverage with defence power. Western countries, particularly the United States, are realizing to their expense that without a fast-developing civil technological base no major power can sustain in the long run its status in the domain of economics, defence and international relations, while rapid advances in civil high technology industries allow latecomers in the international system, such as Japan and South Korea, to challenge the status of established international powers. Japan's success in high technology not only illustrates the repercussions of high technology performance on the status of the country in international relations, but also provides a new paradigm for the relationship between military and civil technologies. Japan, which has hitherto taken a back seat in defence markets, will have at least the potential to challenge the current predominance of the United States, Britain, France and Russia.

With the loss of control over military technologies, traditional suppliers will find it increasingly difficult to influence the course of events in the Third World or to maintain any semblance of international order. As arms production capabilities expand and military autonomy and independence increase, military conflicts may well grow in frequency, duration and severity. Traditional suppliers will find it difficult to impose constraints through arms embargoes or other traditional forms of pressure as a means of conflict management, as the West has found to its embarrassment and shame in the former Yugoslavia. The fear is that the enhanced war-fighting capabilities emerging from indigenous arms production capabilities can result in leaders overestimating the strengths of their military, becoming overconfident and engaging in military adventures that might otherwise not occur. Saddam Hussein's attempt to take on the world in the Gulf conflict in 1991 is a case in point.

Traditional suppliers thus face a crucial dilemma between the short-term economic goal of offsetting procurement costs against the long-term consequences of proliferation. So far all attempts to control the arms trade have been circumvented by short-term considerations. Moreover, the recent attempts at formulating arms trade control policies appear to reinforce the traditional status quo and overlook the newly emerging balance of power and global distribution of military production capabilities. Recognizing the form that the globalization of arms production is taking and what this may mean in terms international relations is crucial for the formulation of arms trade controls in the future. Traditionally restrictions on arms transfers have, with few exceptions, been centred on national decision making and regulating policies. With the growth in the internationalization of arms production and the growing importance of dual use technologies, the conditions required to regulate arms transfers need to change fundamentally. It requires closer international co-operation in the efforts to monitor and control the trade in arms, and adds urgency to the formation of an international transfer control regime.

NOTES

1.  Far East Asia here includes Brunei, China, Hong Kong, Indonesia, Japan, North Korea, South Korea, Malaysia, Mongolia, Myanmar, Philippines, Singapore, Taiwan and Thailand. However, this study will concentrate only on those countries which are significant arms importers and producers, namely China, Japan, South Korea, Taiwan, Singapore, Malaysia and Indonesia.
2.  For a discussion of the impact of military expenditures see S. Deger and S. Sen, *Military Expenditure: The Political Economy of International Security*, Strategic Issue Papers (Oxford: SIPRI/OUP, 1990).
3.  See Tim Huxley, 'South-East Asia's Arms Race: Some Notes on Recent Developments', *Arms Control*, Vol.11, No.1 (1990), pp.69–76; Michael Vatikiotis, 'Measure for Measure: Malaysia, Singapore, Poised to Acquire New Arms', *Far Eastern Economic Review*, 30 April 1992, p.18, Paul Dibb, 'Asians are Arming: A Prospect of Trouble Ahead', *International Herald Tribune*, 26 Nov. 1993, p.6.
4.  For a detailed analysis of the security concerns within the ASEAN region see A. Acharya, *A New Regional Order in South East Asia: ASEAN in the Post-Cold War Era*, Adelphi Paper 279 (London: IISS/Brassey's, 1993).
5.  The Spratly Islands consist of over 230 islets, reefs, shoals and sand banks covering a vast area of about 250,000 square kilometres. Sovereignty over the Spratly Islands is disputed between China, Taiwan, Vietnam, the Philippines, Malaysia and Brunei.
6.  *Jane's Defence Weekly*, 29 May 1993, p.28.
7.  For an excellent discussion of the internationalization of defence production see E. Skons, 'Western Europe: Internationalization of the Arms Industry', in H. Wulf (ed.), *Arms Industry Limited* (Oxford: SIPRI/OUP, 1993), pp.160–90.
8.  For a classification of the forms of internationalization of industrial activities see OECD Industry Committee, *Globalisation of Industrial Activities: Four Case Studies* (Paris: OECD, 1992).
9.  Keith Krause, *Arms Trade and the State: Patterns of Military Production and Trade* (Cambridge: Cambridge University Press, 1992), Ch.3.
10. The global trade in arms fell by 48 per cent between 1987 and 1991, from $46bn in 1987 to $22bn in 1991, representing the worst cyclical downturn in the global defence market since the end of the Second World War. This calculation is based on SIPRI arms trade data, which records the sale of completed weapon systems only. *SIPRI Yearbook 1992: World Armaments and Disarmament* (Oxford: Oxford University Press, 1992), p.308.
11. For a detailed analysis of the restructuring and internationalization of national defence industries see Wulf, op.cit.
12. Several good surveys of this process exist, including M. Brzosk and P. Lock (eds.), *Restructuring of Arms Production in Western Europe* (Oxford: Oxford University Press, 1992), and W. Walker and P. Gummett, 'Britain and the European Armaments Market', *International Affairs*, Vol.65, No.3 (1989), pp.419–42.
13. David Shaw, 'The Emergence of the Third World Aircraft Industry', *Military Technology*, Vol.4, No.4 (1988), p.51.
14. Office of Technology Assessment, *Redesigning Defence: Planning the Transition to the Future US Defence Industrial Base* (Washington, DC: US GPO, 1991), p.69.
15. Reliable sources on defence expenditure data for the region are scarce, and what information does exist diverges widely. For example, some countries in the region do not include internal security expenditures in their defence budgets, while others do, and several countries use special funds to import weapons which are not included in official defence expenditure statistics.
16. Alternative sources of data on Far East Asian defence expenditures can be gleaned from IISS, *The Military Balance 1993–94* (London: Brassey's, 1993) and the US Arms Control and Disarmament Agency (ACDA), *World Military Expenditures and Arms Transfers 1990* (Washington, DC: US GPO, 1990).
17. Figures taken from *The Military Balance 1993–94*, p.226.

llapse of communist insurgency in these two countries by the l[ate] [19]80s. But despite the removal of the communist threat, and the trans[fer of] the bulk of the counter-insurgency role to paramilitary forces, b[oth] Malaysian and Thai armed forces retain at least residual intern[al sec]urity functions: the Malaysian army's planned 'rapid deployme[nt for]ce' will have an obvious utility for intervention in Sabah, should th[e sep]aratist impetus there lead to a serious threat of secession; and a re[cent] upsurge in violence by Muslim rebels in southern Thailand ha[s rem]inded Bangkok that internal security potentially remains a seriou[s prob]lem.[9] Domestic security threats remain a preoccupation for the [arm]ed forces in the Philippines (where both the communist New [Peop]le's Army and Muslim separatists remain active), and to a lesser [exte]nt in Indonesia (where separatist movements still exist in East [Timo]r, Irian Jaya and Aceh). The maintenance of internal security is [also] an important potential function for Brunei's armed forces.

[Mo]st of the ASEAN governments see the development of modern, highly technological armed forces, supported by and paradoxically [suppo]rting a local defence industry, as constituting an intrinsic part of [the ov]erall process of national modernization and industrialization. Pro[vision] for industrial 'offset' work in the purchasing country and for [techno]logy transfer have become vital preconditions for the successful [conclu]sion of arms contracts with several regional countries. Singapore [posses]ses the largest and most diverse defence industry in Southeast [Asia. T]he Singapore Technologies Holdings (STH) conglomerate com[prising] ordnance, aerospace, marine and industrial divisions. STH's [core] companies 'form the backbone of Singapore based and owned [technol]ogy-oriented industries' and perform the 'critical role of groom[ing eng]ineering and technological skills for the country'.[10] Without the [substan]tial domestic market provided by the well-funded Singapore [Armed] Forces, STH could never have developed and prospered. In In[donesia], B. J. Habibie, the minister for research and technology, is [using arm]s acquisition explicitly to further his plans for the development [of capita]l-intensive industries. Indeed, it was apparently Habibie, in[terested] in upgrading Indonesia's heavily-subsidized shipbuilding [industry,] rather than the armed forces who decided in 1992 to purchase a [large par]t of the former East German navy. While the initial price for [the sh]ips was extremely low, Habibie proposed 'transforming the [sale] into a US$1.1 billion . . . project that entails overhauling the [and up]grading 15 shipyards throughout Indonesia, constructing a new [nava]l port . . . and acquiring a pair of oil tankers'.[11] The Malaysian [prime m]inister has said that a project to build a class of offshore patrol [craft fo]r the navy 'will be the springboard for the country's own

18. For a description of this process see C.Z. Lin, 'Employment Implications of Defence Cutbacks in China', in L. Paukert and P. Richards (eds.), *Defence Expenditure, Industrial Conversion and Local Conversion* (Geneva: ILO, 1991).

19. One oft-cited statistic is that China's defence budget has risen more than 10 per cent a year over the past five years – a 70 per cent increase in nominal spending. But if one takes into account that China's retail prices rose by 55 per cent over the same period, then defence budget increases were 3 per cent per annum in real terms. In this light China's defence budget growth appears less alarming.

20. Shunji Taoka argues that the growing anxiety about China's military build-up is vastly overplayed and that in reality its military forces are shrinking. The current edition of *The Defence of Japan*, the annual position paper of Japan's Defence Agency, supports this controversial view. Another significant sign of contraction is the reduction in the size of the People's Liberation Army, which was cut back in the 1980s from 4.7 million to 3 million, and further reductions are in progress. Shunji Taoka, 'A Shrinking Tiger', *Newsweek*, 15 Nov. 1993.

21. Reported in an interview with Sun Chen, the Taiwanese Defence Minister, *Jane's Defence Weekly*, 17 July 1993.

22. US aircraft produced in Japan include the Bell UH-IH Huey helicopter, the Bell AH-15 Cobra helicopter, the Lockheed P-3C Orion patrol airplane, the Boeing 107 Model 11 helicopter, the Boeing CH-47 Chinook helicopter, the McDonnell Douglas Model 500D helicopter, the McDonnell Douglas F-4E Phantom jet fighter, the McDonnell Douglas F-15J and F-15DJ Eagle jetfighter, and the Sikorsky S-61, S-61A and S-61B helicopters.

23. *Jane's Defence Weekly*, 31 July 1993.

24. *Jane's Defence Weekly*, 4 Dec. 1993.

25. US Congress Office of Technology Assessment, *Global Arms Trade: Commerce in Advanced Technology and Weapons*, OTA-ISC-460 (Washington DC: GPO, 1991), p.134.

26. For an account of the relationship between military and civil development objectives in South Korea see 'Climbing the Industrial Ladder', *Jane's Defence Weekly*, 31 July 1993, pp.20–5.

27. Andrew L. Ross, 'World Order and Arms Production in the Third World', in J. E. Katz (ed.), *The Implications of Third World Military Industrialisation: Sowing the Serpents Teeth* (Lexington: Lexington Books, 1986), p.278.

28. J. Fred Bucy quoted in *Defence Science Report 1976*.

29. J. E. Nolan, *Military Industry in Taiwan and South Korea* (New York: St Martins Press, 1986), p.45.

30. Trevor Taylor, 'Defence Industries in International Relations', *Review of International Studies*, Vol.16, No.1 (1990).

31. *Armed Forces Journal*, Feb. 1990, p.62.

32. *Jane's Defence Weekly*, 11 Dec. 1993, p.6.

33. US Congress Office of Technology Assessment, *Redesigning Defence: Planning the Transition to the Future US Defence Industrial Base*, OTA-ISC-500 (Washington DC: US GPO, 1991).

34. Steven Vogel, 'The Power behind "Spin-Ons": The Military Implications of Japan's Commercial Technology', in W. Sandholtz et al., *The Highest Stakes: The Economic Foundations of the Next Security System* (Oxford: Oxford University Press, 1992).

# The ASEAN States' Defence Policies: Influences and Outcomes

## TIM HUXLEY

Since the late 1980s there has been considerable publicity regarding a putative 'arms race' in East Asia, including the ASEAN region. Military expenditure and arms imports in the wider East Asian region have increased quite dramatically in both absolute terms and as proportions of global aggregates.[1] In Southeast Asia, it is evident that the governments of all six members[2] of the Association of Southeast Asian Nations (ASEAN) are determined to develop more substantial defence capabilities. This paper examines the factors which have influenced the ASEAN states' defence policies in recent years, and surveys the impact of these defence policies in terms of trends in military spending and defence equipment procurement in each ASEAN member.

## Influences on Defence Policy

While defence policy-making is undeniably a particularly national issue and an individual examination of each ASEAN member is necessary in order to form an accurate impression of recent developments in the ASEAN region as a whole, there are many commonalities in the factors which have influenced levels of military spending and patterns of defence procurement throughout the region. Further, although it is theoretically feasible to disaggregate the various influences on defence policy in the ASEAN states, any assessment of the importance of particular influences in a chosen ASEAN member is bound to be rather impressionistic. Previous research, though, does indicate that specific *threats* have not been the most important influences on the development of these countries' armed forces: long-term, non-threat factors have generally been far more significant. The importance of these long-term influences is indicated by the fact that the ASEAN states have generally been increasing their defence spending, expanding their armed forces, and enhancing these forces' conventional warfare capabilities since the early 1970s.[3] Recent developments do not, by and large, represent an abrupt break with past trends.

### Domestic Factors

The influences on defence spending and arms acquisiti[...] region include both domestic and international facto[...] portant single domestic factor is almost certainly the a[...] funds for allocation to the defence sector. The 'close a[...] lation' between the ASEAN countries' defence sp[...] economic growth is well-established.[4] Given the nota[...] cess of most ASEAN members, this means that ecc[...] facilitated substantially increased military spending [...] the ASEAN governments have been careful to ensu[...] forces have not been over-lavishly funded: defence[...] generally expanded as quickly as either the ASEAI[...] mies or their governments' total expenditure. Du[...] recession of the mid-1980s, most of the ASEAN g[...] their military spending. In some regional countries, [...] explicitly related future defence spending to econo[...] Singapore, 'the limit for the defence budget is peg[...] GDP',[5] while the Malaysian defence minister has [...] ment is likely to increase defence spending to up t[...] 'from the present 2.5 per cent' over the next ten t[...]

A second, crucial domestic influence on defence[...] the armed forces in political and economic decisi[...] nant military role in politics may contribute to con[...] defence spending, as has traditionally been the c[...] increasingly prominent involvement of senior mil[...] pore's government also seems likely to protect th[...] assigned to defence. But Indonesia's relatively mc[...] and sparse order of battle under the Suharto regi[...] military role in government does not necessarily l[...] penditure. Nevertheless, the military may [...] influence over the allocation of resources to defe[...] not politically dominant: civilian government[...] satisfy the armed forces' requirements in terms[...] order to keep the military contented in their p[...] certainly a significant factor in contemporary M[...] that it has also constrained efforts by Chuan Le[...] tration to reduce defence spending and exerc[...] arms procurement in Thailand since 1992.

Coping with serious internal security threat[...] central concern for defence policy-makers in a[...] cept Singapore. Internal security problems hav[...] as an influence on defence policy in Malaysia a[...]

warship-building industry', which will follow the philosophy and concept of the Proton Saga national car project.[12]

Finally, a vital domestic influence on arms procurement decisions, and one which indirectly probably necessitates greater military expenditure, is corruption – a prominent part of day-to-day business life in the region. The routine payment of 'commissions' to senior Thai military officers involved in procurement has received considerable publicity.[13] Corruption is also probably a significant factor in military procurement in most other regional countries. It has been alleged that various people involved in the negotiations leading to the 1988 Anglo-Malaysian Memorandum of Understanding (MoU), which laid the basis for arms deals worth over £1 billion, 'had been promised financial kickbacks from Britain totalling M$200 million [£40 million]' and that 'a further M$300 million [£60 m] political donation would be given to the ruling Umno Baru party'.[14] The only ASEAN country where corruption is clearly not a significant influence on defence procurement decisions is Singapore, where a complex system of administrative checks and balances, including computerized exercises to produce 'analytical hierarchies' of competing bids for contracts, guards against impropriety.[15]

*International Factors*

Changes in the roles of extra-regional powers have exercised crucial long-term influence over all the ASEAN states' defence policies. The British military withdrawal from Malaysia and Singapore in the late 1960s had a profound effect on the pace of change in these two countries' defence policies. President Nixon's 'Guam doctrine', announced in 1969, affected the region more generally by emphasizing that regional states would have to become considerably more self-reliant in defence terms. This need for self-reliance was underlined in 1973 when the United States withdrew the last of its forces from South Vietnam, and again in 1976 when US air bases in Thailand were closed down. During the 1980s, some ASEAN governments – especially in Bangkok and Singapore – cited the Soviet Union's growing regional role, and particularly its strategic toehold in Vietnam, as a serious security concern. Since the late 1980s the ASEAN states' concern over the changing role of extra-regional powers has focused on the implications of US withdrawal from the Philippines, and the extension of China's, Japan's and possibly India's strategic reach into the region.

From the time of the 1975 communist victories in Indo-China until the late 1980s, all of the ASEAN governments (but particularly those of Thailand and Singapore) claimed to perceive significant security threats emanating from Indo-China. These threat perceptions in relation to

Indo-China were heightened following Vietnam's invasion of Cambodia at the end of 1978. It has often been assumed that there was a fairly direct, almost causal relationship between these dramatic political changes in Indo-China and the substantial increases in the ASEAN states' defence spending and the expansion of the conventional warfare (as opposed to counter-insurgency) capabilities of some of these states' armed forces which occurred during the 1970s and 1980s. However, closer examination reveals that many other factors besides Indo-Chinese developments were influential on the ASEAN states' defence policies, arms procurement and military spending. Although there was genuine concern in the ASEAN capitals (and particularly in Bangkok) regarding events in Indo-China, the spectre of 'regional instability' after 1975 and a more specific 'Vietnamese threat' after the invasion of Cambodia tended to be exaggerated, often providing useful justifications for arms acquisitions and increases in defence spending which politicians and senior military officers saw as desirable in any case for a broad range of other reasons.[16] The Vietnamese military withdrawal from Cambodia and Laos in the late 1980s, the resolution at the international level of the Cambodian conflict, the enfeebled state of the Vietnamese armed forces,[17] and Hanoi's obvious interest in cultivating close ties with its ASEAN neighbours collectively suggest that Vietnam can no longer credibly be considered as a security threat in the ASEAN region. Even the Thai government no longer points to Indo-China as a source of justification for its level of defence spending and military procurement, although the Thai armed forces may still harbour concern about the possibility of Vietnamese re-intervention in Cambodia (perhaps in defence of the persecuted ethnic Vietnamese minority there).

Finally, maritime issues have become increasingly prominent amongst the ASEAN states' security concerns since the 1970s, and have instigated a greater emphasis on the development of their navies. A number of factors apart from conflicting maritime territorial claims or specific threats have spurred greater regional interest in maritime security, including the need to protect 200-mile Exclusive Economic Zones (particularly against unauthorized fishing), and concern over problems of piracy and smuggling.[18]

### The ASEAN States' Defence Programmes

In the early 1990s the ASEAN governments have generally continued to implement defence policies which were in train long before the transformation of the regional strategic environment which has occurred since the late 1980s. This underlines the fact that these defence policies

are generally not merely responses to particular threats but usually reflect long-established, domestically-based rationales overlain by a gradual, long-term response to a regional strategic environment which has been evolving in the direction of greater multipolarity and uncertainty more or less continuously for the last two-and-a-half decades.
The main characteristic of the ASEAN states' defence programmes since the 1970s has been a general movement in the direction of enhanced conventional warfare capabilities. Apart from modernizing their equipment inventories, several of the larger armies in the region have also begun to develop since the late 1980s 'rapid deployment forces', which may have potential utility for internal security purposes as well as external defence. But the development and expansion of the region's navies and air forces, particularly involving the actual or planned acquisition of larger surface warships, more anti-ship missiles, submarines, maritime patrol aircraft and multi-role fighter aircraft useful for both air defence and strike, has been much more striking.

*Indonesia*

Indonesian defence policy remains preoccupied with internal security problems: the armed forces' leadership (which dominates the making of defence policy) sees external threats as remote and minimal. Jakarta stresses 'national resilience', including self-reliance in defence, as the basis for national security. Despite the military's long-standing political dominance, defence budgets have been kept surprisingly low. However, the estimates of Indonesian defence spending by the International Institute for Strategic Studies and the Stockholm International Peace Research Institute, though based on official figures, should be treated with extreme caution. If the IISS and SIPRI figures are taken at face value, they show – incredibly – that Indonesian military spending virtually halved in real terms between the late 1970s (SIPRI) or early 1980s (IISS) and 1991.[19] Lowry provides a much more accurate assessment, pointing to a steady upward trend in defence spending since the late 1980s, after a brief slump in the mid-1980s. Under the 1988–93 five-year plan, defence was allocated 1.9 per cent of expected GNP, or 7.3 per cent of planned government spending.[20] Lowry also admits that even the Indonesian Department of Defence and Security may not know 'the true extent of direct and indirect defence expenditures'.[21] Large parts of Indonesia's military expenditure may be secreted in other areas of the official budget, and the defence budget may be supplemented by 'presidential discretionary funds' and contributions from government- and military-owned businesses: according to one estimate, three times the amount of declared defence spending may be hidden in this way.[22]

Whatever the real size of Indonesia's defence budget, the armed forces' sparse inventory of modern equipment attests to the fact that the government has not funded the defence sector lavishly: there has been a sincere effort not to divert funds from civilian development. Nevertheless, efforts have been made since the 1980s to rebuild the capabilities of the air force and navy, which had been allowed to wither away after the army seized power in the late 1960s. Twelve F-16 fighter aircraft were delivered in 1989–90, and recent contracts cover the purchase of 24 Hawk light fighters, and 39 former East German ships, including 16 corvettes. The addition of the new ships to the nine missile-armed frigates already in service will give Indonesia a substantial and reasonably modern fleet: it will certainly be the most impressive in Southeast Asia. Future plans include the acquisition of at least 12 more F-16s, at least 16 more Hawks, locally-built CN-235 maritime patrol aircraft, anti-shipping missiles for all these aircraft, E-2C airborne early warning (AEW) aircraft, and an additional three submarines.[23]

The reluctance of the United States to continue arming Indonesia in view of its human rights abuses (particularly in East Timor), may encourage Jakarta to turn increasingly to other sources for military equipment. Washington's veto on the proposed sale by Jordan to Indonesia of US-built F-5E fighters in August 1993 prompted speculation that Indonesia might purchase Russian MiG-29s. But in view of the armed forces' strong preference for Western equipment, it is likely that western European sources such as Britain and France will become more important.[24]

*Malaysia*

During the late 1970s and early 1980s substantial increases in defence spending allowed the Malaysian armed forces to expand rapidly and, to a limited extent, to enhance their capabilities for conventional warfare.[25] But funding and other problems soon led to a 'phase of consolidation', with substantially lower defence budgets from 1984 onwards. Defence spending has increased again during the 1990s, with the *development* allocation to defence quadrupling in the Sixth Malaysia Plan (1991–95), compared to the previous Plan.[26] Most of the M$6 bn allocated to defence in the Sixth Malaysia Plan will be spent on projects agreed consequent on the signing of the 1988 Anglo-Malaysian MoU, which marked the beginning of a new effort to upgrade all three services' capabilities, but with the emphasis shifting towards the air force and navy.

Equipment ordered under the terms of the MoU includes 28 Hawk light fighters (armed with Sea Eagle anti-shipping missiles and ALARM anti-radar missiles), two Martello air defence radars and associated command, control and communications facilities, Starburst portable surface-to-air missiles for the army, two missile-armed frigates, and the 'Defence Operations Room' C3I (command, control, communications and intelligence) network.[27] The MoU is also expected to cover the construction of two large army bases, including one for the planned Rapid Deployment Force (RDF). A number of equipment contracts have also been signed recently outside the MoU's ambit, including one for four maritime reconnaissance aircraft.[28] More spectacularly, in June 1993 Malaysia signalled its intention to buy small numbers of two types of advanced fighters, the American F/A-18 (eight aircraft for the strike role) and the Russian MiG-29 (18 aircraft for air defence). A contract for eight F/A-18Ds was confirmed during the following December, with deliveries scheduled for 1997. Confirmation of the MiG-29 purchase was reportedly imminent in early 1994.[29]

Future plans for the Malaysian armed forces include expansion of the army's RDF (presently a reinforced battalion group) into a division by the year 2000. This fully-fledged RDF will require substantial amounts of new equipment, including new armoured vehicles, anti-tank weapons and artillery, and will necessitate the establishment of a helicopter-equipped army air corps. The air force plans to acquire attack helicopters and new transport aircraft, with AEW and in-flight refuelling capabilities as longer-term requirements. The navy is looking forward to introducing a class of as many as 27 locally-built offshore patrol vessels, up to eight submarines, and helicopters equipped for anti-submarine and anti-shipping roles.[30] Whether or not these plans come to fruition will depend to a large extent on the availability of funding under the Seventh Malaysia Plan (1996–2001).

A superficial interpretation of Malaysia's current defence programme is that it is largely a response to China's increasingly aggressive posture in the South China Sea. While apprehension regarding China's regional role cannot be dismissed as an influence, many recent and potential improvements in the Malaysian armed forces' capabilities are almost certainly intended as counters to developments in the Singapore armed forces. A prime example is the new Malaysian emphasis on air defence, which is essentially a belated response to the Singapore air force's ability to devastate the Malaysian air force and command facilities in the first few hours of any conflict between the two countries.[31]

## Singapore

The perceived necessity of deterring Malaysia, and possibly Indonesia, continues to underlie Singapore's defence policy. Singapore's defence policy and deterrent strategy are essentially similar to Israel's, involving reliance on armed forces based on conscripts and reservists, and on the ability to use air power to mount a pre-emptive strike against the enemy. Singapore's intrinsic lack of strategic depth and reliance on Malaysian water supplies means that in a conflict it would need rapidly to seize territory in Malaysia and perhaps also in Indonesia's Riau islands to the south. Defence spending as a proportion of GDP/GNP has consistently been the highest in the ASEAN region, and by the early 1990s was almost as large as that of Indonesia, Malaysia and Thailand in absolute terms. Singapore's dramatic economic growth has allowed a doubling of defence spending in real terms since the mid-1970s.

Despite their utter lack of combat experience and reliance on conscripts and reservists, the Singapore armed forces are in many ways the most impressive in the ASEAN region. Like Israel, Singapore aims to maintain a technological edge over its neighbours in terms of military equipment. Recent arms acquisitions, infrastructure improvements and organizational changes have enhanced the already substantial conventional warfare capabilities of all three services. Current planning for force modernization, encapsulated in the 'SAF 2000' concept, stresses combined arms and combined service operations.

Singapore's air force is undoubtedly the most powerful in the ASEAN region, and probably the whole of Southeast Asia (in view of the decay of Vietnam's air power since the late 1980s). Two precepts seem to underlie planning for Singapore's air force. The first is that Singapore should deploy as many front-line combat aircraft – currently about 120–130 – as do the Malaysian and Indonesian air forces combined. The second, which also applies to the Singapore armed forces more generally, is that Singapore's air force should endeavour to maintain a 'technological edge' over its potential opponents: in the air force's case, this is achieved particularly by using 'force multipliers' such as AEW aircraft, in-flight refuelling tankers, precision-guided munitions, and 'hardened' air bases. Eleven extra F-16 fighters should all be in service by 1995, giving a total of 18, and at least seven more may be ordered. But Malaysia's stated intention to procure MiG-29s and F/A-18s has raised the stakes, and may provide a justification for Singapore's air force to follow up its long-standing interest in the F/A-18 with an order for the type as well as or instead of the extra F-16s. However, less glamorous but nevertheless effective A-4 strike aircraft and F-5E interceptors will probably continue to provide the bulk of the air force's combat strength until around the year 2010. Local industry has provided thoroughgoing upgrading programmes for both these types, including the re-engining of the A-4s. More E-2C AEW aircraft may be ordered, and Singapore may be a customer for the Israeli-developed Phalcon combined AEW and communications-intelligence system (carried in a converted Boeing 707).[32] The air force's role in directly supporting the army and navy has been increasing in the early 1990s. A squadron of Israeli-built remotely-piloted vehicles provides real-time intelligence for the army, and eight F-5Es have been converted to a reconnaissance configuration. Four Fokker Maritime Enforcer patrol aircraft, now entering service, will be under the navy's operational control. Three new squadrons comprising additional support and attack helicopters were also being formed in 1993.[33]

The army is being fundamentally reorganized, the bulk of its combat forces being grouped into three combined arms divisions, each composed of a mixture of professional, conscript and reservist troops, and each including an armoured brigade. A rapid deployment force, including a heli-mobile, and increasingly amphibious, elite 'Guards' brigade is reportedly being set up covertly. In the longer term, a mechanized division may be established. Army firepower is being increased in many areas: the army's AMX-13 light tanks have been thoroughly refurbished; up to 350 M-113 armoured personnel carriers are being upgraded, half of them being converted into armoured infantry fighting vehicles; a small number of new French-built AMX-10 armoured vehicles has been bought, and US Army surplus M60 main battle tanks may follow; the locally-developed FH-88 155mm howitzer has re-equipped several artillery regiments and older 155mm artillery has been upgraded. Future artillery purchases may include 105mm guns and the Multiple Launch Rocket System (MLRS).[34]

Singapore's navy has also been restructured. Fast attack craft, including the six heavily-armed missile corvettes delivered since the late 1980s and six smaller, recently-upgraded missile-armed craft, have been grouped into one flotilla, with smaller craft being assigned to the newly-established Coastal Command or transferred to the Police Coast Guard. The five landing ships have been upgraded, and two major equipment programmes are under way: six minesweepers are under construction, and up to 12 offshore patrol vessels, with anti-submarine warfare capability, are planned. The navy hopes to order two submarines (in the first instance) in the mid-1990s, and hovercraft capable of carrying 200 troops each may be acquired for amphibious operations.[35]

### Brunei

Brunei's military expenditure is the smallest in the ASEAN region, unsurprisingly in view of the Sultanate's small population (about 280,000). But on a per capita basis Brunei spends even more than Singapore on defence.[36] Such high defence spending, budgeted at around US$390 million in 1992, has been made possible by the Sultanate's massive revenue from royalties on mineral fuel exports. Funding is available on such a scale that the Brunei's Ministry of Defence usually has difficulty in spending more than 60 per cent of its allocated budget. Two reasons might help to explain this 'underspend': the constraints which a small population with little exposure to modern technology imposes on the armed forces' ability to expand; and, since the late 1980s, an unwillingness or inability to make defence procurement decisions.[37]

Brunei's defence planning has been driven since the 1970s primarily by the long-term need to become more self-reliant in security in anticipation of the eventual withdrawal of Britain's Gurkha garrison from the Sultanate. The maintenance of internal security has remained the principal potential operational role of the Royal Brunei Armed Forces. But concern over external threats has also played a part in the formulation of Brunei's defence plans, focusing principally on the perceived need to deter interference by Malaysia. Problems in relations between the Malaysian federal government and the Sabah state government since the late 1980s have not helped to allay Brunei's concern over the threat from Malaysia, despite the superficial improvement in relations between Kuala Lumpur and the Sultan's government. Brunei has also become concerned since the late 1980s over developments in the South China Sea, where it is one of the three ASEAN claimants in the Spratlys. Although Brunei's territorial claim is relatively minor, and no Bruneian forces have been stationed in the Spratlys to support it, the Sultanate is clearly intent on increasing its ability to defend its maritime resources within its Exclusive Economic Zone.[38]

Despite considerable publicity concerning supposed arms 'contracts' agreed by Brunei since the late 1980s, virtually no major new military equipment has been ordered or delivered for several years, apart from 20 French-made armoured vehicles which entered service in 1990. In October 1989 Mrs Thatcher and the Sultan signed a 'Defence Protocol' covering the purchase by Brunei of combat aircraft and missile-armed naval vessels, reportedly costing B$800 million (about US$400 million). This was Brunei's largest ever defence agreement, and was alleged to have been granted to Britain partially as recompense for the continuing Gurkha presence. At the same time, it was reported that Brunei would buy CN-235 maritime patrol aircraft from Indonesia and training aircraft from Italy.[39] It was widely assumed at the time that the 1989 Protocol would at the very least automatically result in firm orders for 16 Hawk fighters and three Vosper-Thorneycroft missile corvettes. But in September 1990 it was announced that the 'competition' to supply warships had been reopened, and that five shipyards (only two of which were British) would be competing. Why this should have happened is unclear, but the establishment in 1990 of a strategic planning cell to make considered and impartial recommendations to the Sultan regarding defence matters almost certainly reflected his concern over the conflicting and partial advice which he had recently received from various advisers. In November 1990 it was reported that a contract for Hawks would be 'delayed indefinitely' because of the reopening of the warship competition: the defence ministry did not apparently possess the resources to manage two contractual processes simultaneously.[40] Problems with the CN-235's performance delayed this contract as well. Although firm orders for all these equipment items have been expected imminently since 1989, by September 1993 no contracts had been signed. Until these existing procurement programmes are sorted out, no progress can be expected with regard to the Sultanate's interest in buying various other equipment, including more Rapier surface-to-air missiles, and 105mm artillery.[41]

## Philippines

Since the closure of the US bases in 1992 the Philippine government has faced the daunting task of expanding the Armed Forces of the Philippines' (AFP) capabilities to enable them to fulfil an external defence role. The US withdrawal also involved the virtual curtailment after 1991 of the substantial military aid (approximately US$200 million annually) which had been given as 'compensation' for the US presence, and the end of the tax-free fuel supplies which the AFP had received from the American bases. The Philippines' weak economy, implying an inability to replace the US military assistance and to fund a substantial new procurement programme, is the main constraint on the reorientation and re-equipment of the AFP. Manila's defence budget for 1993 of roughly US$800 million amounts to only about one-third of the amounts spent by Malaysia, Singapore or Thailand. The government has proposed a special budgetary allocation of US$1.6 billion to upgrade the AFP's capabilities, but this will be spread over fifteen years.[42]

Reflecting the Philippines' geographical configuration, the economic importance of its maritime resources such as fishing grounds, the two major oilfields being developed off the island of Palawan (which will make the Philippines almost self-sufficient in oil by the year 2000), and the increasing tension and militarization of the South China Sea, the reorientation of the AFP involves a much greater emphasis on the navy and, to a lesser extent, the air force. Simultaneously, though, the AFP will be required to maintain pressure against three major internal security threats: the communist New People's Army (NPA), Muslim secessionist rebels in the south, and right-wing military mutineers and private armies. The Philippine National Police was supposed to have taken over the counter-insurgency role by 1992, but the unexpected resilience of the NPA (still about 10,000 strong in 1993) has led to the postponement of this transfer of responsibility.[43]

Tight financial constraints have forced the scaling down of the earlier, relatively ambitious plans for the modernization of the AFP which were formulated in 1991 on the assumption that the United States would hold on to Subic Bay for another decade and that its military assistance would continue at a high level. The navy has had to trim its corvette refurbishment programme and by mid-1993 had been forced to reconsider contracts to buy small numbers of modern fast attack craft from Spain and Australia and support vessels from China. Significant recent naval acquisitions have been limited to twelve second-hand gunboats donated by South Korea, and eight coastal patrol craft and two logistic support vessels from the United States. The air force has had successively to abandon plans to buy token numbers of F-16 fighters, second-hand Israeli Kfirs, and Czech L-39s. In July 1993 President Ramos promised that the air force would be modernized and that a scheme to refurbish the handful of F-5A/B fighters in service had been approved. The requirement for new fighters may now be filled by ex-South Korean F-5Es. So the Philippines' conventional defence capabilities will probably remain negligible for the rest of the 1990s – the AFP will certainly be incapable of defending the Philippines' Spratly claims. Until the economic situation improves, the best that Manila can realistically hope for is an improved capability to control low intensity problems such as poaching of fisheries, piracy and smuggling.[44]

*Thailand*

The army's dominant political role has been the main influence on the development of the Thai armed forces since the 1930s. Although the demonstrations in Bangkok in May 1992 forced the army to step back from direct political involvement, it is still too early to assert that the army's direct political role has ended permanently. But in any case the army remains an important political force even under the new civilian administration, which will need to fund the development of the armed forces' 'professional' role as a necessary part of its programme to depoliticize the military. Although the personnel strength of the armed forces is to be reduced by 25 per cent between 1992 and 2002, the new government's first defence budget (for fiscal year 1992) was 14 per cent higher than that for 1991.[45]

Important changes were already planned for the Thai armed forces even before the political events of 1992. By the late 1980s mass surrenders had led to the virtual collapse of the Thai communist party's insurgency. Simultaneously, the Thai army's disappointing performance against Vietnamese forces on the Cambodian border in February 1987 and against the Laotian army in the battle of Ban Romklao between November 1987 and February 1988 highlighted its derisory capabilities in the external defence role. These developments underlined the vital need for just the sort of modernization and reorganization programme, aimed at improving the army's conventional warfare capability, which had already been initiated in late 1986.[46] This new emphasis on conventional warfare also benefited the air force and navy: although the army traditionally saw them as subsidiary arms, their support role was clearly much more important in the context of larger scale, conventional warfare than it had been during the counter-insurgency era. Under the essentially civilian Chatichai administration (1988–91), the air force and navy were assigned important roles in defending new industrial areas along Thailand's eastern and southern seaboards.[47] The emphasis on enhancing conventional warfare capabilities was maintained despite the withdrawal of Vietnamese forces from Cambodia in 1989: it was evident that domestic factors, combined with a general concern over the expansion and modernization of nearby countries' armed forces (including China's, Myanmar's and even Malaysia's)[48] and the contraction in the United States' regional military presence, were more important influences on Thai defence policy than consideration of particular threats. While the Thai armed forces' modernization has necessitated substantial increases in defence spending, this has fallen as a proportion of GDP since the late 1980s owing to rapid economic growth.[49]

The 1992 regime change left most of the Thai armed forces' re-equipment plans fundamentally unchanged. The emphasis on procuring naval and air force systems remains. The navy, benefiting from its non-involvement in the suppression of pro-democracy demonstrations in 1992, as well as from its increasingly important role in protecting maritime resources in the context of a declining US naval presence, saw its budget double between 1986 and 1993. China is supplying six frigates at 'friendship prices', all of which will have been delivered by 1995. Two of these ships will be delivered with Western electronics and weapon systems, and it is hoped to upgrade the others to a similar standard. The next major procurement programme involves a Spanish-built helicopter carrier ordered in March 1992. The carrier's air group will comprise S-70B Seahawk helicopters and probably also Harrier fighters. The carrier, when delivered in 1995-96, will provide a power projection capability, currently possessed only by one other Asian navy – India's. The navy also seems likely to strengthen its land-based air power with 30 ex-US Navy A-7 strike aircraft. Future plans include the acquisition of small numbers of German frigates, submarines, and possibly a second carrier.[50]

The Thai air force's next major infusion of combat aircraft will comprise a second batch of 18 F-16s, due for delivery in 1995. Ultimately, the air force would like as many as 72 more F-16s, but budgetary limits will almost certainly prevent such a large order. Financial constraints and the possibility of part-payment in rice underline the potential for a deal with Russia to buy MiG-29s. A new air defence radar network will be operational by the mid-1990s, and plans call for four E-2Cs in the AEW role. British Hawks may fill the requirement for up to 40 new attack aircraft with an anti-shipping capability.[51]

Despite its pro-China orientation in geopolitical terms, the Thai army has been disappointed with the quality of the Chinese arms, particularly the T-69 main battle tanks, which it bought at bargain prices during the 1980s. This has led to a renewed emphasis on procurement from Western and other non-Chinese sources. During the 1990s the army plans to acquire new artillery (including the MLRS) and possibly a replacement for the T-69s. Russia may become a source for some army equipment, including helicopters.[52]

The irrational multiplicity of equipment performing similar roles in the Thai forces' order of battle betrays the important part which 'kickbacks' have traditionally played in Thailand's defence procurement process. The consequences – seen, for example, in the extremely poor in-service performance of equipment such as the Cadillac Gage Stingray tanks bought in 1987 – have frequently been disastrous. While defence funding has continued at a high level in the aftermath of the political setback suffered by the military in 1992, it is clear that the armed forces cannot expect such lavish provision to continue indefinitely in the new, civilianized political environment. Under pressure from the civilian government, the military leadership has been attempting to get better value for money from spending on defence equipment. Serious attempts have been made to reduce the role of corruption in defence procurement by introducing greater 'transparency' into the decision-making process. The first example of this new policy was the decision in 1993 to purchase 20 Bell 212 helicopters for the army rather than more expensive or untested alternatives.[53]

### Intra-ASEAN Defence Relationships: Co-operation, Competition and Latent Conflict

One striking feature of recent military developments in the ASEAN region is that they have resulted from purely and unabashedly national defence programmes. There is no evidence of any co-ordination of these developments: for example, there have been no joint initiatives in arms purchasing or arms production, or in developing compatibility between regional countries' military orders of battle. This may seem surprising, particularly as many previous analyses have exaggerated both the actual significance of, and the potential scope for, defence co-operation between ASEAN members. It is, however, difficult to discern which amongst the proliferation of agreements on various forms of defence co-operation between ASEAN members are actually significant. Certain pairs of ASEAN members have undeniably co-operated successfully, and to mutual benefit, on particular military matters. After the end of Jakarta's 'Confrontation' policy in the mid-1960s, Indonesia and Malaysia co-operated against communist insurgents in the area of their mutual border in Borneo. Indonesia has co-operated bilaterally with Malaysia, Thailand and the Philippines to ensure the security of their maritime frontier zones against low intensity threats such as piracy. Exchanges of military intelligence are believed to have taken place regularly between various ASEAN members in connection with counter-insurgency operations. The Singapore armed forces makes constant, high intensity use of training facilities in Thailand, Brunei, Indonesia and, until the closure of the US bases there, the Philippines. Singapore has also sold arms to Thailand.[54] But the contribution made to national or regional security by some other forms of defence links within ASEAN lies more in the realms of confidence-building than in functional co-operation towards practical objectives. This is particularly true in relation to the supposed 'defence co-operation' between Singapore and Malaysia. Most significant military co-operation between the two countries takes place under the auspices of the Five Power Defence Arrangements (FPDA), which also involve the United Kingdom, Australia and New Zealand. Within the extra-regional partners' defence establishments there is ready acknowledgement of the FPDA's central role to keep open channels of communication regarding defence between the potentially adversarial regional members. Singapore's defence minister has spoken explicitly of the confidence-building role of intra-ASEAN military co-operation.[55]

The absence of multilateral defence co-operation between ASEAN's members, and the widespread lack of substance (other than in the sense of confidence-building) in bilateral defence co-operation indicate the most widely underestimated influence on defence policies in the region.

This is the competition and latent conflict which undoubtedly persists between various ASEAN members. There is a wealth of evidence to support the idea that over the last 20–25 years this competition has led to a process of 'interactive weapons acquisition' involving most ASEAN members.[56] 'Non-threat factors', notably military and national prestige in relation to ASEAN neighbours but also 'supplier pressures' from the defence industries of the United States and Europe, have provided much of the impetus for this process. Huisken pointed out that such interactive acquisition seems to have manifested itself particularly in the purchase by most Southeast Asian navies of missile-armed fast patrol boats during the 1970s.[57] From the early 1970s there was also evidence of a more specific variety of the phenomenon, as Southeast Asian air forces acquired various types of US-built combat aircraft: several ASEAN governments successively decided to buy second-hand A-4 ground attack aircraft (Singapore, Indonesia and Malaysia) and new F-5E interceptors (Malaysia, Thailand, Singapore and Indonesia). In the mid-1980s Thailand, Singapore and Indonesia all opted to buy multi-role F-16 fighters.

'Threat' factors also play a part in interactive weapons acquisition within ASEAN. Certain ASEAN governments base their defence planning and military force structures to a greater or lesser extent on the need to deter, or assert military power against one or more of their ASEAN neighbours. This is particularly clear in the case of Singapore arming itself to deter Malaysian aggression or interference,[58] but tensions between various other combinations of ASEAN members (including Malaysia and every other member of the Association) also have important implications for the defence policies of the states involved.[59] Whether or not interactive arms acquisition by Singapore and Malaysia can be classified as an 'arms race' depends on how the term is defined, but a bilateral 'arms dynamic',[60] involving a fairly intense process of competitive military procurement, infrastructural development and operational planning, and aimed at maintaining the military status quo between the two states, certainly does exist. In the absence of a resolution of the mutual suspicions which continue to cloud intra-ASEAN relations (for instance, between Malaysia and Thailand), the increasingly convincing conventional warfare capabilities of the ASEAN states' armed forces may stimulate the expansion of this bilateral 'arms dynamic' to include other countries in the region.

## NOTES

An earlier version of this paper was published as a chapter in the author's *Insecurity in the ASEAN Region* (London: Royal United Services Institute for Defence Studies, 1993).

1. Desmond Ball, *Trends in Military Acquisitions in the Asia-Pacific Region: Implications for Security and Prospects for Constraints and Controls*, Working Paper 273 (Canberra: Strategic & Defence Studies Centre, Australian National University (hereafter SDSC), 1993), pp.1–2.
2. Brunei, Indonesia, Malaysia, the Philippines, Singapore and Thailand.
3. Tim Huxley, *The ASEAN States' Defence Policies, 1975–81: Military Responses to Indochina?*, Working Paper 88 (Canberra: SDSC, 1984).
4. Ball, op.cit., p.3.
5. *Defence of Singapore 1992–1993* (Singapore: Ministry of Defence, 1992), p.46.
6. *Straits Times*, 13 July 1993.
7. Sukhumbhand Paribatra, 'Thailand: Defence Spending and Threat Perceptions', in Chin Kin Wah (ed.), *Defence Spending in Southeast Asia* (Singapore: Institute of Southeast Asian Studies [hereafter ISEAS], 1987), pp.75–108.
8. Interviews, Kuala Lumpur, July 1993.
9. Rodney Tasker, *Far Eastern Economic Review* (hereafter FEER), 2 Sept. 1993, pp.20–1.
10. Bilveer Singh, *Singapore's Defence Industries*, Canberra Papers on Strategy and Defence 70 (Canberra: SDSC, 1990), p.57.
11. Adam Schwarz and Mark Clifford, FEER, 13 May 1993, p.54.
12. *Business Times* (Singapore), 23 Dec. 1992.
13. See, for example, Tai Ming Cheung, FEER, 2 July 1992, p.13.
14. *Observer*, 7 May 1989; FEER, 18 May 1989, p.14; Tai Ming Cheung, FEER, 8 June 1989, p.30. Allegations regarding corruption in Malaysian defence procurement were also rife in the early 1980s. See K. Das, FEER, 4 Dec. 1981 and Harold Crouch, FEER, 20 Oct. 1983, pp.50–1.
15. Interviews, Singapore, July–Aug. 1993.
16. For a much fuller analysis, see Huxley, *The ASEAN States' Defence Policies, 1975–81*.
17. According to one recent analysis, the Vietnam People's Army will, for the foreseeable future, 'remain a poor man's army capable of defending Vietnam's territorial integrity and maintaining internal security but little else'. See Carl Thayer, 'All-People's National Defence: the Vietnam People's Army under Doi Moi', Paper presented at 'Workshop on Arms and Defence Planning in Southeast Asia', ISEAS, Singapore, 18–19 June 1993, p.70.
18. Huxley, op.cit., pp.23–5. On piracy, see Amitav Acharya, *A New Regional Order in South-East Asia: ASEAN in the Post-Cold War Era*, Adelphi Paper 279 (London: International Institute for Strategic Studies, 1993), pp.37–40.
19. See composite table in Acharya, p.65.
20. Bob Lowry, *Indonesian Defence Policy and the Indonesian Armed Forces*, Canberra Papers on Strategy and Defence 99 (Canberra: SDSC, 1993), pp.23, 31.
21. Ibid.
22. Astri Suhrke, 'ASEAN: Adjusting to New Regional Alignments', *Asia Pacific Community*, Vol.12 (Spring 1981), p.27.
23. Prasun Sengupta, 'Indonesia's Force Modernisation: Strategies and Plans', *Military Technology*, Vol.16, No.11 (1992), pp.36–40.
24. *Straits Times*, 11 Aug., 10 and 23 Oct. 1993.
25. Huxley, op.cit., pp.34–42.
26. *Sixth Malaysia Plan 1991–1995*, p.62. As a proportion of the planned development budget, defence spending increased from 4.2 per cent to 10.9 per cent. But Malaysian defence expenditure has both a 'development' and an 'operating' component each year, so the substantial increase in the development component does not mean that 'total defence spending' will quadruple or that 'defence spending will grow from 4.2 per cent to 11 per cent of the budget' during the 1991–95 period, as claimed by other authors.

27. *New Straits Times*, 16 Sept. 1991 and 1 Feb. 1993; David Saw, 'Malaysia Looks Beyond Its Deal of the Decade', *Armed Forces Journal International*, June 1992, p.32–3.
28. *Flight International*, 11 Sept. 1991.
29. *New Straits Times*, 30 June 1993; *Air International*, Dec. 1993, p.291; *Flight International*, 15 Dec. 1993, p.291.
30. Saw, op.cit., p.33; Abdul Razak Abdullah Baginda, 'Malaysia's Armed Forces in the 1990s', *International Defense Review* (April 1992), pp.305–9; Prasun Sengupta, 'The Malaysian Navy in Transition', *Military Technology*, Vol.16, No.4 (1992), pp.70–7; *Flight International*, 21 April 1993; *New Straits Times*, 6 and 7 July 1993.
31. Tim Huxley, 'Malaysia and Singapore: A Precarious Balance?', *Pacific Review*, Vol.4, No.3 (1991), pp.208, 212.
32. David Saw, 'Singapore Defence', *Military Technology*, Vol.15, No.3 (1991), pp.14–15; David Saw, 'Politics and Defence Modernisation in Southeast Asia', *Military Technology*, Vol.16, No.4 (1992), pp.19–21; *Aerospace Yearbook 1993* (Singapore: Asian Business Press, 1993), p.60; *Flight International*, 28 July 1993, p.31 and 24 Nov. 1993, p.31, *Air Pictorial*, Aug. 1993, p.357.
33. Interviews, Singapore, July–Aug. 1993; *Aerospace Yearbook 1993*, p.60.
34. Saw, 'Singapore Defence', pp.13–14; Saw, 'Politics and Defence Modernisation in Southeast Asia', p.22; Prasun Sengupta, 'Singapore and the Army 2000 Plan', *Military Technology*, Vol.16, No.7 (1992), pp.71–6; interviews, Singapore, July–Aug. 1993.
35. Prasun Sengupta, 'South East Asian Naval Programmes. Part III', *Naval Forces*, Vol.14, No.1 (1993), pp.30–1; David Saw, 'Defence Spending in Southeast Asia', *Military Technology*, Vol.16, No.2 (1992), pp.20–2.
36. Figures for the other ASEAN members published in *The Military Balance* together with recent official Brunei sources indicate the following approximate per capita military expenditure figures for 1990 in US dollars: Brunei, $862; Singapore, $619; Malaysia, $94; Thailand, $35; Philippines, $14; Indonesia, $9.
37. Interviews, Brunei and Singapore, July–Sept. 1990.
38. See Tim Huxley, *Brunei's Defence Policy and Military Expenditure*, Working Paper No. 166 (Canberra: SDSC, 1988).
39. *Borneo Bulletin*, 28 Oct. 1989.
40. *Jane's Defence Weekly*, 1 Sept. 1990; *Financial Times*, 21 May 1991; *Flight International*, 5 Nov. 1990 and 4 Sept. 1991; interviews, Singapore, July–Aug. 1993.
41. Saw, 'Defence Spending in Southeast Asia', p.18.
42. John McBeth, FEER, 9 Sept. 1993, pp.29–30; *Asian Defence Journal* (Nov. 1992), p.11.
43. McBeth, op.cit., p.30.
44. Saw, 'Defence Spending in Southeast Asia', p.16; Sengupta, 'South East Asian Naval Programmes. Part III', pp.29–30; Robert Karniol, *Jane's Defence Weekly*, 7, 11 and 21 Nov. 1992, 22–4 and 27 Feb. 1993; *Straits Times*, 10 Dec. 1992, 24 June, 2 July and 13 July 1993.
45. *Straits Times*, 12, 22, 23 and 30 Oct. 1992; *Asian Defence Journal* (Nov. 1992), p.97.
46. Jacques Bekaert, 'The Royal Thai Army', *Asian Defence Journal* (March 1987), pp.4–18; David Saw, 'Thailand: Preparing for the Future', *Military Technology*, Vol.12 (1988), pp.48–58.
47. *Jane's Defence Weekly*, 24 Dec. 1989; *Straits Times*, 14 Aug. 1990; *Asian Defence Journal*, Sept. 1991, p.87.
48. See comments by Thai defence minister, *Straits Times*, 23 July 1993.
49. *Military Balance 1992–1993*, p.221.
50. David Saw, 'The Royal Thai Navy – Now a Regional Player?', *Asian Military Review*, No.1 (May/June 1993), pp.28–32; *Straits Times*, 12 June and 9 Nov. 1993; Rodney Tasker, FEER, 21 Oct. 1993, pp.30–31.
51. Saw, 'Politics and Defence Modernisation in Southeast Asia', p.23; *Aerospace Yearbook 1993*, pp.65–6.

52. Saw, 'Defence Spending in Southeast Asia', p.23; Saw, 'Politics and Defence Modernisation in Southeast Asia', p.24; *Flight International*, 21 July 1993.
53. *Straits Times*, 22 Feb. 1993; Rodney Tasker, FEER, 20 May 1993, pp.21–2; *Asian Defence Journal* (Sept. 1993), p.36.
54. Huxley, *The ASEAN States' Defence Policies, 1975–81*, pp.47–51.
55. Interviews in Kuala Lumpur and Singapore, July–Aug. 1993; *Straits Times*, 25 Aug. 1992.
56. The term is Ron Huisken's. See *Limitation of Armaments in South-East Asia: A Proposal*, Canberra Papers on Strategy and Defence 16 (Canberra: SDSC, 1977), p.35.
57. Huisken, op.cit., pp.49–50.
58. See Huxley, 'Singapore and Malaysia: A Precarious Balance?', pp.204–13.
59. See Acharya, pp.30–2 for a list of territorial disputes between Malaysia and its neighbours. These disputes are probably most accurately interpreted as symptoms of, rather than explanations for, intra-ASEAN tensions.
60. See Barry Buzan, *An Introduction to Strategic Studies* (London: Macmillan, 1987), pp.69–131 for a pertinent discussion of 'Arms Racing and the Arms Dynamic'.

# China: Arms Transfer Policies and Practices

## GERALD SEGAL

The proliferation of conventional weapons is one of the most important items on the post-Cold War agenda, but the major arms exporters have distinctive mixes of policies and practices. China's distinctiveness begins with the fact that, with the exception of Germany, in the past four years it appears to be the only major arms exporter not to see a decrease in both the percentage and volume of its transfers in a rapidly shrinking market. In 1992 China ranked third among exporters of major conventional arms to the developing world and fourth overall.[1] China is also distinctive because, by virtue of its place in the heart of Asia, its indigenous arms production affects arms transfer policies of other states in East and South Asia. Thus China needs to be understood as an arms producer in the widest sense: both as exporter and as stimulus to the imports of its neighbours. Third, China is distinctive in that it is a developing country with a far less sophisticated arms industry than any of the other major suppliers. Chinese exporters have stressed the utility of cheaper and less sophisticated technology and this has meant that it is limited to certain kinds of markets. China is unique among major exporters in not being able to sell to most developed countries.

Of course, these distinctive features are subject to major changes which must also be assessed. China's ability to increase its market share depends to an important extent on how extensively Russia sells arms from its bargain basement clearance and how much it produces weapons for export at inexpensive prices. For much the same reason that China itself is buying weapons from Russia, China might find its market niche is undercut by Russian policies. China might also find that its ability to sell lower technology systems is insufficient in the new marketplace, especially after the Gulf War demonstrated the utility of smarter weapons. China may find itself pushed further down market or into closer collaboration with states such as Russia to co-produce more sophisticated weapons. Finally, China is also finding itself under increasing pressure to constrain its arms transfers. China has found that arms transfers, like the posession of nuclear weapons, is part of the reason why it is treated like a great power. But if the other great powers become more serious about limiting arms transfers, pressure on China to join in will be increased. China also finds that its attitude to arms transfers is part of a broader choice between pursuing a more independent or interdependent foreign policy. This choice is tied up with choices about how far and fast to pursue reform at home and connections with the international market economy. China's choices about arms transfers are therefore part of broader decisions about openness in foreign policy and its commitment to reform.[2]

## The Patterns of Chinese Exports

The basic data concerning Chinese arms transfers are available in SIPRI and CRS annual studies.[3] China is a major player in the arms market, now ranking third among exporters to the developing world and fourth overall. In 1987 and 1988 China ranked fourth among exporters to the developing world and fourth overall. In 1989 and 1990 China ranked fifth among exporters to the developing world and fifth overall. In the 1988–92 period taken together, China ranked third among exporters to the developing world and fifth overall. This relative stability in ranking, however, masks some more pronounced swings as China adjusted to changing political and market conditions. China's market share for exports to developing countries was 8.8 per cent in 1988 and nearly double (16.4 per cent) five years later. In the meantime it dropped to a low point of 3.9 per cent in 1989 when China's share of total arms transfers was just 2.4 per cent. In sum, China now ranks, along with major European arms exporters (Russia, Britain, France, Germany) as second rank exporters behind the United States. China is more like France and Britain than Germany in the sense that the vast majority of French and British arms transfers are to the developing world. Thus the second major feature of Chinese transfers is that Peking is almost totally dependent on markets in the developing world. In the 1988–92 period all of Chinese arms transfers were to the developing world by far the highest percentage of any major arms exporter. This is easily explained by the lower quality of Chinese arms exports and thus its inability to make much of an impact on richer states seeking more sophisticated technology. Third, China, like most arms exporters, depended heavily on markets in the Middle East. In the 1987–91 period nearly half of Chinese arms exports went to the region, with East Asia and South Asia splitting much of the rest. But in the 1988–92 period 68 per cent of Chinese transfers were to Asia and only 29 per cent to the Middle East. The top five importers of Chinese weapons during this later period were (in order) Pakistan, Thailand, Iran, Bangladesh and Saudi Arabia. The fourth major pattern of Chinese transfers is that Peking is not always the largest arms supplier to its major markets. China accounted for 55.5 per cent of the Pakistani market, 45.3 per cent of the Thai market, 26.8 per cent of the Iranian market, 81.5 per cent of the Bangladeshi market and only 9.8 per cent of the Saudi market. Myanmar (ranked sixth among China's export markets) took 80 per cent of its arms from China. North Korea (ranked seventh) acquired just under 10 per cent of its arms from China. Iraq (ranked eighth) acquired only 4.7 per cent of its arms from China. Thus China rarely opens up markets, but in many cases it is a major supplier and its policies are important to the management of regional arms races. Fifth, China has also managed to avoid undue dependence on any one state for its exports. It was thought following the end of the Iran-Iraq War that China would fade as an arms exporter, but it has been able to find new markets in Asia while retaining one in Iran. Iraq disappeared because of the UN embargo in 1990, but China is well placed to return when Iraq is eventually allowed to re-arm. Unusual deals such as the medium range ballistic missile (MRBM) agreement with Saudi Arabia suggests China is prepared to be flexible in its approach and is able to sell to various sides in a complex conflict zone.[4] As we shall see below, Chinese motives are complex and changing. Finally, China has transferred a wide range of weapons. The image of China as primarily a small arms supplier has not been accurate for some time, especially when considering exports to Asian states. The major feature of Chinese exports to the Gulf region was the large number of aircraft and tanks, while the MRBM deal with Saudi Arabia demonstrated that China was willing to sell weapons that no other power was prepared to provide. In brief, China has shown that it is willing to sell virtually any conventional weapon in its arsenal.

Of course, Chinese weapons are generally less modern and effective than those sold by the developed states. Chinese equipment is clearly not first rate, but then it is something more than third rate. As Iraq discovered in its confrontation with a coalition of powers with modern Western arms in 1990–91, when up against modern arms Chinese equipment is not of much use. But as the preceding Iran-Iraq War had demonstrated, when the conflict was against a less modernized enemy, war could be waged with Chinese arms. China has apparently won market share for its weapons by compensating for poor quality with lower prices. Little hard evidence is available about the prices China charges, but it is churlish of those such as Thai officials to complain about the poor quality of Chinese arms when they obtained theirs at bargain prices, no doubt including heavy pay-offs to corrupt colleagues. As the deals with Thailand suggest, China's low tech arms may make it harder to win contracts with armed forces seeking prestige weapons, but

Chinese equipment will do when a major motive is to find a dealer willing to pay bribes.

It should also be noted that China has an important impact on the pattern of arms exports simply by virtue of its existence as the dominant power of Asia. Even if China did not export any weapons, its indigenous arms production would be a major factor in Asian arms races. It is impossible to understand fully the pattern of the arms trade in Asia without understanding Chinese policy.[5] If only by virtue of its size, China must be considered by nearly every Asian power who acquires weapons. Pakistan and India consider how China might use its power in the case of renewed fighting in the sub-continent. ASEAN states are especially concerned about China's extending naval and air power. Managing a future crisis on the Korean peninsula depends to a large extent on Chinese capabilities and intentions. And one of the most critical factors in Japanese considerations of its post-Cold War defence policy is the nature of its relationship with a China that continues to increase the size of its defence budget. Indeed, the fact that China continues to modernize its forces, to use force in the South China Sea, to increase its defence spending, and to test its nuclear weapons, is a vital factor in Asian arms races. While it is true that China's arms are not first rate, most of China's neighbours could be overwhelmed by sheer numbers when reinforced by a few more modern systems. China's acquisition of modern equipment from Russia led to increased tension in the South China Sea and encouraged the United States to sell F-16s to Taiwan. While it is true that China's weapons procurement is now stressing more quality than quantity, recent trends also indicate greater concern with weapons with longer range and greater mobility. Various reports suggest China is seeking closer co-operation with the Russian defence establishment on possible co-production of newer weapons.[6] China has apparently acquired in-flight refuelling technology from Iran, but is still having major problems in deploying the system because of the complexity of skills required.[7] As the range and lethality increase, so China's arsenal at home becomes as much a source of concern as its exports abroad.

## Why China Exports

It is perhaps harder to understand Chinese motives for arms transfers than it is in the case of any other great power.[8] China is still ruled by a communist party, and aspects of national security continue to be more tightly wrapped in secrecy. Analysis is complicated by the fact that the study of China is surrounded by highly productive rumour mills, many of which can be traced to Hong Kong. Given that we are so wary about even the basic data on the scale of arms transfers, we need to be all the more cautious about suggesting unambiguous motives for Chinese behaviour. Needless to say, with such uncertainties about policies and motives, any attempt to control Chinese behaviour will be difficult to formulate.

These problems are evident when considering what is said to be a major motive for Chinese exports – the desire by Chinese officials to make money for themselves and their families.[9] It is often argued that the so-called Red Princes and Princesses – the children of the ageing leaders of China – are key players in China's complex network of arms export corporations. As China's economy has become more open to market forces, Chinese leaders and their children have been able to create vast empires and amass equally large fortunes by selling arms abroad. The anecdotal evidence that the Red Princes are involved in the arms trade cannot be disputed, although it remains impossible to know just how much money has been made and how specific decisions on arms transfers are taken. What is far more difficult to assert is that Chinese arms transfers cannot be controlled because of such nepotism. It is true that the network of arms export corporations is more complex than it was in the former Soviet Union, although as China becomes more of a market economy a more proper comparison should be made to such middle powers as France and Britain. The number of Chinese arms exporters is not particularly larger than those in France and Britain, although the familial nature of the links to the ruling elite in China may make the power of these corporations harder to assess. There is undoubtedly pressure from the corporate level to increase exports and for other parts of government to lift restrictions, but this is as true in market economies as it is in China. Competition between corporations, whether in China or the capitalist world, also adds to the pressure to increase sales. But whether analysts speak of a military-industrial-complex in the West, or Red Princes in the East, there are limits to personal avarice as a motive for arms sales.

The key to this question is whether the government, if it so chooses, can limit arms transfers. Ultimately we are concerned with the motives of government, even though the motives of corporations and individuals may be contributing factors. If the question is asked whether the Chinese government is any less able to control the motives of its corporations and individuals than those in France, Britain or the United States, the answer must be, not really. Although China is increasingly becoming more of a market economy, the control of the internal and external means of production and communication is probably tighter than in the West. Tanks and aircraft are at least as hard to make and market in China as in the West. The raw materials for such equipment remains within the state sector of the Chinese economy. Negotiation with foreign customers requires major support abroad which fledgling Chinese firms cannot develop without state support. In short, the Red Princes can export arms only because the state wants them to do so. There are no doubt times when some deals are pushed harder, or are more difficult to halt, because of the pressure of well-connected family members. These qualifications have their parallels in the United States, such as electoral politics fuelling F-16 exports or corporate contributions to election war chests. But the bottom line is that in China, as everywhere else, arms transfers can be halted by a determined government. The Red Princes, like many others, made vast amounts of money from arms exports to Iraq, but China, like everyone else, ceased arms supplies after a United Nations resolution was agreed (although China abstained in the vote). Suggestions that Chinese arms exports should be treated more leniently because of the role of the Red Princes is to indulge in ethnic chic.

The role of the Red Princes can be seen, at least in part, as merely one segment of a change in Chinese motives in the 1980s that put far more stress on the economic benefits of arms transfers. But by the 1990s this notion that Chinese arms transfers were primarily for economic reasons was increasingly out of date. In the days before it was opened to economic reform in the late 1970s, China was said to export arms primarily for political reasons. Weapons were 'sold at friendship prices' in order to support revolutionary causes or friends in coalitions against whatever superpower was deemed to be the major threat. In short, China made little money from arms transfers. For a decade after the late 1970s when China's economy became increasingly market oriented, there was a much remarked shift to arms sales rather than simple transfers. Yet analysts have found it difficult to assess just how much money was being made on individual deals and who was earning the money. There has been much speculation that the Chinese People's Liberation Army (PLA) was obtaining important extra-budgetary allocations because the arms exporters it controlled were able to retain large parts of the profits. Some of these funds were said to have been plowed back into research and development of new equipment for the PLA.[10] The rise of the Red Princes seems to be both part of this process and part of the reason why revenues to the PLA might have been falling in recent years. There is no way to obtain an accurate picture of this problem.

Even if the PLA still earns money from arms sales, the figures are unlikely to be anything like large enough to balance cuts in the defence budget in the early and mid-1980s. And even if the state as a whole pocketed the profits, the figures are miniscule as a percentage of China's rapidly rising foreign trade. To be sure, making money from arms sales was better than giving away equipment at friendship prices, but one must be cautious about suggesting such a change was crucial for Chinese foreign or defence policy. More significantly, the search for profit took China into new markets, most notably the Middle East. The vast majority of Chinese sales (as opposed to transfers) were to Iran, Iraq and Saudi Arabia. As some of these markets dried up in recent years, China has been able to make money from major deals with Thailand and Burma, and this in a region where China usually 'sold at friendship prices'. Even if the Middle Eastern markets re-open later in the 1990s, it is unlikely that the scale of the transactions will make profit the only major motive for transferring arms. At a minimum, China will remain very interested in deals which mean that they can obtain samples of foreign technology, as they seemed to have done in obtaining in-flight refuelling from Iran. China will also welcome the opportunity to see their weapons tested on the battlefield and learn how best to modernize Chinese equipment as a result.

While profit remains a factor in China's arms transfers in the 1990s, its relative importance has been diminished in recent years above all because the strategic environment in which China operates has been revolutionized by the ending of the Cold War. Arms transfers have taken on added importance as a political tool for increasing China's international standing. China is now in a much more fluid international environment where it recognizes that it will be far harder to play off other great powers. In such an atmosphere of increased paranoia and uncertainty, China can justify far more arms transfers as being in the national interest, although the specific type of national interest may vary.

China's most important national security consideration might be defined as helping to support friendly neighbours. On this definition, some 54 per cent of Chinese transfers in the 1988–92 period were for such political motives. Of this, North Korea and Pakistan are the most unambiguous cases, although for different reasons. North Korea, though, is of decreasing importance as it is no longer needed in a competition for influence with the Soviet Union, and it has even been a complicating factor in normalizing relations with South Korea. Pyongyang's unreformed domestic economy became an embarrassment to China, and its nuclear weapons programme risked drawing China into unwanted conflict in the region. One can expect Chinese arms transfers to North Korea to decline even further as political calculations lead

Peking to see an increased need to push Pyongyang towards a peaceful reunification of the two Koreas. However, should Sino-American relations deteriorate, China may feel that in the short term it makes sense to help defend North Korea as a communist state, at least until a succession can be arranged to a more moderate and reforming regime. North Korea also has its uses as a channel for Chinese arms exports that otherwise might cause problems in China's relations with the West. Persistent reports of such use of North Korea for missile sales to the Middle East helps muddy the waters of Chinese policy and Western policy responses.[11]

Chinese transfers to Pakistan are likely to hold up far better. Pakistan has been seen as a key point of pressure on India, and despite the rapid changes in power balances in the region, this rationale still holds. India is no longer closely aligned with the Soviet Union and Sino-Indian relations have been improving.[12] China has no reason to wish to see conflict in Kashmir, but neither does it particularly wish to see India achieve its objectives there. India and China share a concern with uncertainty in a potentially Islamic Central Asia, but China knows that Pakistan will be a significant actor in this region and that close ties are important. China would be strongly opposed to dismembering Pakistan in the event of a free-for-all in Central Asia, since Peking would then fear for the stability of its own Central Asian territory. As Pakistan finds it harder to obtain arms from a United States that is wooing India and worried about Pakistan's nuclear weapons programme, so there are likely to be demand as well as supplier arguments for continuing arms transfers to Pakistan. The reported supply of M-11 missiles may be only part of a much more complex series of weapons being provided. Co-production deals for a type 2000 main battle tank or a K-7 jet trainer, for example, are likely to continue as these two countries see the benefits of co-operation at a time when the advanced Western countries seek to isolate and pressurize both states.[13]

The remaining portion of Chinese transfers to neighbouring countries are much smaller and more complicated. During the Afghan war of the 1980s China sold weapons to the CIA and donated others directly to Pakistan for the mujahidin in the largest covert operation since the Second World War.[14] The Chinese transfers to Afghanistan have mostly been small arms, and to all intents and purposes Afghanistan has ceased to exist as a single state. Given the deepening chaos in Afghanistan, it is possible that China will become drawn into supporting one faction, and with increasingly powerful arms. But this looks like being a guerrilla war for some time to come, where China recognizes that the threats to its own security are minor and at the furthest reaches of its frontiers. Dealing with Afghanistan will probably, therefore, be part of a more general concern with the fate of Central Asia.

The 5.3 per cent of Chinese exports to Myanmar (Burma) do not really qualify as part of a concern with national security. These sales to a pariah regime are far more to do with making money and helping control the flow of arms and drugs in China's southwest. China has little interest in Burmese battles with Thailand or Bangladesh that are made more possible by the provision of arms. China might be said to have some interest in the victory of a more reformist regime in Rangoon, and thus support for the present junta can be seen as counter-productive. But China is more afraid of the ethnic disintegration of Burma under a less ruthless military regime because the drug barons would be harder to control. As it stands, Chinese officials are said to profit to some extent from the illicit trade in the frontier region, but with some confidence that the scale of the problems is under control. Nevertheless, although most of China's arms deal with Burma is to be counted more as for money than for national security, concerns about the future persist.[15] In particular reports that China is helping Burma build a naval base on the Andaman Sea coast which may eventually also service Chinese ships in a blue-water role lead to worries that China does have major, long-term, political objectives in South Asia.[16]

A broader definition of China's national security in the Asian region would take in transfers to such countries as Thailand (19.3 per cent in the 1988–92 period). But, as has already been suggested, the recent Chinese deals with Thailand have a great deal to do with the Thai armed forces seeking suppliers willing to pay bribes for weapons that are unlikely to be used except against internal dissent. The fact that Chinese weapons are of poor quality and difficult to maintain would only be a matter of concern if Thailand was planning to use them against external enemies. With the easing of tension in Indo-China, the Thai armed forces are settling down to the more prosaic interest of earning their share of the illicit trade that goes on with Cambodia and Laos. China sees Thailand as a friend in ASEAN and a way of channelling aid to the Khmer Rouge. But the diminution of concern with Vietnam means that China needs Thailand less than in the 1980s. It is true that Thailand is one of those ASEAN states less worried about the Chinese threat in the South China Sea, but overt Chinese support for Thailand as a way of putting pressure on Malaysia to back off its claims in the South China Sea would run serious risks of harming China's position in Southeast Asia as a whole. In sum, Thailand is a case where China has a mixture of political and economic motives for arms transfers, with the latter of increased importance in recent years.

As one moves further from Chinese territory, one might expect the political and national security motives to decrease in importance. This is correct so long as one assumes that China sees its national security primarily in Asian terms, but in recent years China has become even more sure that such parochialism cannot be sustained. The disintegration of the Soviet Union has made China more aware of the need to play on an international stage and has freed it of the obsessional worry about Soviet strategy. As China now fears a single American superpower and as Sino-American relations deteriorate, so China sees the need to stress its global role as a way of deterring US pressure and compelling Washington and the West to take China seriously in the absence of the need for unity with China on an anti-Soviet basis.

China's attempt to prove that it has become more, rather than less, important in the post-Cold War world depends on its ability to demonstrate that it is a global player. China has quickly learned that threats to proliferate nuclear weapons in the Islamic world (Algeria or Iran), makes Chinese policy a matter of major concern in the West. Threats to block the use of the United Nations Security Council to sanction collective action against the likes of Iraq, Libya or Serbia, makes the wooing of China more important in the post-Cold War world. Similarly, Chinese adherence to the Missile Transfer Control Regime (MTCR) or co-operation among the P-5 to limit arms transfers to the Middle East becomes a matter high on the international agenda. China's conventional arms transfers are, like China's nuclear weapons, key parts of the rationale for why China must be treated as a great power.

For these reasons China can rightly see its arms transfers to the Middle East as important political steps that help ensure that China is taken seriously and its concerns not trampled in pursuit of a US and Western-defined new international political order. Chinese transfers to the likes of Iran may not have begun for primarily political reasons, but in the post-Cold War world such transfers can now be seen as having primarily political rationales. This is not to say that China necessarily feels that, like the superpowers in the Cold War, they could manipulate arms sales to support allies against the ideological enemy. China, as a one-time arms seller to both Iran and Iraq, is far too pragmatic for any such illusions of direct influence. Reported sales of M-9 missiles to Syria are also not made with any great expectation of greater influence in the Middle East peace process, but China is fully aware of the worry that such sales engender in the United States and the West.[17] Peking may hope that arms transfers may lead to civilian construction contracts and may win some extra votes in international institutions. China also knows that the risk that it might resume arms sales to Iraq and sell with less discrimination in the Middle East as a whole is useful in helping to limit the

American willingness to revoke Most Favoured Nation status and allow a sharp deterioration in Sino-American relations. Of course, should Sino-American relations take a serious turn for the worse, China will feel more free to sell what it wants in the Middle East.

Thus it seems that the primary motive for China may simply be to sell arms in order to worry the United States and the West. China's threat to break the P-5 process on limiting arms transfers to the Middle East did not stop the United States from selling F-16s to Taiwan, but the broader concern with China as a geopolitical power helped to keep President Bush anxious not to see a rapid deterioration in Sino-American relations. The American decision to allow the sale of communication satellites to China in September 1992, just after the announcement of the F-16 deal, suggested that China could not win all the battles but that the general strategy was working. The fact that China quit the P-5 conventional arms talks on the Middle East but was generally restrained in its reaction to the F-16 sale for fear of harming President Bush in the run-up to the November election, suggests China is able to play a subtle great power game when it wants.

There is little reason to expect China to change course. Russian arms sales to China, and US and Russian sales to the Middle East suggest that efforts to control the transfer of conventional arms are in serious trouble. Just as China was not the first to open most arms markets, so it will not be the first to pull out. China will sell arms where money is to be made and where the political costs in doing so are low. Of course, where the political gain is evident, even if in the negative form of causing worry for others, then China will certainly be reluctant to curb its arms transfers. China understands that it is part of what Europeans might term a concert of great powers – a complex balance of power among several key actors. The trick for China, and for the rest of the international community, is that this mainly political strategy of transferring arms requires China to be credible about joining in international efforts to control arms proliferation. If China is never seen to be likely to join international arms control arrangements, then there will be less reason to bargain with China and less reason to co-operate. Thus for the same motives that China transfers arms, China must also co-operate with efforts to control the spread of conventional arms.

### Dealing with the China Problem

China is a middle-sized power and a middle-sized problem for those wishing to control the proliferation of conventional arms. If arms control is to succeed, it must involve China, but it is unlikely that China will be primarily to blame if arms control fails. China has dragged its feet as attempts have been made to strengthen the MTCR, control arms transfers by the P-5, or implement the United Nations Arms Register. But none of these efforts has failed simply because China has held back, and China can equally be said to have been unco-operative because the other powers have also undermined these international accords.

China can and does take part in international arms control efforts when it is pushed sufficiently hard, when the risks involved in agreeing are low, and when the benefits of agreeing are high. Thus China eventually agreed not to block sanctions and an arms embargo against Iraq in 1991, signed up to the NPT in 1992, accepted to be bound by the terms of the MTCR in 1992, and agreed to sanctions and an arms embargo against Serbia later that year. In 1992 China also remained sceptical in its approach to the Chemical Weapons pact and, as we have already noted, withdrew from the Middle East P-5 process.[18] These agreements and expressions of doubt, as with policies related to the management of the international economy, are part of a gradual movement in China towards accepting international interdependence. And yet the transition is obviously painful and fitful as the Chinese domestic debate about reform staggers forward. As the succession struggle in China approaches, these debates about reform and the degree of interdependence become more acute and difficult.[19] The Chinese seem to have a particular problem with the concept of a 'regime' in international affairs (as in the MTCR), and this may in part be explained by the different cultural approach of the Chinese to international law in general.[20] China's willingness to test the limits of definition in the MTCR may therefore be something more complicated than sheer duplicity. China's ambivalence and caution about conventional arms control is essentially yet another manifestation of domestic debates about reform and interdependence, and at a time of already evident uncertainty about the post-Cold War pattern of international relations.

While there are a wide range of efforts underway to contain the conventional arms race, it makes little sense to try to understand how to deal with China by starting with solutions rather than problems. Dealing with the China problem in conventional arms control can be broken down into two main areas. First, there is the problem of China and Asian security.[21] China is both a major supplier to states in the region and, by virtue of its own presence and power, a major source of insecurity. China has already undertaken major unilateral efforts to reduce the size of its armed forces in the 1980s and the signs are that the number of troops on PLA rolls will continue to decline. This process was crucial to the development of Sino-Soviet détente and was enhanced when the Soviet Union itself disintegrated. The result was a

China more secure in its frontiers than at any time in several hundred years. Troops are now being moved away from the northern frontier and far more attention is being paid to the need to have more modern and mobile forces. Possible threats include unrest in Central Asia, naval action in the South China Sea, and preparing for a possible arms race with Japan. The lessons of the 1990–91 Gulf War taught China the virtues of modernity and mobility in war, and forces are being streamlined and modernized as a result. Major deficiencies in equipment are being remedied by selective imports from Russia, assistance from Israel, and a long-term research and development programme. Should Russia and China agree to co-produce weapons in the future, China would have filled a major gap in its defence industry and seriously strengthened its position in the arms export business.[22]

These developments would not necessarily be seen as antithetical to conventional arms control if they were undertaken more slowly, with a stable defence budget, and with less stress on air and naval force projection. So long as China continues to develop this more dangerous defence policy, and as it does so in a region mostly devoid of multilateral arms control and replete with latent and sometimes active tensions, China will be among those most obstructive to regional arms control. The fact that China remains largely a revanchist power bent on territorial acquisition (for example Hong Kong, Taiwan, South China Sea and other minor territorial disputes), means it has less reason to support arms control. Chinese arms purchases from Russia and discussions about more long-term defence co-operation are part of the reason why the United States decided to sell F-16s to Taiwan, thereby fuelling an arms race. Of course, the F-16 sale in turn aggravates those in the Chinese system determined to resist Western pressure on arms sales and supports the more hardline factions set against reform and inter-dependence.[23]

To be fair to China, there is little arms control on the Asian agenda so far. In a region better known for its nationalism than its multilateralism, Chinese irredentism and suspicion often appear to be a problem because China is such a major player in Asia and involved in so many sub-regional discussions. Arms control in Northeast Asia is only at the stage of academic fora, and for a long time it was the United States more than China which blocked any progress, while Chinese détente with South Korea was crucial in shaping the virtuous cycle of détente in the region. In Central and South Asia, there is not even this minimal level of discussion of conventional arms control, while China has nevertheless played its part in détente with India.

Where China does loom as a larger problem for conventional arms

control is in Southeast Asia. Efforts to contain disputes in the South
China Sea have clearly been hampered by Chinese determination to discuss anything but sovereignty. China has also used oil exploration (by an
American firm) and an aggressive naval patrol policy to extend its territorial claims when political and military conditions are propitious. China
is not inclined to surrender its objectives of acquiring territory unless it
meets direct and powerful counter-pressure. The acquisition of in-flight
refuelling and new aircraft from Russia suggests that China is prepared
to use force in this dispute and eschew effective arms control. The Taiwan problem also involves contested sovereignty, and China's military
modernization has helped provoke Taiwan, like others in Southeast
Asia, to acquire their own modern weaponry. Put at its most stark,
China is highly unlikely to accept any form of arms control that limits its
ability to re-take Taiwan, and this despite the fact that the growing economic co-operation across the Straits has helped build confidence in a
more peaceful solution. More worrying in the long term is the risk of a
Sino-Japanese arms race and the lack of any multilateral arms control to
head off the threat. As China acquires more modern hardware, concern
grows in Japan that China's increased ability to project power will force
Japan to do the same. If China was to deploy effective in-flight refuelling, an aircraft carrier, or even Aegis-type ships capable of providing air cover for troop carriers, this would encourage worries that China
wants to control sea lanes, resources, islands, or even threaten sanctions
against Japanese trading partners or Japan itself. Japan is a major sup-
porter of greater transparency in international arms control, while
China hides behind an obfuscating definition of national security.
Therefore, it was a pleasant surprise to see that China complied with the
terms of the UN Arms Register in 1993, despite earlier opposition to the
plan. China may simply be on an arms control learning curve.

   In the absence of any major arms control initiative such as a more
ambitious P-5 process for Asia, the prognosis for conventional arms
control in Asia is gloomy. China is less of a problem in this region as an
arms exporter than by virtue of its revanchist and unco-operative behaviour. Although a P-5 process for Asia is probably hopeless and
greater transparency would help only at the margins, the real difficulty is
how to deal with the political roots of the disputes that involve China.
Whether it is the Korean conflict or the South China Sea, each has its
own dynamic requiring an à la carte approach to arms control.[24] But the
root of Chinese policy remains an unsettled debate about how much
interdependence it should accept and how much of the irredentist
agenda should be abandoned. These are all issues tied up in the basic
debate about reform in China, and therefore well beyond the reach of
negotiators on conventional arms control.

But in the second major area of Chinese arms proliferation – the Middle East and beyond – there is more room for optimism. As we have seen, Chinese motives for arms transfers to these regions are now a mix of some monetary reward and much political symbolism. The political impulses can be satisfied to a great extent by a drawn-out process of negotiations at the P-5 level where China is a major player, but not the only obstacle to a deal. In fact, this is more or less where we stand today. China decided to boycott the P-5 process after the United States decided to sell F-16s to Taiwan, but it can hardly be argued that the P-5 process was otherwise on the brink of a breakthrough. The United States announced a new round of aircraft sales to the Middle East in between the announcement of the F-16 deal with Taiwan and the Chinese decision to pull out of the P-5 process.[25] Unless China is challenged with a firm agreement by the other big four arms exporters, there is little prospect that China will feel compelled to accept a curb on its arms exports. Where agreements have been reached, such as on the MTCR, China will continue to test the limits of the accord as it contests the evaluation of the range of its weapons. Uncontrolled export of modern aircraft will encourage China to stretch the terms of the MTCR because it is seen as a pact that artificially tries to deal with only a limited range of weapons. Yet China is unlikely to transfer MRBMs as it did to Saudi Arabia, for that would be venturing far beyond current practice. China wishes to be a nuisance without becoming defined as the problem. Agreements on transparency in arms transfers in this region are much less likely to be opposed by China, if only because China's own territory will not be covered. Indeed, this might be the area to begin serious arms control designed to test Chinese sincerity in limiting the proliferation of conventional arms. Now that China has normalized relations with Israel and is more involved in the Arab-Israeli peace process, it is more inclined to be co-operative in this region. Concern with Islamic forces in Central Asia is an additional factor that might lead China to be more co-operative with multilateral arms control in the Middle East.

In sum, China can be pressed into taking arms control more seriously, but the process is every bit as complex as it was when engaging the Soviet Union during the Cold War. The West has enormous influence with China on trade, and China has already shown that it can be swayed when the United States exerts sufficient pressure. China is also deeply concerned that COCOM type restrictions will remain in place and even be tightened. There are certainly good arguments for denying China access to certain technologies, even if it means limits on Western trade with China and damages the prospects for the economy of Hong Kong.[26] Aid to China can also be restricted, or at least tied to performance indicators, even in the field of human rights. Although China has denied that it will respond to such pressure, there is growing evidence that sustained pressure yields incremental results.[27] China can also be influenced through the provision of support to China's rivals, as the F-16 sale to Taiwan has demonstrated. A change in the American and Japanese attitude to Vietnam may fall into the same category.

Of course, China can, and has, responded to such pressures in ways that often harm Western interests. The saga of the F-16 sale to Taiwan is not yet over, but its complexity demonstrates that China has options to pursue. Withdrawal from the P-5 process may be classed as a negative act, but China also has the more 'positive' option of buying more hardware from Russia, or even the much-discussed Ukrainian aircraft carrier. China can spread nuclear weapons technology, block the use of the United Nations Security Council, and even foment regional unrest by resuming support and arms for the likes of the Khmer Rouge. In short, China is hard to push around, even though a good case can be made that it is essential to make clear to China that its irredentist and independent policies will not always be tolerated. Just as it took a long time to persuade the Soviet Union that it could not win a struggle with the West, so a similar arsenal of co-operation and conflict will have to be used in relations with China.

The expectations of success in limiting China's independent policy, even in the Middle East, should be restrained. Even if the international system were more stable and more amenable to arms control building on an emerging political consensus, China is not ready for such sweeping multilateralism and interdependence. China is a revanchist power in Asia and a dissatisfied power on the global level. This dissatisfaction derives not so much from communist ideology, as was the case in the past, as from a nationalism that distrusts others who talk about internationalism when they really mean maintaining the status quo. To be sure, China has gradually grown more accommodating to arms control and it is a less dissatisfied power than it once was. But the process of change is slow. It may take the passing of a generation (or two) before China is ready for significant multilateralism and interdependence. In the meantime, China's nationalism and sense of great power status can be turned into limited accords on a case-by-case basis.

### NOTES

An earlier version of this paper was presented to a conference at the Carnegie Endowment, November 1992.

1. The statistics used for this study are drawn from the *Sipri Yearbook* of 1993 (Oxford: Oxford University Press, 1993), unless otherwise noted. There is no agreement on

statistics used in the study of arms transfers. Figures produced by the United States Arms Control and Disarmament Agency are too out of date to be of much use in these post-Cold War conditions. The Congressional Research Service (CRS) Report for Congress, *Conventional Arms Transfers to the Third World, 1984–92* by Richard Grimmett (July 1993), is up to date but is sharply at variance with Sipri data. CRS data show the volume of Chinese arms transfers to the developing world falling between 1990 and 1992, although China's percentage of the market was steady at 4.7 per cent. Sipri shows the volume of Chinese transfers increasing in terms of volume and the percentage up from 7 per cent to 17.4 per cent. CRS figures are for all arms, not just major conventional arms, and are in constant 1992 US$m instead of constant 1990 US$m used by Sipri. Sipri uses a much more complex system for valuing arms transfers and has a long track record in producing such figures. Sipri figures are not intended to represent the real money received by China – something that cannot possibly be known. These discrepancies in figures are not insignificant. They suggest different trends, and the problem cannot simply be dismissed by arguing that we are interested in trends more than absolute numbers. If we were to adopt CRS figures, it would be harder to argue that Chinese arms transfers are of much importance. Those who prefer to use CRS data ask us to trust the validity of their data gathered from intelligence sources without being able to provide any indication of why they believe Sipri data to be wrong. The track record of manipulation of official American data, whether during the Cold War or the Gulf War, suggests we need to be cautious about accepting such data without challenge. This has been a matter of particular concern during the Bush administration when official policy was to suggest China was less of a problem for international security.

2.  This is the theme of Chapter 2 of Gerald Segal *et al.*, *Openness and Foreign Policy Reform in Communist States* (London: Routledge for the Royal Institute of International Affairs, 1992).

3.  See also R. Bates Gill, *Fire of the Dragon* (Geneva: Program for Strategic and International Security Studies of the Graduate Institute of International Studies, 1991) and his 'Curbing Beijing's Arms Sales' in *Orbis* Summer 1992. See also Richard Bitzinger, *Chinese Arms Production and Sales to the Third World*, RAND Note N-3334-USDP (Santa Monica: RAND, 1992).

4.  Yitzhak Shichor, *A Multiple Hit: China's Missile Sales to Saudi Arabia*, SCPS Papers No.5 (Kaohsiung, Taiwan: Sun Yat-sen Center for Policy Studies, 1991).

5.  See also Gerald Segal, 'Managing New Arms Races in Asia/Pacific', in *The Washington Quarterly*, Vol.15, No.3 (Summer 1992).

6.  Tai Ming Cheung, 'Ties of Convenience', a paper for the Chinese Council on Advanced Policy Studies, Taipei, June 1992 and an article in *Far Eastern Economic Review*, 3 Sept. 1992, p.21.

7.  For some discussion of these issues see *International Herald Tribune*, 24 Aug. 1992.

8.  For an earlier discussion of Chinese policy on arms transfers see Anne Gilks and Gerald Segal, *China and the Arms Trade* (London: Croom Helm, 1985).

9.  John Lewis, Hua Di, Xue Litai, 'Beijing's Defense Establishment: Solving the Arms-Export Enigma', *International Security*, Vol.15, No.4 (Spring 1991).

10. Yitzhak Shichor, 'Defence Policy Reform,' in Gerald Segal (ed.), *Chinese Politics and Foreign Policy Reform* (London: Kegan Paul International for the Royal Institute of International Affairs, 1990).

11. *Asian Defence Journal* (June 1992), p.120.

12. Zheng Ruixiang, 'Improving Sino-Indian Relations', *The Pacific Review*, No.1 (1993).

13. *Far Eastern Economic Review*, 6 Feb. 1992.

14. Steve Coll, 'Secret CIA Escalation in '85 Tipped Afghan Balance', *International Herald Tribune*, 21 July 1992.

15. John Bray, 'Burma: Resisting the International Community', *The Pacific Review*, No.3 (1992).

16. A Kyodo report on 17 Sept. 1992 in BBC/Summary of World Broadcasts/Far East/1489/i.

17. *International Herald Tribune*, 4 April 1992; *Jane's Defence Weekly*, 20 June 1992; *Defense News*, 16 March 1992.
18. On the chemical weapons issue see *Defense News*, 24 Aug. 1992, p.12.
19. Gerald Segal, 'China and the Disintegration of the Soviet Union', *Asian Survey* (Sept. 1992).
20. For a discussion of some of these issues see Harry Gelber, 'China, Strategic Forces and Arms Proliferation', a paper for the CAPS conference in Taipei, June 1992.
21. For a general discussion see Robert Scalapino, 'Northeast Asia – Prospects for Cooperation', *The Pacific Review*, No.2 (1992).
22. Ellis Joffe, 'Modernizing Chinese Defence Policy', a paper for the CAPS conference, June 1992.
23. For some speculation on this process see François Godement, 'Policy Dynamics', *Far Eastern Economic Review*, 17 Sept. 1992.
24. On à la carte security see Gerald Segal, 'Northeast Asia: Common Security of *à la carte*', *International Affairs*, Vol.67, No.4 (Oct. 1991) and 'The Consequences of Proliferation in Asia', a paper for the IISS annual Conference, Seoul, Sept. 1992.
25. *Financial Times*, 16 Sept. 1992.
26. On the issue in general see William Schneider, 'The Emerging Pattern of Arms Export Controls Affecting Advanced Technology', in *Contemporary Southeast Asia*, Vol.14, No.1 (June 1992).
27. Simon Long, 'The Tree that Wants to be Still', *The Pacific Review*, No. 2 (1992).

# Nuclearization or Denuclearization on the Korean Peninsula?

## DARRYL HOWLETT

For a short period prior to the announcement by the Democratic People's Republic of Korea (DPRK) on 12 March 1993 that it was withdrawing from the Non-Proliferation Treaty (NPT), movement towards denuclearization of the Korean Peninsula appeared inevitable.[1] Since the announcement, this assumption has been shown to be premature. Moreover, subsequent developments have indicated the possibility of a more disconcerting trend: the spread of nuclear weapons throughout the Northeast Asia region. While it is possible to envisage that the nuclearization of the region might create a favourable security arrangement based on deterrence, such an outcome appears very optimistic. Even assuming an alternative optimistic scenario, whereby the Republic of Korea (ROK) and Japan refrain from acquiring nuclear weapons because of their security guarantees with the United States, this restraint could not be expected to remain indefinitely. A more pessimistic scenario might therefore see a 'proliferation chain' envelop the region. The initiation of such a nuclear arms race would undoubtedly prejudice stability in the region and critically undermine the nuclear non-proliferation regime.

Northeast Asia already has three nuclear weapon states – China, Russia and the United States – impacting upon its security. An increase in the number of states in the region with nuclear weapon capabilities would inevitably add complexity to existing relationships. Moreover, any regional deterrent system would need time to evolve, which may not be available. Uneven development of nuclear warhead and delivery capabilities could provoke preventive action to reduce perceived vulnerabilities. Brinkmanship during crisis situations may not lead to restraint but to the implementation of pre-emptive strategies. Finally, this situation is likely to exacerbate a range of overlapping regional threat perceptions stemming partly from the Cold War and partly from much earlier rivalries. Re-establishing the trend towards denuclearization in the region is therefore one of the primary challenges confronting the international community.

## Denuclearization?

### The DPRK and Nuclear Rapprochement

The DPRK signed the NPT on 12 December 1985. Under Article III.4 of the Treaty, the DPRK should have negotiated an INFCIRC/153 safeguards agreement with the International Atomic Energy Agency (IAEA) within eighteen months of signature. However, the agreement was not concluded until January 1992 and did not enter into force until 10 April 1992.[2] The DPRK handed over documents related to design information of its nuclear facilities and an initial materials inventory on 4 May 1992.[3] Since that date, the IAEA has attempted to verify the completeness of North Korea's materials inventory by conducting a series of *ad hoc* inspections. In the intervening period, between NPT signature and entry into force of the safeguards agreement, there was continued speculation about the DPRK's nuclear intentions. For its part, the DPRK persistently declared that its nuclear programme was geared to peaceful purposes. The country also stated its concern about United States' nuclear weapons allegedly based in the ROK and gave this as a reason for delaying negotiations with the IAEA over safeguards. This particular basis for the DPRK's objection to signing its mandatory safeguards agreement was removed on 27 September 1991 when President Bush announced that all ground-launched and sea-launched tactical nuclear weapons would be withdrawn back to the United States. When in October 1991 the ROK declared its territory nuclear weapon free, the way was open for reciprocal initiatives from the DPRK to underpin these movements towards denuclearization of the Korean Peninsula.

Throughout this key period, another significant element of the denuclearization process was initiated. Between September 1990 and December 1991 the two Koreas witnessed an unprecedented improvement in their bilateral relationship. Whereas previous attempts at *rapprochement* had largely floundered, notably in 1972 and between 1985 and 1986, the early 1990s improvement appeared more substantive and far-reaching. The dialogue was conducted with a high level of political involvement and produced a series of agreements which addressed the very crux of the inter-Korean security situation. In September 1990, the ROK and DPRK began a series on inter-Korean High-Level Talks, with the prime ministers from both states participating for the first time. On 13 December 1991 the two states signed an Agreement on Reconciliation, Non-Aggression, and Exchanges and Co-operation, which provided a strong foundation for their continued political *rapprochement*. This was followed on 31 December 1991 by a Joint Declaration on the Denuclearization of the Korean Peninsula, which established eight principles for achieving this objective. These included: a statement preventing either state from testing, manufacturing, storing, deploying, receiving or using nuclear weapons; an intention to make the Peninsula nuclear weapon free; a prohibition on enrichment and reprocessing technology; and a commitment to use nuclear energy solely for peaceful purposes.[4]

By the middle of 1992 the denuclearization process appeared to be moving satisfactorily towards the ultimate objective, the total elimination of nuclear weapons from the Korean Peninsula for all time. As a result of the DPRK's initial declaration to the IAEA, much of the uncertainty that had surrounded its nuclear programme was apparently lifted. A picture emerged of the extent of the DPRK's nuclear capabilities and the reasons underlying its pursuit of particular technologies.

*The DPRK's Known Nuclear Capabilities*

The DPRK developed a nuclear infrastructure based on the principle of self-reliance. Although it had assistance at key stages from the former Soviet Union, China and the IAEA, the DPRK consequently sought to reduce its external nuclear dependence. Ultimately this meant a focus on indigenous nuclear research and development, particularly on the use of a natural uranium and plutonium fuel cycle. The DPRK's nuclear energy programme originated in the mid-1940s and developed at the laboratory level throughout the 1950s as a result of joint research projects conducted with China and the former Soviet Union.[5] However, a programme on an industrial scale did not begin in earnest until the early 1960s when the Nuclear Research Centre at Yongbyon was established. This Centre concentrated initially on basic research on nuclear physics and reactor technology. In 1965 construction started on a Soviet-designed IRT-2000 type research reactor, the supply of which included an agreement for the spent fuel to be returned to the Soviet Union. This supply relationship between the two states also yielded the transfer of a small critical nuclear assembly for the Institute of Nuclear Physics at Yongbyon. In 1977 the research reactor and the critical assembly were placed under IAEA INFCIRC/66, or non NPT-type, safeguards and both facilities have been inspected regularly ever since.[6]

In the late 1970s a major indigenous nuclear energy programme was started. This utilized the same technology which provided the United Kingdom with the plutonium for its early nuclear weapons, the natural uranium-fuelled, gas-cooled, graphite-moderated ('Magnox') reactor.[7] In 1979 work started on a small 5MW(e) research reactor of this type. This reactor went critical on 14 August 1985 and became operational in 1986. Prior to the DPRK's initial declaration to the IAEA, several reports had suggested the existence of this larger reactor at Yongbyon.

These reports also indicated that a reprocessing facility was located close to the site of the larger reactor, fuelling speculation that the country had a dedicated weapons programme.[8] During the 1970s, the DPRK also conducted several experiments on a range of nuclear processes at the Yongbyon Nuclear Centre. These included ore conversion, fuel fabrication and the exploration of reprocessing techniques using laboratory hot cells for hardly irradiated materials. This research formed the basis for the next phase of nuclear development which, according to the facilities declared to the IAEA, involved a large capital investment and a major leap to full-scale industrial facilities.

In addition to the two facilities already under IAEA INFCIRC/66 safeguards, the DPRK declared the following facilities:

> A sub-critical facility at the Kim Il Sung University in Pyongyang; a nuclear fuel rod fabrication plant and storage in Yongbyon; an experimental nuclear power reactor (5MW) of the Institute of Nuclear Physics in Yongbyon; and a radiochemical laboratory of the Institute of Radiochemistry under construction in Yongbyon and declared to be designed for research on the separation of uranium and plutonium and waste management and for the training of technicians.[9]

The DPRK also declared two uranium mines, two plants for producing uranium concentrate, and stated that two much larger nuclear power reactors were under construction. One had a 50MW(e) capacity and was under construction in Yongbyon. The other was a 200MW(e) plant under construction at Taechon in the North Pyongan Province.[10] It was expected that the 50MW(e) plant would be completed by 1995, with the larger plant scheduled to be finished a year later. Further nuclear power plants were planned.

Another element of the DPRK's nuclear strategy indicated by the new information was an interest in more advanced nuclear processes. The DPRK stated that it embarked on its gas-cooled reactors because access to uranium enrichment or heavy water production technology was unavailable. However, the DPRK was aware that its indigenous technology was obsolete and would eventually need replacing. This had led to some initial research on fast-breeder reactors and on mixed oxide (MOX) fuel for use in light water reactors (LWR). The drawback to an LWR programme was also recognized: the DPRK would need to import the reactor technology and gain access to an assured supply of fuel. This would mean an increased dependence on external suppliers and inevitable conflict with the principle of self-reliance.

*Doubts about Inspection and Denuclearization*

This was the extent of knowledge about the DPRK's nuclear programme that stemmed from the initial declaration made to the IAEA. On this basis, the IAEA initiated a series of inspections to verify its completeness and thereby further the denuclearization process on the Korean Peninsula. Yet instead of producing an agreed account of the DPRK's nuclear programme, the inspections gave rise to several anomalies requiring clarification. Even at the time of the IAEA Director-General's visit to the DPRK in May 1992, and before the inspection procedures had been implemented, questions concerning the radiochemical laboratory (which the Director-General stated would usually be called a reprocessing facility in IAEA terminology) were repeatedly raised. Concerns were also expressed about the leap in reprocessing technology that the DPRK made when it went straight from basic research to large-scale construction: there was no indication of an intervening pilot plant stage to prove the technology before moving to a larger facility as had been the case in other programmes, and suspicions were raised that such a plant existed but had not been declared to the IAEA (though the United Kingdom made a similar technological leap in the early stages of its nuclear development).[11]

While the IAEA sought to resolve these questions, problems began emerging within the inter-Korean dialogue. As part of the effort by the ROK and DPRK to further their bilateral nuclear understanding, the two countries had established a Joint Nuclear Control Commission (JNCC) on 19 March 1992 to verify the Joint Declaration on Denuclearization. While several initial meetings of the JNCC were held, differences over the kind of bilateral inspection mechanism to be implemented stalled discussions. The DPRK wanted inspections which simultaneously addressed mutual suspicions. The DPRK delegation offered the ROK access to the Yongbyon nuclear complex in exchange for the DPRK being allowed to inspect all US military bases in the South. This contrasted with the ROK's proposal, based on the principle of reciprocity, whereby the DPRK also opened its military bases for inspection.[12] The issue of whether special inspections should be incorporated into the bilateral inspection mechanism was also disputed. Whereas the ROK insisted that special inspections (which would allow the inspected party 24-hour prior notification but no right of refusal) were a vital component of the bilateral inspection system, the DPRK maintained that such procedures were outside the scope of their agreement.

In late 1992 both the ROK and the United States became concerned about the uncertainties over the DPRK's nuclear programme. Because of the lack of progress on bilateral inspections, a decision was taken to resume their joint Team Spirit annual military exercises, which had been suspended in 1992, unless there was a satisfactory resolution to these issues. The DPRK interpreted the resumption of Team Spirit as a threatening action and responded by breaking off all talks except those in the JNCC and demanded the cancellation of the exercises. Although discussions continued in the JNCC between 14 October 1992 and 25 January 1993, the DPRK's position remained unaltered: there would be no progress on bilateral inspections unless Team Spirit was stopped. On 26 January 1993 South Korea and the United States announced that the exercises would go ahead as planned on 9 March 1993.[13] Immediately before the exercises were resumed, the DPRK placed its troops on a semi-war footing and remained in this state of readiness for sixteen days.

## Nuclearization?

### The IAEA and Nuclear Safeguards Anomalies

In early 1993 the IAEA stated that it was unable to discharge fully its safeguards responsibilities in the DPRK. This was because of anomalies related to the composition and amount of plutonium in the materials inventory, and because of information suggesting that there might be nuclear facilities in the country which had not been declared to the IAEA. It has been reported that three different quantities of americium-241 (am-241) were found in the plutonium sample the DPRK declared to the IAEA. This indicated that the DPRK possibly reprocessed spent fuel from its 5MW(e) research reactor in 1989, 1990 and 1991.[14] This contrasted with information supplied to the IAEA that the country separated plutonium once in 1990, and once in 1975 when it reprocessed a small amount from the IRT-2000 research reactor. It is known that although the 5MW(e) reactor started operating in 1986, it has suffered from operational difficulties. Because of these difficulties, the DPRK says the reactor still contains the fuel that was loaded into the core when it first started up.[15] Until this can be internationally verified, there will inevitably be uncertainty about whether the reactor has been unloaded and the spent fuel reprocessed to produce plutonium. To dispel concerns that additional fuel loads have not been irradiated in the reactor, it is important that the IAEA is allowed to inspect the unloading of the current fuel to verify the operating history of the reactor and make an estimation of the total amount of plutonium it has produced.

Information about the exact quantity of nuclear material in North

Korea remains safeguards confidential, in keeping with all other inventories supplied for IAEA inspection. The DPRK has acknowledged that it produced small quantities of plutonium as a result of experimental work at the radiochemical laboratory. This in itself is not prohibited under the NPT, providing it is acknowledged and placed under safeguards. Only if fissile material, such as plutonium, is removed from safeguards and intentionally diverted to nuclear weapons does it become a prohibited activity. The IAEA must satisfy itself that this has not occurred. As in the case of Iraq, another way a state party to the NPT could violate its safeguards and non-proliferation obligations would be if it pursued an undeclared clandestine programme designed to manufacture nuclear weapons. It is therefore equally important for the IAEA to determine that the DPRK has declared all its nuclear facilities, otherwise suspicions will remain that a clandestine programme exists. Because of the difficulties the IAEA has had in verifying the completeness of the DPRK's initial material inventory, the IAEA Board of Governors decided on 25 February 1993 to initiate a special inspection in an attempt to clarify the inconsistencies and gain access to additional sites suspected of being undeclared nuclear waste sites.[16] The IAEA Board set a deadline of 25 March 1993 for completion of the special inspection. The DPRK refused to allow the inspection to take place. Instead, the DPRK insisted that the IAEA had become a tool of the United States and that the two suspected sites were military bases and therefore not open to inspection.

## The DPRK's Withdrawal from the NPT

On 12 March 1993 the DPRK announced its intention to withdraw from the NPT under Article X.1. This was the first time an NPT Party had formally made such an announcement. It came in the form of a letter by the DPRK's Minister of Foreign Affairs, Kim Yong Nam, addressed to the Ministers of Foreign Affairs of the other NPT Parties and to the President of the UN Security Council. The letter stated that the decision had been taken 'in connection with the extraordinary situation prevailing in the DPRK, which jeopardizes its supreme interests'. It specified the resumption of the US-ROK 'Team Spirit' military exercises and the demands by the IAEA for a special inspection as the reasons for its decision.

On 1 April 1993 the IAEA Board passed a resolution charging the DPRK with non-compliance of its safeguards agreement and submitted the issue to the UN Security Council as required by Article XII.C. of the IAEA Statute and Article 19 of INFCIRC/403, the DPRK's NPT safeguards agreement. On 2 April 1993 the three NPT Depository States,

Russia, the United States and the United Kingdom, issued a statement requesting the DPRK to retract its withdrawal and honour its safeguards agreement with the IAEA. On 11 May 1993 the UN Security Council adopted Resolution 825, which called for the DPRK to reconsider its NPT withdrawal decision and respect its non-proliferation obligations. The Resolution also made it clear that the Security Council would consider further action if necessary. By the end of May 1993, the DPRK had emerged as a test case for the new-found resolve of the IAEA in the post-Iraq, post-Cold War world. The lessons learned by the IAEA from its experiences over Iraq and the verification of the disarmed status of South Africa, were all put into operation in the DPRK. The IAEA was thus able to introduce new detection techniques for dealing with potential clandestine nuclear weapon programmes and call on the support of the UN Security Council when it was unable to discharge fully its NPT safeguards responsibilities. Coupled to this, the DPRK's withdrawal also reinforced concerns about its nuclear intentions.

*The DPRK's Motivations and Intentions*

The lack of certainty over the DPRK's nuclear capabilities has resulted in two contrasting views of the country's future intentions. The first view maintains that the country has something to hide: a militarily significant nuclear weapons infrastructure which has already produced enough fissile material to construct one or more nuclear weapons. The second view is more cautious in its assessment of the DPRK's capabilities and intentions. This view asserts that the DPRK has suffered resource and technical difficulties with its nuclear programme and is using its ambiguous nuclear status to bargain with the United States and other states and extract concessions from them. Those assessments which point to a weapons programme focus on the nature of the DPRK's choice of reactor technology, which has largely been abandoned elsewhere as too costly and inefficient for energy production although it is considered appropriate for plutonium production.[17] In addition, reports have suggested that the DPRK has conducted experimentation with conventional high explosives designed for nuclear detonation purposes.[18] Moreover, concern has also been expressed about recent improvements in the country's ballistic missile capability. The DPRK is considered to have developed the Scud B ballistic missile together with a recently improved variant which is reported to have a greater range.[19] Estimates of the range of the Scud variant, sometimes referred to as the Nodong-Ho missile, indicate that it could reach targets up to a distance of 1,000 km. This would place several population and industrial centres in Japan, including Osaka, Kyoto and Tokyo, within the target range of the missile. Although there is nothing to suggest this missile has been designed to carry anything other than a conventional warhead, its potential to carry nuclear ordnance has done little to reduce the tensions caused by the uncertainty over the DPRK's nuclear capabilities.

If a nuclear weapons programme does exist in the DPRK, what are the motivations behind it and what ends does it serve? Past studies of the DPRK's nuclear programme have suggested several competing explanations relating to strategic, economic and political factors. There are solid grounds for assuming that strategic calculations underpin much of the DPRK's recent activities in the nuclear area. The major problem with any strategic analysis, however, is that the kinds of rational calculation normally associated with nuclear strategy may not be appropriate in this case. It is conceivable that any DPRK weapons programme is geared to regional concerns and is a response to moves by the ROK or even Japan. There is no doubting that mutual distrust has infused the security concerns of both Koreas for more than forty years. During the 1970s the ROK, fearing that the United States' security guarantee to protect its territory was eroding, embarked on a clandestine nuclear weapons programme. Although this programme was later abandoned under pressure from the United States and in 1975 the country ratified the NPT, it may have provided the stimulus for a similar programme in the DPRK. Statements emanating from the DPRK have also indicated an underlying concern about the intentions of Japan in the Northeast Asia region. This reflects traditional rivalries between the two states, evident well before the DPRK was formed.[20] However, a counter trend is also discernible. Because the DPRK is seeking to bolster its economy, the attraction of developing formal relations with Japan is considerable. Japan is a ready source of economic assistance, although it also has a strong interest in seeing an early resolution to the DPRK nuclear issue. Japan has consequently linked its assistance to the DPRK's continued abidance to the NPT and progress on nuclear inspections.[21]

Some analysts have suggested that the strategic motivation for the programme may have become more significant because of developments associated with the end of the Cold War. The demise of the Soviet Union and the resultant decline in solidarity among the remaining socialist states has left the DPRK isolated within the international community. These changes have meant that the country can no longer rely on the security guarantees provided under its old alliance relationship with the former Soviet Union, and possibly even China. The DPRK may also be concerned that its conventional forces would be unable to deal with a combined assault by the ROK and the United States, which might involve nuclear capabilities. As one analyst has contended, 'The conviction that the United States and South Korea, the two supposed enemies of the DPRK, might be unwilling to exclude the use of nuclear weapons in the event of war seems to contribute directly to the North Korean desire to have nuclear weapons for their own security.'[24]

Several assessments have indicated that the DPRK's economy may be failing dramatically. There are persistent reports of resource scarcities, food shortages and difficulties over international trading relationships, especially with the DPRK's traditional trading partners, China and Russia. There appears to be a debate in the DPRK between those supporting opening the economy to outside investment and those stressing the importance of continued indigenous socialist development. The concern of the latter group is that by opening up the economy, society would be adversely affected by liberalizing forces. The concern of the former group is that, without outside assistance, the economy will simply collapse. If this were to happen there is concern within the region that it would have destabilizing effects on an already fragile regional situation with refugees from the north flooding southwards or across the Sea of Japan.[23] Another motivation for a DPRK nuclear weapon capability may therefore stem from problems associated with economic development. It is estimated that the DPRK is currently spending approximately 22 per cent of its Gross National Product (GNP) on defence. This contrasts with a figure for the ROK of around 3.8 per cent of a far larger GNP. One suggestion has therefore been that the DPRK has attempted to reduce its defence expenditure, which is unsustainable in the long term, by pursuing a nuclear weapons capability as 'a relatively low-cost "strategic equalizer" in its military competition with the South'.[24]

Other analysts have focused more on the domestic political situation in the DPRK, in particular the possibility that recent actions are a means for uniting the nation against an external threat to reduce criticism of economic problems and aid a dynastic transition. Since the late 1980s the DPRK leadership has been undergoing transition from Kim Il-Sung to Kim Jong-il, from father to son. There is uncertainty over how far this transition has reached, whether it has gone smoothly, and whether Kim Jong-il will follow the same policies as Kim Il-Sung. Coupled to these domestic issues, the whole political future of the DPRK in the post-Cold War world remains unclear. It is thought that the regime operates a highly centralized bureaucratic system, but 'is not monolithic and does have substantial elasticity and adaptability'.[25] The nature of the regime consequently allows for internal political struggles to occur, including over the nuclear issue. Ultimately, however, ensuring the future of the regime itself may be a major motivation for the

DPRK in the nuclear area. While some analysts agree that domestic factors are a crucial element in explaining recent developments, for others 'regime security' provides only part of the picture.[26] According to this view, the real issue is the nature of the Korean unification process and which of the two Koreas will ultimately gain control over the Peninsula.[27]

### Dilemmas for the Nuclear Non-Proliferation Regime

While there may be strong motivations for the DPRK to consider a nuclear weapons option, there is as yet no hard evidence that this option has been taken. What is clear is that the DPRK's actions in the nuclear area have raised fundamental dilemmas for the nuclear non-proliferation regime.

#### *Exploiting Nuclear Ambiguity*

The DPRK has seemingly used its ambiguous nuclear status to enhance its international bargaining position. Just as South Africa's strategy during the Cold War sought to use its ambiguous nuclear position and, later, its operational capabilities, to obtain security guarantees, so the DPRK appears to be exploiting its status for similar ends.[28] What is also apparent, however, is that there are significant differences between the two situations. One difference is that while South Africa decided that the end of the Cold War negated the need for a such a strategy, it is possible the DPRK feels more compelled to pursue this course precisely because the Cold War has ended. While it is conceivable that the DPRK originally adopted an ambiguous nuclear strategy to gain security guarantees from either China or the Soviet Union during the Cold War, the motivation today may be greater because of doubts about existing guarantees.

Another potential difference concerns the nature of the capability and its potential role. South Africa decided to acquire a rudimentary nuclear explosive capability when it perceived itself to be diplomatically isolated and territorially threatened. It was never known for certain that South Africa had actually developed such a capability, although there was considerable speculation over its existence. According to the strategic doctrine it declared after the past existence of the nuclear explosive programme was announced, South Africa decided that it did not need a deliverable weapon for use against perceived enemies. Rather, South Africa's limited capability was designed to influence potential allies. For the DPRK, the capability and role could conceivably be different due to its radically changed international circumstances. Although similarly perceiving itself to be diplomatically isolated and territorially threatened, a rudimentary capability might not be considered sufficient if the role envisaged was to deter an attack, as the DPRK lacks potential nuclear protectors. Yet it seems unlikely that any nuclear weapon programme that the DPRK could implement alone would provide a nuclear weapons stockpile sufficient to deter a superpower such as the United States. Similarly, if it became conclusively known that the DPRK had developed a small stockpile of a few weapons, the possibility of direct action to deal with it would inevitably increase. At least according to one assessment, this vulnerability does appear to be understood by senior military personnel within North Korea.[29]

If the ultimate objective is to obtain security guarantees and other concessions, such as economic assistance, then it may not be necessary to have a functioning capability at all, only the required infrastructure. The key question for the DPRK would therefore be the converse of the South Africa case: whether the infrastructure would be sufficient to influence perceived enemies rather than potential allies. The suggestion is that it may have had some success, but the bargaining has undoubtedly been reciprocal. Engaging the United States in direct talks on 'an equal and unprejudiced basis' has undoubtedly been one of the DPRK's central objectives.[30] The first round of bilateral talks occurred in New York in June 1993 and resulted in the DPRK agreeing to suspend its withdrawal from NPT. The two states also agreed the following principles which, in terms of ensuring the long-term security of the DPRK and the central role of IAEA safeguards, were very significant: 'assurances against the threat and use of force, including nuclear weapons; peace and security in a nuclear-free Korean Peninsula, including impartial application of fullscope safeguards, mutual respect for each other's sovereignty, and non-interference in each other's internal affairs; and support for the peaceful reunification of Korea.'[31]

A second round occurred in Geneva in July 1993 where the possibility was raised of the DPRK rescinding its withdrawal in exchange for guaranteed access to LWR technology. Both states also acknowledged the need for a strong nuclear non-proliferation regime and the importance of implementing the Joint Declaration on Denuclearization.[32] A third round of talks was scheduled for September 1993 but were called off when the United States stated that future progress on issues affecting both states hinged on developments between the two Koreas. This did not prevent further bargaining, however, as both parties sought simultaneous compromises over outstanding issues.[33]

*The DPRK's Challenge to Non-Proliferation Policies*

The DPRK has once more raised the sensitive issue of how to respond to non-compliance with non-proliferation norms and obligations. In the case of another NPT party found to be in non-compliance with its obligations, Iraq, there were other issues involved which dictated the choice of compliance procedures, ultimately involving military force. The DPRK's non-compliance raises less clear-cut choices. The DPRK insists that it has not violated the NPT and that threatening circumstances forced it to take the extraordinary action of serving notice of withdrawal from the NPT. Yet the DPRK has also been unwilling to allow international verification procedures to clarify certain anomalies in its nuclear programme that have come to light. What can be done in such cases?

One point to note is that if the DPRK does formally withdraw from the NPT the IAEA's right to conduct a special inspection would be nullified as would its routine safeguards rights under INFCIRC/153. However, the IAEA would still have the support of the UN Security Council. This support is stipulated within the IAEA's legal constitution and is reinforced in a UN Security Council Declaration of 31 January 1992 which identified the proliferation of nuclear weapons as 'a threat to international peace and security'. This Declaration highlighted the importance of implementing fully effective IAEA safeguards and that the members of the Security Council would 'take appropriate measures in the case of any violations notified to them by the IAEA'.[34] As such, it is the UN Security Council which becomes the ultimate arbiter for determining cases of non-compliance with the NPT and with IAEA safeguards. Once a case of non-compliance has been decided, the UN Security Council may then use all means at its disposal to secure compliance. Normally this would be understood to mean a graduated series of responses, beginning with diplomacy, then sanctions and, ultimately, military force. The dilemma for the nuclear non-proliferation regime is that any movement up the ladder of responses beyond diplomacy threatens to undermine the very foundation on which it is based: consensus between the parties.

The NPT is a multilateral treaty voluntarily entered into by states. But as a particular kind of treaty, it is also important to develop the voluntary consensus which provides the Treaty's foundation and defines its purposes. As has been pointed out, these purposes have traditionally been viewed as threefold:

1. to express clearly agreed norms of behaviour, and to define clearly the boundaries between what is therefore acceptable and unacceptable international conduct;

2. to provide an opportunity, and by extension a motive, for governments to make a credible public demonstration of attachment to those norms and acceptance of obligations implied by those boundaries; and

3. by showing publicly which nations are and are not willing to accept such obligations, to distinguish between those which thereby merit different standards of treatment by treaty parties.[35]

If all states party to the Treaty accept and abide by these purposes then the voluntary consensus underpinning the NPT is strengthened. Equally, that consensus can easily be weakened where one or more parties are charged with non-compliance, but are actually innocent although unable to convince the other parties; or, conversely, if the offending party or parties are guilty of non-compliance but manage to avoid any penalty owing to the limitations of the Treaty.[36] Both alternatives raise important questions about the most appropriate response to the DPRK.

Within the Northeast Asia region there appears to be a consensus among states party to the NPT that the diplomatic route offers the best option for dealing with the DPRK. In particular, the culture of the region demands that if the DPRK is to be persuaded to rescind its NPT withdrawal, its leadership must be allowed to do so without loss of face. Those parties outside the region, however, have expressed unease about the precedent this would establish, especially if major concessions which affected nuclear inspections were granted. One significant measure of compliance or non-compliance is whether an NPT party abides by its safeguards obligations. The DPRK was found to be in non-compliance with these obligations. If the country was seen to do this with complete impunity then the entire global safeguards system would be undermined. Another possible step to deal with cases of non-compliance, short of more stringent measures, would be to suspend the offending state from the IAEA. There is provision within the IAEA Statute to do this for members which are considered to have transgressed the organization's general principles. Under Article XIX.B, the DPRK could be suspended from the privileges and rights of IAEA membership if it was found to have 'persistently violated the provisions of this Statute or of any agreement entered into by it pursuant to this Statute . . .' [37] However, to suspend the DPRK from the IAEA would close a very significant diplomatic channel for resolving the dispute over safeguards access. If, ultimately, the diplomatic route does not yield the desired outcome, pressure for more stringent measures would undoubtedly grow. The next stage of the ladder would then be to implement sanctions. In the case of the DPRK, the possible imposition of sanctions against it has already been shown to have severe problems. Such a strategy would require the involvement of all Northeast Asian states if sanctions were to have any chance of success and several key states in the region have indicated their strong reservations about imposing them. There are also doubts about what impact sanctions would have on an economy like the DPRK's which is largely isolated from the normal international trading arrangements. Moreover, some states in the region are concerned that a total breakdown in the DPRK's economy could produce devastating consequences for the region as a whole.

Movement up the ladder of responses to the use of military force provides the biggest dilemmas of all. While there is undoubtedly a need to strengthen the nuclear non-proliferation regime in cases of non-compliance, and the use of military force could provide an enforcement capability of last resort, this is the response that can do the most damage to the global non-proliferation consensus.[38] Apart from the difficulties of determining the international legal basis for sanctioning the use of force in the absence of overt military aggression from the DPRK, there are also the following practical problems. First, there are the difficulties associated with target identification and destruction. While it may be conceivable that precision targeting strategies could be used to deal with known nuclear facilities, this strategy would not be suitable for clandestine nuclear locations, especially if they are hidden in deep underground bunkers. Second, even if the known facilities could be targeted, there are the potential radiological consequences stemming from attacks on operating nuclear facilities.[39] Finally, attacks of this kind would run the risk of initiating a much larger conflagration involving the whole Peninsula.

So if the circumstances under which military options could conceivably be used are limited, where does this leave the non-proliferation regime? Probably where it has always been: dependent on the consensual support of the parties to move forward on measures designed to strengthen it. Fortunately, in the aftermath of what occurred in Iraq, a consensus has emerged that the regime needs strengthening. At the global level, this has enabled improvements in IAEA safeguards and export controls, and allowed the UN Security Council to take a more prominent role within the regime. More can still be done, but it is at the regional level where many of the significant challenges lie. None is more pressing than Northeast Asia.

### Constructing an Enduring Northeast Asia Security Relationship

Re-establishing the trend towards denuclearization is a prerequisite for an enduring security relationship in this region. This will inevitably require a resolution to the DPRK's nuclear situation as a first step.

Because of what has occurred over safeguards, the DPRK will have to assure the region and the rest of the international community that it is prepared to abide by its non-proliferation obligations in the future: this means that the IAEA must be allowed unhindered access, including provisions for special inspections, to all the DPRK's nuclear facilities. If agreed, this would provide a solid foundation for further measures, especially bilateral inspection procedures, designed to address the ROK-DPRK relationship. However, it seems likely that if these measures are to proceed, the ROK may have to modify its initial position on reciprocal inspections and instead move progressively towards special inspections.[40]

A further stage of the denuclearization process would involve the establishment of a regional organization for dealing with nuclear energy issues. Whereas in Europe the European Atomic Energy Community (EURATOM) exists, Northeast Asia has no similar overarching regional organization.[41] Consideration would need to be given to the procedures by which the regional organization was linked at the global level to the IAEA, and at the bilateral level, to the JNCC established by the ROK and the DPRK.[42] This development might also coincide with moves to create a Nuclear Weapon Free Zone (NWFZ) in the region,[43] although there may be problems associated with such a zone that could prove intractable.[44] As part of building confidence among the states of the region, and in an attempt to reduce threat perceptions, the establishment of a formal dialogue on security issues in Northeast Asia could provide positive benefits. The states involved might initially include the two Koreas, Japan, China, the United States and possibly Russia and Canada. This forum might become a regular annual fixture in the calendar and provide a conduit for discussing broad security issues such as nuclear questions, crisis management structures, conventional force arrangements and confidence building measures. Finally, because security appears to have been a major factor determining the DPRK's stance, it is imperative to give consideration to new types of positive and negative security assurance. While these might be developed at the global level to enhance the assurances already given, more specific ones might need to be designed for the Korean Peninsula. The dilemma here, however, is that any regional assurances might be seen to reward the DPRK for its behaviour over safeguards. The issue of security assurances has also placed the United States in a difficult position. Because of its security relationship with the ROK, embodied in the 1953 Mutual Defense Treaty, the United States must assure the South of its continued support in any confrontation with the North. This explains the resumption of the 'Team Spirit' exercises, and it led President Clinton in the Autumn of 1993 to warn the DPRK that an invasion of the ROK would be considered an attack on the United States. At the same time, the United States has also sought to send the right security assurance signals to the DPRK.[45] But while the DPRK has welcomed the cancellation of 'Team Spirit' and the withdrawal of US tactical nuclear weapons from the ROK, it still requires further assurances that its political autonomy as a state will not be threatened or that it will not be destroyed by a joint US-ROK military invasion.[46] An enduring regional security arrangement will probably require that these issues are addressed.

## Conclusion

The DPRK's action has precipitated concerns which have resonated throughout the entire fabric of the international security structure, especially the nuclear non-proliferation regime. This suggests two important conclusions: first, that the end of the Cold War has eroded some of the established verities of the nuclear non-proliferation regime and demonstrated its potential fragility; and second, that the DPRK, although today more isolated and in a position of relative weakness, has been able to exploit these concerns over nuclear proliferation and enact a powerful strategy designed to enhance its bargaining leverage within the international community. These developments consequently pose two major challenges for non-proliferation policies: how to minimize any leverage that might be sought by states which threaten to go nuclear or exploit an ambiguous nuclear status; and how to strengthen compliance procedures while not undermining the existing non-proliferation consensus.

### NOTES

1. The terms nuclearization and denuclearization used in this article refer to the spread of nuclear weapons or, conversely, their removal or disarmament, and not to the use of nuclear energy for civil purposes.
2. See *Safeguards Agreement between the Democratic Republic of Korea and the International Atomic Energy Agency (INFCIRC/403)* (Vienna: IAEA, 1992).
3. 'Democratic People's Republic of Korea (DPRK) submits initial report to IAEA under comprehensive safeguards agreement in connection with the Non-Proliferation Treaty', IAEA press release (Vienna: IAEA, 5 May 1992).
4. For an overview of the *rapprochement* between South and North Korea and the High-Level Talks see Seong W. Cheon, 'National Security and Stability in East Asia: The Korean Peninsula', in Darryl Howlett and John Simpson (eds.), *East Asia and Nuclear Non-Proliferation*, Papers from the Twelfth PPNN Core Group Meeting held in Japan November 1992 (Southampton UK: Mountbatten Centre for International Studies for the Programme for Promoting Nuclear Non-Proliferation [PPNN], 1993), pp.38–47.

5. Tae-Hwan Kwak and Seung-Ho Joo, 'The Denuclearization of the Korean Peninsula: Problems and Prospects', *Arms Control: Contemporary Security Policy*, Vol.14, No.2 (Aug. 1993), p.68.
6. 'The North Korean Nuclear Program', *ENSP News Release* (Monterrey, CA: Monterrey Institute for International Studies, 1 June 1993).
7. 'North Korea's Nuclear Power Programme Revealed', *Nuclear News* (July 1992), p.2.
8. See Andrew Mack, 'Is Pyongyang the Next Proliferator?', *Pacific Research* (Feb. 1990), p.6; and Leonard S. Spector, *Nuclear Ambitions* (Boulder, CO.: Westview Press, 1990).
9. 'Democratic People's Republic of Korea (DPRK) submits initial report to IAEA under comprehensive safeguards agreement in connection with the Non-Proliferation Treaty', IAEA Press Release, 5 May 1992 (Vienna: IAEA, 1992).
10. Ibid.
11. See, Margaret Gowing, *Independence and Deterrence: Britain and Atomic Energy 1945–1952. Volume 2, Policy Execution* (London and Basingstoke: Macmillan, 1974), pp.402–23, especially p.407.
12. Seong W. Cheon, op.cit.
13. However, throughout this period the IAEA continued with its *ad hoc* inspections in North Korea.
14. Am-241, a decay product from Pu-241, begins building up again after it is removed during reprocessing and can effectively date reprocessing activities. Mark Hibbs, 'Isotopics Show Three North Korean Reprocessing Campaigns since 1975', *Nuclear Fuel*, 1 March 1993, p.3.
15. It is possible that the core could contain between 5 and 10 kilograms of plutonium (or enough for one or two nuclear weapons). See David Albright, 'North Korea Drops Out', *Bulletin of the Atomic Scientists* (May 1993), p.10.
16. The IAEA had conducted six inspections in North Korea prior to the request for a special inspection. *IAEA Board of Governors Reviews Agency's Inspections in the Democratic People's Republic of Korea (DPRK)*, reproduced in *PPNN Newsbrief*, No.21, First Quarter 1993 (Southampton: Mountbatten Centre for International Studies for PPNN, 1993).
17. Another problem with 'Magnox' reactors is that the spent fuel produced from the reactor can only be stored for a very short period as its decay is rapid and therefore it must be reprocessed.
18. For a chronology of these reports see 'The North Korean Nuclear Program', op.cit.
19. Peter Hayes, 'International Missile Trade and the Two Koreas', Program for Non-proliferation Studies, Monterrey Institute of International Studies, *Working Paper No.1*, March 1993.
20. See for example Statement by Ambassador Pak Gil Yon at the General Debate of the First Committee of the 48th Session of the UN General Assembly, New York, 22 October 1993.
21. Since the end of the Second World War there had been no formal relations between Japan and North Korea. Formal normalization talks between the two states began in January 1991 in Pyongyang. A follow-up meeting was held in Tokyo and all subsequent meetings have occurred in Beijing. Apart from resolution of the nuclear issues, other preconditions for Japan's diplomatic normalisation with North Korea are that such normalisation should not unduly affect its relations with South Korea and that it leads to peace and stability on the Peninsula. Yoshio Okawa, 'North East Asia and North Korea', in John Simpson and Darryl Howlett (eds.), *The Future of the NPT: The 1995 Review and Extension Conference* (Basingstoke and London: Macmillan Publishers, forthcoming).
22. Song Young Sun, 'The Korean Nuclear Issue', *Working Paper 1991/10*, Dept of International Relations, Australian National University, Canberra, Australia, p.3.
23. Yoshio Okawa, 'North East Asia and North Korea', in Simpson and Howlett (eds.).
24. Andrew Mack, 'Nuclear Dilemmas: Korean Security in the 1990s', in Pak Chae-Ha,

Nam Sung-Woo and Eugene Craig Campbell (eds.), *A New World Order and the Security of the Asia-Pacific Region* (Seoul: Korea Institute for Defense Analysis, 1993), p.283.

25. Peter Hayes, 'North Korea's Nuclear Gambits', *Director's Series on Proliferation*, No.2, Lawrence Livermore National Laboratory, 1993, p.31.

26. 'What is at stake in North Korea is not merely the survival of the Kim regime, but that of the state itself – that is, governmental institutions, as well as the country's present social structure'. Paul Bracken, 'Nuclear Weapons and State Survival in North Korea', *Survival*, Vol.35, No.3, p.147.

27. Ibid., pp.147–8.

28. For an analysis of South Africa's nuclear strategy see Darryl Howlett and John Simpson, 'Nuclearization and Denuclearization in South Africa', *Survival*, Vol.35, No.3, pp.154–73.

29. See Hayes, op.cit., p.30.

30. According to Peter Hayes, two issues dominate DPRK thinking: first, the DPRK wants the United States to recognize the DPRK politically and until 'it is confident that the United States is willing to coexist with the North Korean regime, the North is unlikely to abandon its nuclear weapons program'; and second, the North wants to end the nuclear threat to its survival which it perceives is posed by US nuclear weapons. Hayes, op.cit.

31. *Joint Statement of the Democratic People's Republic of Korea and the United States of America*, New York, 11 June 1993; see also, Seong W. Cheon, 'North Korea's Nuclear Problem: Current State and Future Prospects', *Korean Journal of National Unification*, Vol.2 (1993), pp.93–4.

32. Cheon, op.cit.

33. The United States requested access to already inspected locations to ensure continuity of safeguards, access to other locations, and further exchanges with the ROK over bilateral inspections. The DPRK asked for cancellation of future 'Team Spirit' exercises; renunciation of the threat to use nuclear weapons; and guarantees that the country would not be subject to a policy of repression because of its political system.

34. *UN Security Council Declaration on Disarmament, Arms Control and Weapons of Mass Destruction, 31 January 1992*, reproduced in *PPNN Newsbrief Number 17*, Spring 1992, (Southampton: Mountbatten Centre for International Studies for PPNN, 1992).

35. Ian Smart, 'Compliance with the NPT', Paper presented to the Programme for Promoting Nuclear Non-Proliferation (PPNN) Core Group Meeting, Baden bei Wien, Austria, November 1989.

36. Ibid.

37. *Statute of the International Atomic Energy Agency*, reproduced in Darryl Howlett and John Simpson (eds.), *Nuclear Non-Proliferation: A Reference Handbook* (Harlow: Longman, 1992), pp.143–55.

38. Some advocates of a more stringent non-proliferation regime argue that 'a repertoire of military options' should be developed for dealing with situations where 'all other remedies have been exhausted'. See Peter W. Rodman, 'A Grown-Up's Guide to Non-Proliferation', *National Review*, 5 July 1993, p.36.

39. For a discussion of the issues raised see Bennett Ramberg, *Nuclear Power Plants as Weapons for the Enemy: An Unrecognized Military Peril* (Berkeley, Los Angeles & London: University of California Press, 1980).

40. Seong W. Cheon, 'North Korea's Nuclear Program: Current State and Future Prospects', *Korean Journal of National Unification*, Vol.2 (1993), p.104.

41. For consideration of the issues raised by such regional organizations see Darryl Howlett, 'Regional Nuclear Co-operation and Non-Proliferation Arrangements: Model from other Regions', in Darryl Howlett and John Simpson (eds.), *East Asia and Nuclear Non-Proliferation*, pp.63–75.

42. John Simpson, 'Nuclear Capabilities, Military Security and the Korean Peninsula: A Three-Tiered Perspective from Europe', *Korean Journal of Defense Analysis*, Vol.4, No.2 (Winter 1992), pp.11–32.

43. See William Epstein, 'Nuclear Security for the Korean Peninsula', *Korean Journal of Defense Analysis*, Vol.4, No.2 (Winter 1992) pp.64–8; and Jozef Goldblat, 'Nuclear Weapon-Free Zones: Lessons from the existing Agreements', in Darryl Howlett and John Simpson (eds.), *East Asia and Nuclear Non-Proliferation*, pp.56–62.
44. The geographic remit of a North East Asia NWFZ could prove difficult to negotiate and China, Russia and possibly the United States might not be supportive of such a zone and decline to sign any additional protocols relating to nuclear weapon states. See Simpson, op.cit., p.25.
45. See the statement by Assistant Secretary of State, Richard Solomon, in January 1991. He stated that the United States posed 'no nuclear threat to North Korea. The United States has provided a solemn assurance that it will not use nuclear weapons against any non-nuclear weapons state party to the NPT. This assurance applies except in the case of an armed attack on the United States or its allies by such a state associated with a nuclear weapons state. We have stated that the assurance applies to all non-nuclear weapons states parties to the NPT, including the DPRK, if they meet the assurance criteria'. Quoted in Ronald F. Lehman, 'A North Korean Nuclear Weapons Programme', *Security Dialogue*, Vol.24, No.3, p.263.
46. Hayes, op.cit., p.32.

# Notes on Contributors

**Colin McInnes** is Defence Lecturer in the Department of International Politics, University of Wales, Aberystwyth.

**Mark Rolls** is Lecturer in Comparative Asian Politics, Department of Political Science and Public Policy, University of Waikato, New Zealand.

**David Arase** is Lecturer in the Department of Politics, Pomona College, California.

**Darryl Howlett** is Senior Research Fellow at the Mountbatten Centre, University of Southampton, and Information Officer for the Programme for Promoting Nuclear Non-Proliferation.

**Tim Huxley** is a Senior Lecturer in the Centre for South-East Asian Studies, University of Hull.

**Gerald Segal** is Senior Fellow in Asian Security Studies, International Institute for Strategic Studies, London.

**William T. Tow** is Reader in International Relations, Department of Government, University of Queensland, Australia.

**Susan Willett** is a Research Fellow in the Centre for Defence Studies, King's College, London.

**Mike Yeong** is a consultant in Asia-Pacific affairs, and wrote this article whilst a Research Fellow at the Institute of Southeast Asian Studies, Singapore.

The editors wish to thank Donna Griffin for her cheerful and friendly assistance in wordprocessing the manuscript, and Mark Smith for preparing the index.

# Index

Afghanistan 163–4
Asia-Pacific economic co–operation
  (APEC) 32, 58
Arms trade 2, 5, 6–8, 112–135;
  demand trends 117–26; exports
  to Far East Asia 122–3;
  implications of 132–3;
  industrialization and 126–30;
  security issues of 112; state
  strategies in 130–2; supply
  trends 113–7, 130
Association of Southeast Asian
  Nations (ASEAN) *see also*
  ASEAN states 2, 3, 6–7, 30,
  35, 54–5, 58, 65–6, 81, 83–4,
  85–8, 90, 91, 96, 123, 129, 136,
  137, 139, 140, 164; origins of
  66; problems of 67–8, 73–6;
  purpose 66–8; security co-
  operation and 4, 65–79, 102,
  151–2; Thai security and 103–5
ASEAN states (*see also* Brunei,
  Indonesia, Malaysia,
  Philippines, Singapore,
  Thailand) defence policies of
  135–55; influences on defence
  policies of 136–40; US and
  27–30, 32, 139
Australia 29

Brunei 27; defence policy of 145–7
Burma *see* Myanmar

Cambodia (Kampuchea) 4, 95, 96;
  conflict with Vietnam 4–5,
  69–70, 80, 81–4, 94, 140;
  elections in 88–9; Khmer
  Rouge 82, 85, 88–90, 91, 96,
  100, 101; security of 90–1;
  Thailand and 100–101, 105
China 2, 4, 19, 20–3, 67, 74–5, 80–1;
  arms control and 166–71; arms
  exports of 7–8, 125, 156–73;
  arms exports and national
  security 165–6, 168, 171;
  military capacity 21–2, 52–3,

69, 119–20, 167–8; nuclear
  weapons and 22; Paracel and
  Spratly Islands and 52, 69, 87;
  role in ASEAN region 143;
  Thailand and 96, 97, 102–3,
  106–7, 149–50, 164; US and
  34–5, 53; Vietnam and 82,
  83–4, 85–6, 87–8
Cold War, Asia Pacific region and
  end of 1, 8–9, 84, 68–9, 70, 182
  190

Democratic People's Republic of
  Korea (DPRK) *see* Korea,
  North

Five Power Defence Arrangements
  (FPDA) 29, 68, 151

Gulf War 45–6, 168

International Atomic Energy Agency
  (IAEA) *see also* Nuclear Non-
  Proliferation Treaty; North
  Korea and 175, 176, 177, 178,
  180, 181, 186, 187, 188, 189
India 159, 163
Indo-China *see* Cambodia, Laos,
  Thailand, Vietnam
Indonesia 27, 28–9, 68, 73, 75, 115,
  122, 126, 130, 138, 152
  defence policy of 141–2

Japan 116, 159; defence expenditure
  117–8, 122, 125–6, 129, 131–2;
  domestic politics 1, 47, 59–61;
  economic policy 54, 57–8; Gulf
  War and 45–6; North Korea
  and 51–2, 181–2; nuclear
  weapons and 55–6, 174;
  peacekeeping operations and
  47; post-war policy 44–5;
  regional security and 2, 3, 4,
  8–9, 34, 53–4, 69, 169; Russia
  and 49–51; security policy of
  44–64; US and 44, 45, 56–8

Kampuchea *see* Cambodia
Korea, North (DPRK) 22, 29, 34;
    China and 162–3; Japan and
    48, 51–2, 181–2; motivations for
    nuclear programme 181–5;
    nuclear energy programme
    176–9; nuclear policy 8, 51–2,
    174–93; NPT and 174, 175,
    180–1, 186–8; South Korea and
    175–6,178, 189; US and 24–25,
    185, 189
Korea, South (ROK) 34, 115, 168,
    174; arms exports and 125;
    defence expenditure 126, 129,
    130, 131; North Korea and 51,
    175–6, 178, 189; US
    commitment to 16–7, 24–7,
    178–9 182, 189–90

Laos 95, 149

Malaysia 27, 28, 31, 68, 73, 122, 127,
    138, 139, 146, 149, 152 164;
    defence policy of 137, 142–3,
    144, 151
Missile Transfer Control Regime
    (MTCR) 165, 167, 170
Myanmar (Burma) 72, 74, 95;
    Thailand and 101–2, 106, 149;
    China and 164

Non-Aligned Movement 81
Nuclear Non-Proliferation Treaty *see*
    nuclear weapons
Nuclear weapons (*see also* Japan,
    North Korea) 8, 31; non-
    proliferation regime 184–90;
    Nuclear Non-Proliferation
    Treaty 20, 50, 55, 167, 174,
    175, 180–1, 186; South Africa
    and 184

Pakistan 157; China and 163
Paracel and Spratly Islands 52, 69,
    146, 148
Paris Peace Agreement (1991) 4, 68
Philippines 27, 32, 68, 69; defence
    policy 147–8

Republic of Korea (ROK) *see*
    Korea, South

Russia (*see also* Soviet Union) 34,
    68; China and 156, 159, 168
    Japan and 49–51

Singapore 27–8, 32, 67, 73, 115, 138,
    143; defence policy 120–2, 126,
    127, 129, 130, 137, 143–5, 151,
    152
Southeast Asian Treaty Organisation
    (SEATO) 27
Soviet Union 2, 30, 69, 82, 85, 86,
    139, 160, 165

Taiwan 32, 53, 115; defence policy
    121–2, 126, 127, 129, 130, 169
Thailand 27, 32, 67, 68, 74, 84, 90,
    137, 138, 152, 157; ASEAN and
    103–5; Cambodia and 100–1,
    105; China and 102–3, 105, 106,
    164; Communist Party in 94;
    defence policy 106–7, 122,
    148–50; Indo-China and 95–6,
    97–101, 104; Japan and 105–6;
    Myanmar and 101–2, 104, 106;
    security policy of 5, 94–111,
    140; US and 105; Vietnam and
    99–100, 104

United Nations 46, 47, 89, 161, 186,
    188
United States; arms trade and 123–4,
    152; ASEAN and 27–30;
    Asian–Pacific security and 1–2,
    2–3, 10–43, 53, 56–7, 129–30,
    139, 163, 170; Bush
    Administration 12, 14, 175;
    China and 20–3, 31, 34–5
    165–6; Clinton administration
    2, 10–11, 14–18, 19, 20, 24,
    30–1, 36; Japan and 23–4, 31,
    56–8; North Korea and 24–7,
    31–2, 33 185, 189; Philippines
    and 147; South Korea 24–7,
    178–9, 182, 189–90;
    Thailand and 29, 149, 150;
    Vietnam and 86–7; Vietnam-
    Cambodia conflict and 82–4;
    Vietnam War 80–1

Vietnam 4, 52, 67, 69, 72, 74, 95;
    Cambodia and 4–5, 69–70, 80,

81–4, 84–5, 87, 94, 140; security
policy of 85–88, 91; Thailand
and 99–100 149; unification 81
Vietnam War 80–1

Zone of Peace, Freedom and
Neutrality (ZOPFAN) 27, 66,
68, 73, 103